NO PLACE TO HIDE

NO PLACE TO HIDE

HOW I PUT THE BLACK
IN THE UNION JACK

ERROL CHRISTIE
WITH TONY MCMAHON

First published in Great Britain
2010 by Aurum Press Ltd
7 Greenland Street
London NW1 0ND
www.aurumpress.co.uk

Photographs: p.ii, courtesy of *Mirrorpix*; p.44, courtesy of *Mirrorpix*;
pp.98-99, courtesy of *Mirrorpix*; p.102, courtesy of *Mirrorpix*;
p.201, courtesy of *PA Photos*; p.204, courtesy of *Boxing News;*
pp.224-225, courtesy of *PA Photos*.

A catalogue record for this book is available from the British Library.

ISBN 978 1 84513 513 3

1 3 5 7 9 10 8 6 4 2
2010 2012 2014 2013 2011

Text design by Saxon Graphics
Typeset by Saxon Graphics

Printed by MPG Books, Bodmin, Cornwall

to Havelin Wolf – a true warrior

CONTENTS

FOREWORD
BY STEVE BUNCE

I first saw Errol Christie fight in Blackpool. It was 1976 and I was there to watch a friend try and win the National Schoolboy title. Every year, the Schoolboy finals were held at Pontin's holiday camp. Errol had been the king of Blackpool for four years and that was about as good as it got back then.

It was a good year, 1976. Herol 'Bomber' Graham won and a kid called Colin Derrick, who was terrifying, also gained a title. At that time, the Schoolboy champion-

Errol Christie with Steve Bunce.
Sean Keating/P4P Event Photography

ships involved as many as 5,000 boxers and started out at the smallest regional level. Most cities were divided into four and a boxer would have to win seven, eight or even nine times to get to Blackpool – it was the hardest title to win. Errol's name kept coming up even before I had seen him fight – that happens with great boxers – and during the Blackpool years, none were better than Errol Christie of Coventry.

Errol went on to set a record by winning ten British amateur boxing titles to place his name for ever in the *Guinness World Records*. It will stay that way because changes to the championship formats mean that it is now impossible to win more titles. It seemed Errol was simply destined to be a world champion in the 1980s. Thankfully, this book will ensure that Errol Christie is not dismissed lightly: he deserves to finally take his place next to the best in British boxing history.

Some of Errol's fights will not be forgotten in a hurry, while others have already vanished from memory. It's a brutal game, the boxing business, and Errol talks about it like a true survivor. The highs and the terrible lows are all here. This is no fairy tale, unlike so many celebrity boxers' books; at the same time it's not the latest misery memoir either. A true fighter's tale, it hits from the heart.

The end of Errol's boxing career was not so sweet, though, and I was there again. It was a bleak night in Manchester's Free Trade Hall in 1993. The opponent was a tough but limited fighter called Trevor Ambrose, with a history in martial arts; the type of boxer that Errol, the old Errol, would have taken care of in a few one-sided rounds. But at this late point in his boxing life, Errol was chasing a lost cause and like most fighters in the dying days of their careers, he simply refused to accept that the great boxing dream was over. He was stopped in two rounds. That was the end and it felt like my report in the *Daily Telegraph* was a living obituary. It was the only report of Errol's last fight in a national newspaper – even his local paper in Coventry had given up by then.

It is when the neon goes out that a boxer's life can get very, very messy. Errol missed out on the glory he had been promised for so long, and his fall from the ring was harsh. Since that defeat, Errol has been a busy boy, but I suspect that he has just been filling in the holes in a life that he was once promised: he has worked as a comedian, he put a coat on to work the doors and he sold dodgy gear in markets. He kept popping up on various radars and his work training white-collar warriors has placed him back inside boxing. Today he visits schools to talk about his experiences on the streets, his life near the grime and the crime. His words on knife crime make a hollow mockery of the Mayor of London's bleats and the insulting photo-savvy sound bites of any other politician with an agenda rammed up his or her backside. Errol's words have soul and that is a Cov' thing, trust me.

It's all in the book. It's all here and it's all part of the same amazing and moving journey.

This book is about Errol's mission, his passion and his struggles on both sides of the ropes. It takes him from Coventry to Las Vegas, from a serious working-class background to celebrity status, and from fights in tiny clubs to the world's finest boxing stages. At times, it is brutal and sad. Errol met every challenge heart-first and never went on the missing list – he stood, as we say. He never ran because he knew from the start that when you're a true fighter, there's simply no place to hide.

INTRODUCTION

I strode out of the changing room at Wembley Arena to find myself in the midst of a baying mass of faces. A lynch mob might have been a better description. In any other fight, the roar of the crowd would have been a blessing; it's a mighty sound that gets any fighter's adrenalin flowing, ready for the ordeal ahead – but not tonight.

Few of my supporters had dared to turn up and so I was left alone to contend with the enemy's fans. The barrage of abuse was just one stormy growl, a hurricane of hate. Luckily, I couldn't make out any of the insults being lobbed at me. From the PA stacks 'Eye Of The Tiger', the pumping anthem chosen by my management to herald my arrival, was blaring.

On every side, thousands of pumped-up, pop-eyed white men from West Ham screamed for their man.

'Kaaaaaayyyyyylooooorrrrr!!!!!'

In pubs all over the East End of London, National Front supporters had been proclaiming for weeks that I was about to get a sound beating from their boy. That uppity black bastard Errol Christie, with his cocky Muhammad Ali shuffle, needed to be taught a lesson: put back in his box and sent packing back to Coventry. I was determined not to give them that satisfaction.

As I walked towards the ring, the spotlights above burning into me, I thwacked my gloves together. My manager, Burt McCarthy, had been demanding this fight for months and now, there I was, facing a man whose fan base represented everything I despised: the sort of men who had chased me home from school every day of every week from as early as I could remember.

Around the ring was a double line of cops: the enemy, the boot boys in uniform, as I'd always seen them. To the forefront of their minds must have been the recent riots at the Broadwater Farm Estate, where a police constable had been stabbed to death. This was 1985 and, after four years of calm, rioting had returned to

Britain's streets. No doubt most of the police present that night wanted my white opponent to win.

Back home in Coventry, watching the event unfold on the telly, were my long-suffering parents: Mum, a God-fearing, church-going woman with a sharp tongue, and my violent, undiagnosed schizophrenic of a father. They'd been warned by leaders of the black community not to attend in person because of the likelihood of violence. Immigrants from Jamaica, with their crumpled clothes and 'Yes, Massa' attitude, they had arrived in the 1950s only to be ripped off by every smooth-talking swindler England could throw at them. They never enjoyed coming to see me fight, but then I hadn't really made much of an effort to get them along. This climb up the boxing ladder was my achievement alone.

The Coventry of my youth was a pressure-cooker environment of constant tensions and violence. In a city where the car factories were closing down and angry young people found themselves with no job, no future and no hope at all, they wanted someone to blame. Younger readers might find it difficult to recognise this strange England, but it seems like barely yesterday to me. The story of my generation of black youth has often been overlooked: we weren't like our parents – grinning colonials off the *Windrush*, prepared to believe whatever they were told. We were an angrier, far more impatient bunch of kids, who eventually set our cities alight during the long hot summer of 1981.

Throughout my youth I encountered attitudes to colour, even when I became a successful professional boxer, which would make jaws drop today. To be told, as I was, by a leading voice in the boxing world that I would have to accept less money on account of my pigmentation would probably shock most boxers now. Back then, it was pretty much par for the course.

People like me were the first black faces to appear on the nation's TV screens in any guise other than figures of fun, servants or extras. Small victories back then mean that today's black youth can demand a respect that we ourselves were denied.

Boxing saved my life. It brought me into contact with celebrities, gangsters and royalty. The sport gave me some of the highest highs I have ever experienced but also laid me low to the point where I wondered whether it was worth going on. Within these pages are genuine heroes who lifted me up and asked for little or nothing in return, and also the worst of villains: people who used me – and other fighters – as a throwaway object.

That fight with Mark Kaylor, on 5 November 1985, was the culmination of two decades of struggle, violence and pain. It was the night when I took on my tormentors, those who tried to crush my spirit and destroy my body, the date that defined my life. Before that day, I had climbed a mountain. Afterwards, I fell into a sad and shadowy underworld – a place where declining boxers brush shoulders with all kinds of criminals, thieves and pimps, just to survive.

The cast is all here – boot boys and skinheads, rudies and black yuppies, violent gangland members and corrupt cops, preachers and women talking in tongues, boxing promoters and managers … Let's go meet them.

1

THE CHRISTIE FAMILY

'So in between the sleepless nights
You dream that you are winning fights
But then it happens, dreadful thing
A wave appears too big to swim
You're drowning, you're drowning'

'Drowning' — The Beat

The Christie family: me *(far left)* next to Michael *(back left)*, Mum *(centre)*, Des *(back right)*, Wesley *(far right)* next to Andy and little Simon *(middle)*. In later life, Annette *(front left)* scratched her face out deliberately.

Errol Christie, personal collection

Mum and Dad on their wedding day.
Errol Christie, personal collection

The Christie brothers: Michael *(far left)*, me and Wesley at the back,
Simon in the centre and Andy *(far right)*.
Errol Christie, personal collection

The Christie brothers go to church.
Errol Christie, personal collection

'**W**ho broke di bloody key?'

In one hand, Dad held the broken half of a key. The other half was stuck in the lock on the driver's side of his builder's van. Dad himself had split the key in half by trying to open the door too forcefully. That was Ralph Christie, all brute force and ignorance. But in that confused and tortured mind of his things were very different.

'I said, who broke di bloody key?'

My younger brothers, Andy and Simon, knelt on a bunk bed in our cramped, dank bedroom and clutched their stomachs, laughing at Dad.

'Dad thinks we broke the key!'

Simon and Andy savoured Dad's bewilderment from what they mistook to be the safety of the bedroom. Meanwhile, I crept down the stairs on the tips of my toes to take a closer look. My old man was on good form today, completely barking. None of us had been near his van when the key broke so there was no way on earth that any of us were to blame, but the reality completely escaped him.

His grumbling grew louder and louder. That familiar harsh and uncompromising Jamaican growl made the walls of our small house vibrate. Dad was jabbering away angrily about what he would do to the culprit when he got hold of him. An almighty retribution lay in store.

The stairs creaked slightly as I held onto the banister and made my way down, praying to the Lord Jesus that Dad wouldn't see me. The Lord Jesus was on the wall nearby – a blond, blue-eyed saviour, who gazed disinterestedly down on me from a framed picture. He hadn't the slightest intention of getting involved – not even when our Dad was punching his children for no good reason.

We Christie brothers feared our father, though we also mocked him and strangely enough, like all good Christian boys, we kind of honoured him or at least we tried to do so. 'Honour Thy Father and Thy Mother,' they told us at the Church of God, but if your dad happened to be a maniac who was prone to thumping the living daylights out of his own flesh and blood, well, it was a tough call.

'Ay, bloody boy,' those were the words that terrified us most. They meant a sound walloping was coming to whoever got in the way of his bloodshot stare. If he fixed one of his sons in his sights, the big leather belt would be yanked off and an undeserved tanning meted out. Not that we ever dreamt of striking our own father back. No matter that we boys were fighting men his size on the streets, his person was sacred. In this terraced house, on Cheveral Avenue in Coventry's Radford district, the demented madman was God.

Nothing he was muttering at that moment in the back yard made any sense. In an attempt to catch a glimpse of our tormentor, I leant over the banister as far as I could go. That proved to be my grand undoing. Immediately, the bull-like head turned and snorted in my direction.

'Ay, you bloody boy, come 'ere!'

Now, I was done for. Locked, his eyes and mine. Rage on his side, fear on mine. Staring straight at me, it was almost as if he was staring through me to some imaginary enemy, out to undo him, that he must destroy. Now began the chase.

Dad turned from the van and prepared to charge. His belly might have protruded over his trousers, his legs may have been puffy and his arse enormous, but like an old steam engine, he powered slowly into action and once his feet got going, he could outrun any of us. I'd even seen him sprint after my oldest brother Des, who was almost a grown man. Once he'd managed to delude himself that a head start on Dad would save his ass from being whipped, but soon enough the old man bore down on him and dispensed his cruel and warped idea of justice: a shower of thumps and Jamaican cusses.

I didn't fancy sharing the same fate, not that day nor any other. Without glancing back, I flew up the stairs as he shrieked behind me, 'Bloody boy, come back 'ere!'

To save myself, I had to think fast: that meant sacrificing my two younger brothers. As I got to the landing, I pushed open the bedroom door. Simon and Andy were still kneeling on the bed, unaware of the grim threatening creature hurtling towards them. Turning rapidly on my heels, I darted into the toilet and bolted the door. Inside, I sat quietly on the bowl and waited to see if Dad would fall for the open-door decoy.

Of course, I knew exactly what would happen if he did. My plan went like clockwork: the pathetic yelps of my two younger brothers, begging for mercy, could be heard through the wall. Unfortunately for Andy and Simon, this God knew no mercy. Now that Dad had seen them, he completely forgot about me. No longer in his field of vision, I was as good as non-existent. My poor brothers screamed out our well-rehearsed response to his fists: 'No, Daddy! No, Daddy! *Nooooooo!*'

While they whimpered and begged for him to stop, I spotted my chance to escape. Out of the toilet I crept, and with a few leaps, I was downstairs and through the front door to the safety of the road outside. It would take a while for this latest episode to calm down. Fifteen years of age and more than capable of looking after myself, I headed off for the squats of Hillfields. In that drug-infested, hooker-riddled district, I'd find some peace and quiet, plus a good night's sleep.

The only positive thing I can say about my father's liberal use of his fists was that it prepared me, Errol Christie the fighter, for the worst the boxing ring could throw at me. Pain was like an old friend, I would tell people: I knew it well. To experience pain was to be reminded of home, sweet home.

Having been at the receiving end of Dad's punches, it seemed almost inevitable that all the Christie boys would come to don boxing gloves, with varying degrees of success. Wesley and I would go professional, as welterweight and middleweight fighters respectively. Michael, Simon, Andy and Des went some distance as amateurs. All this made possible, in part, by a father who ensured fighting was such an integral part of our lives from day one.

So, who was Mr Christie senior? The first thing to say is that Jamaica was written all over him, a crude toughness shared by thousands like him who came off the boats in search of a better life. In the 1950s, the Empire cried out to the colonies for cheap labour and its loyal subjects had come running.

Back in his homeland, Dad had grown up illiterate and earned a meagre living by digging up yams – that long, potato-like staple of the Jamaican diet. To get the fare to England, he'd gone down on his hands and knees, and dug up an entire field of yams – then hidden them away to sell later at the market. Bright and early the next morning, he returned to his secret stash, only to find somebody else had spirited it away. Such bad luck dogged my father in everything he did; things never seemed to go completely right for him.

So, he went back under the blazing sun, sweating away to harvest as many yams as he could. This time he got them to market and, amazingly, made enough money for the big journey: Mr Christie was coming to England.

My dad was a man of few words, hence the frequent use of his fists, which was an easier and more direct way of expressing himself. Sometimes, though, he found himself in the uncomfortable position of having to answer questions. This happened when he got to Immigration in England and was asked what he did for a living. Not really knowing what to say, having never had what you might call a formal occupation, he simply spat out: 'Mi dig up yams, me tek a market, gu [go] sell.'

The year was 1956 and most probably the immigration officers had no idea what he was talking about. Often I've wondered what words they must have exchanged as he shuffled off.

'What the fuck's a yam?'

'Dunno, mate.'

England, his new home country, should have been Dad's salvation. Instead, it was a place that would drive him mad. Jamaicans came to the motherland to help rebuild the economy, but having persuaded men like my father to go there, it wouldn't give them a place to sleep. Up went the 'No Blacks, No Dogs' signs in the B&B houses as he trudged from door to door, looking for somewhere to lay his head.

Sick and tired of not being able to find a room, my dad ended up renting a bed. Not the room around it, just the bed itself. The dingy converted living room was shared with several other sleepers who were in pretty much the same situation. Having found himself regarded on the same level as a dog, Dad dreamt of having his own house. Not a council house either; his very own place, just like a respectable British person. He would have a stake in the motherland that nobody could take away from him.

In those days, men travelled from Jamaica first and brought their families over later. But my dad didn't have a wife and, back in England, no queue was forming for the vacancy of Mrs Christie. He'd have to convince a woman from Jamaica to come and join him to start a family in his new home. In one of our few proper conversations before he died, my old man told me how he managed to snare himself a wife.

'When mi's in England, mi can't get no woman, so mi send home 'n hasked Miss Mary if she know anybody she can send over for mi to marry.'

Miss Mary was his mother. She dutifully scouted around and found one possible candidate but once the poor girl heard a few details about my old man, she reconsidered and made a hasty exit. A man who couldn't read or write, with no job or savings, wasn't a great prospect for any woman, then or since. Somehow, though, Miss Mary found a willing partner: a pretty twenty-two-year-old called Havelin Wolf.

Little did she know what life lay ahead: if only she'd been given a glimpse of her future, maybe she'd have torn up the one-way ticket and stayed in the Caribbean. But no, Havelin Wolf arrived and soon my parents-to-be were arguing like cat and dog; they didn't get on one bit.

In frustration, she once yelled at him: 'Should I gu back?' Sullenly, he stared at her. No way could he let her escape now and he had the perfect words to keep her grounded: 'Me already paid for the wedding licence.' So that was that – a marriage made in hell.

Mum was more educated than Dad. In the early days, before she was totally crushed by her family, there was a touch of the Hyacinth Bouquet (that posh lady from the BBC sitcom *Keeping Up Appearances*) about her: all airs and graces. Not that her family was all that wealthy, but they'd had enough money to give her an education, which was more than my Dad got. He was more like Onslow, Hyacinth's fat and dirty brother-in-law.

Mum often called Dad 'illiterate' and it was true. Picking yams, he'd never needed to read or write. And back in those days, he didn't have to operate a computer at work. His inability to read and write could be kept a secret: all he was required to do on shift was lift his tools and put his back into it.

Insanity, not illiteracy, was Dad's main problem. My father was mad – really, really mad. Years later, the medical profession finally diagnosed the old man as a complete schizophrenic. I remember the day my mum phoned to tell me.

'Dem say you father mad.'

'Yeah, Mum – like I hadn't figured that out,' I replied, holding back a big sigh.

To my way of thinking, it was scandalous that he hadn't been sussed out much earlier on: before he beat us like runaway slaves might have been handy. Looking back, it seems in the sixties and seventies as if the brain doctors assumed people of certain pigmentation were naturally hot-tempered and volatile. A black man could behave in a way that would have landed a white man in a padded cell. Growing up, Dad's madness was clear as day to me, but it took until the early eighties before he was put on the right medication – by which point most of us had already left home and so we never got to experience the newly pacified Mr Christie.

In fairness to any readers with Jamaican roots, I know that violent ultra-disciplinarian fathers often come as part of the Afro-Caribbean family package, but our dad didn't just reserve his physical outbursts for us kids; Mum wasn't to be left out either. My earliest memory is of sitting in a high chair in the kitchen and watching, open-mouthed, as my father threw hot milk in my mother's face. The reason for his action remains a mystery to this day, but it set the tone for the years ahead.

Mum soon realised she'd taken a wrong turn, but in those days there was no going back: you made your bed and you really had to lie in it for good. Maybe she dreamt of a man with refined manners and plenty of money who might sweep her off her feet and whisk her away. Instead, she was lumbered with the Christie clan. Her way of handling this disagreeable situation was to develop an acid tongue, one that lashed out at us in her most bitter moments:

'Unu good for nuttin' … Unu bad breed kroff [tramp].'

'Unu wutless.'

'Unu worse than dog.'

Perhaps seeing a mini-version of Dad in me, Mum was on my case from morning till night. If I cleaned anything, it wasn't anywhere near clean enough. When I tried to help out in the kitchen and wash the cups and plates, they were still dirty. Mum would look down at a little boy desperate for approval and quickly sum me up:

'Bad breed kroff.'

Once too often a victim of that caustic, unforgiving tongue, my brother Andy now rarely speaks to Mum. In recent years, though, I've come to see her as a warrior who had to fight every day of her life: carrying the burden of a husband who combined petty frustration with insanity while doing her best to keep order in a house crawling with boys, who grew increasingly uncontrollable.

From the moment she set foot in Britain, back in 1956, her humiliation started. The British Government promised new arrivals £2 – money that would pay for a rent deposit or food to get started after they'd arrived. So, Mum went down to the local Labour Exchange, as they used to call the DSS in those days, but found herself in a large queue of very angry people, most of them white men.

Some sort of commotion seemed to be in progress, with people tearing up bits of paper and throwing them in the clerk's face. He seemed unmoved by all of this. My mother had no idea what was going on and wondered if she should leave, but then she remembered how much she needed the money – she was cold and hungry. Her turn came to face the clerk.

In a less-than-friendly tone, he asked why she'd come to the country. She gave him her story. Then he asked to see her passport, but she didn't have it. Dismissively, he shook his head: Mum would have to go away and come back with her passport. So, the next day she returned – only this time the Labour Exchange was eerily empty. But the same clerk was there and as she approached, he stared in stony contempt. He examined the passport and then asked her how she got to Britain.

'I came by plane,' she replied.

'Why didn't you come by a cheaper way?' he asked, holding Mum's passport between forefinger and thumb as if it was covered in filth. 'Could have used the rest of the money to help yourself now.'

He slid the passport back across the counter to Mum and then announced that she wouldn't be getting her £2. That was it, he had decided. Presumably he often made decisions like this, hence the ugly scenes when Mum first set foot in the Labour Exchange. Fighting back tears of hurt, she took her passport and quietly left. As she walked down the street, she resolved never again to ask the British Government for money. The State could keep its £2 and any other handouts: she would make her own way.

Back in the 1960s, Mum encountered a lot of racism. One of our Irish neighbours in Coventry routinely referred to my mother as 'Chocolate' and not in a particularly endearing way, either. He also told her to go back to where she came from, even though he himself wasn't English. Clearly, the irony was lost.

Often she'd have to go down to the garage to pick up fuel to put on the fire, central heating being absent in the Christie household. But every time she wandered out, a little boy in a house opposite would yell: 'Oi, golliwog!' Had my mother known what a 'golliwog' was, the insult might have had greater impact.

Unfortunately for this mini-racist, Mum asked my older brother Des what the word meant and he hit the roof. Des was still at school and about the same age as the name caller, but considerably stronger. A little later, it emerged that Des had given the kid a rather sound kicking – so much so, that he and his Dad appeared at our front door to complain about it. The kid's cardigan was ripped down the front. His dad was full of indignation, puffed-up with a righteous swagger: how dare my brother do this to his son? Roughly translated, how dare a black kid do this to a white kid?

Now that my mother had been enlightened about the word 'golliwog', she was in no mood to apologise, though. Not in any way did she resemble the fuzzy-haired black cartoon character with a big, smiling red-lipped mouth that used to adorn Robertson's jam jars in Britain back then – and still did so until as late as 2001. Mum was definitely no golliwog. Bristling, she squared up to the father of the nasty child and told him that if Des had done this, then clearly he'd been provoked beyond endurance. Of course, she was really referring to herself.

We never saw that father and son again but, listening in the wings, I realised then that the only language a racist understood was two tight fists that could jab and cross until he was on his knees, begging for mercy. That was an early lesson for Errol Christie.

At the time Coventry was as far from politically correct as you could get, but although the city would make a huge impact on me, the Christie family didn't start out there. We actually began life further north in Leicester. It was in that city, on 29 June 1963, that I was squeezed out of my mum into a world where people of my colour were still fighting for their civil rights. It's hard to believe that such giants as John F. Kennedy, Malcolm X and Martin Luther King were still breathing as I made my first gurgling sounds. Within six months of my birth, JFK was riddled with bullets. A decade later, I would attend a school named after him.

Long before Mum gave birth to me, she'd been working as a machinist. It was heavy and demanding work. One day, she tripped and fell. As a direct result, she lost the baby that she was carrying. The pain of the miscarriage was too much to bear and so she left the factory to retrain as a nurse.

My dad also forged his own link with the National Health Service. He began work miles away in Coventry as a 'brickie' on the new Walsgrave Hospital. Not far from the Walsgrave, the Coventry and Warwickshire Hospital was also being rebuilt, having been callously blown to bits by the Luftwaffe during the First World War. The Third Reich also managed to level Coventry's cathedral, a crime that still scars the city to this day.

Previously, Dad worked as a metal basher for the Royal Mint in Birmingham, but he swapped making coins for the construction site and backbreaking work for hours on end. Soon it became clear, though, that the daily commute from Leicester to Coventry wasn't good for a man as seriously confused and mentally unstable as my dad. He wasn't patience personified to start with, either.

Tired of the long journey to and fro, one day he announced that we would up sticks and move on to live in Coventry. I was six years old at the time and it seemed the start of a fine adventure, but my mother had cousins in nearby Birmingham who began whispering serious warnings in her ear:

'Don't go to live there, Havelin. You'll be sorry, that no place for black people.'

Wise advice, as it turned out – which my parents chose to completely ignore. Instead, fingers in their ears, they packed their bags and moved on. Coventry might have been the making of me, but those words of warning should have been heeded, for we were relocating to the skinhead capital of England, a National Front paradise.

But before we encountered any Coventry boot boys or fascists, there was another enemy to contend with: mortgage brokers. Determined never to have to go from door to door, looking for somewhere to sleep only to be turned away, my parents wanted to buy their own house in Coventry. Dad had slaved away on building sites and put enough money aside for the deposit, but as with the yams he'd stashed to get the fare to Britain, he was to lose this bit of wealth too.

Enter a slick mortgage broker. Sharp-suited and silvery tongued, this criminal talked financial babble to my parents. Dad must have resembled a gigantic sitting duck, an easy target to be conned. Unable to read or write, and like many first-generation immigrants, he was completely in awe of any authority figure that crossed his path, even a mortgage broker. Instead of seeing through this slimy conman, the unprincipled trickster became Dad's new 'massa'. After all, he had smart clothes and well-shined shoes, slicked-down hair and a contrived posh accent. My father never stood a chance.

The deposit was soon handed over, never to be seen again for Dad was sweet-talked out of months of savings and it crushed him. Back to the building site he went to start all over again. With hate-filled intensity, he created another nest egg and this time he made sure that he got himself a place to call home. Cheveral Avenue, in the Radford district of Coventry, was to be the

Christies' new base of operation.

If ever there were any other black families on Cheveral Avenue, they must have been lying low. From day one, all I saw was a sea of white faces. Often kids are unaware of the stupidity of adults and my brothers and I took to the streets and played around without a care in the world. My first realisation that things wouldn't go so easily with our new neighbours came a few weeks after moving in.

I was in the back yard playing with a dirty old football, lost in my childish thoughts. About six at the time, I was already keen on sports. My eyes didn't leave that ball as I balanced and booted it around. Suddenly, I had the eeriest sensation of being watched. Slowly I gazed upwards to find a whole row of pasty-white faces staring at me, as if I was in a zoo, along the fence. As the years went by, this was a feeling that was to become all too familiar. One of the adults was even pointing directly at me.

As a black child, I was cute but deadly, clearly an object of curiosity and revulsion at the same time. Possibly the only black faces these people had ever seen were on television. Not on mainstream shows and certainly not presenting the news, though. Blacks on TV were usually servants and slaves – bit parts in *Tarzan* movies. Worse still, every Saturday night we had the indignity of the BBC's *Black and White Minstrel Show*, during which white singers and dancers 'blacked-up' to play us. Those were surreal times, indeed.

I wasn't 'blacked-up', though: I was for real. And I was their neighbour. The looks on the faces along that fence spoke of falling property values and fears for their daughters. They were right to worry about the latter, maybe the former too. Guys like me, once we got out of short trousers, would leave coffee-coloured babies all over Coventry. White mothers would hold their heads in shame at what their daughters pushed in their prams, but that was way ahead in my future.

Smiling awkwardly, I looked back at the white faces. I was just a youngster with no idea how much hatred and loathing was behind those curious eyes. My mother must have seen this scene unfold from the kitchen, where she was probably re-washing the cups and saucers I'd cleaned in an attempt to get on her right side.

She rushed out and put on her poshest Jamaican accent:

'Git away, this is the Christie residence!'

In an instant, they popped out of view.

Me and my brothers and sisters came up with nicknames for our new neighbours based on the colour of their cars. So, there was blue man, yellow lady and so on. It was pretty inoffensive stuff. What we didn't realise was that our neighbours in turn were thinking of nicknames for us, also based on colour and not quite so inoffensive. The first whiff of trouble came from a nasty family (we'll call them the Pughs in the hope that they've cleaned up their act in the last thirty years).

The son in that brood took to jumping on our fence and shouting 'Nigger!' at the top of his voice. He would then speed off as fast as his little legs could carry him, down through the so-called 'entries' – the grassed-over alleyways behind our houses. In the years ahead, this hidden world was where all our fights and alter-cations would take place.

The Pugh kid's behaviour made me start to realise that my life would be one long battle against hatred. If I went outside, net curtains twitched feverishly in the neighbouring houses. Looking up quickly, I'd see a white face at a window rapidly disappear, a glimpse of fear in their eyes. Initially, this bugged me but then, realising it wasn't going to change, I secretly started to enjoy their rage; the illogical pain these people were inflicting on themselves. Shame they decided to inflict it on us as well.

Day after day, the Christies were out in the yard, playing. At this point, I should introduce my brothers and sisters. As I have already mentioned, Desmond was my oldest brother and he would be the first to leave home. Like me, he entered the boxing ring and won three big fights, but his career never took off, unlike mine. Des was always a wheeler-dealer, with a scheme on his mind to make money and improve himself.

As a kid, he got mixed up in petty crime and spent a short spell in borstal. I would visit him behind bars and ask what it was like, while thinking it would be hell on earth, of course. Des would smirk and lean back. 'Like being on holiday', he'd reply. 'Room to yourself, good mates, regular meals, colour telly, lots of activities and the warders are quite nice.' No wonder he kept going back.

Michael was the next oldest. He had a mild voice and a mature outlook, definitely the sanest of us all, with a droll sense of humour. We needed to laugh at the dreadfulness of our predicament, so I resorted to corny gags and goofing around while Michael would make sarcastic observations.

Once in my teens, after I'd demolished a racist with my fists, I was briefly terrified by the brutality of what I'd done. I remember Michael put his hand on my shoulder and on looking down at the mess, observed: 'Well, you did hit him rather hard.' Then he unveiled a wonderful smile – his smiles made even the worst situations seem all right. Today, there's a church congregation in Tottenham, north London, that's lucky to have him as their minister.

Wesley was next oldest and the brother who came closest to matching my achievements in boxing. Like Des, he too ended up in borstal and adapted to the system as best he could. But that spell inside messed up his early career in the ring. Boxing requires an almost military discipline, which I had and always felt my older brother lacked. He did become British Welterweight Champion under the name 'Lloyd Christie' but later sank into obscurity. Now he owns a scrap-yard.

The next brother down in age was me and what marked me out early on was a willingness to open doors that were supposed to be closed to black kids like us – which led me to the door of the Territorial Army on one occasion. Confronted by a scruffy ghetto boy, they didn't even bother with the niceties.

'What are you doing here?' barked the white officer. If he hadn't been in a uniform with epaulettes and officer's stripes, I'd have done to him what I did to anybody who talked like that to me on the streets. Needless to say, I never got near their parade ground.

Then there was Andy. We were close as little kids, inseparable even. In our earliest years at infant school, I had to drag him to the gates when the bullying in the playground got too much. I'd try and guide him, keep his spirits up, and the two of us would fight the bullies, shoulder to shoulder. But eventually he reacted to the unrelenting hostility we faced as a family by hanging out with the local bad boys; becoming a bit of a tearaway led to him being placed in care.

Andy was fostered by a white couple and rejected his own family name: 'I'm not a Christie,' he once announced to me. For a while, he was hardly able to accept Mum as his real mother. That was unacceptable to me: even though she made many mistakes, Mum also fought night and day for us. Often there was no money or food in the house, but she kept the Christie family going.

Next down was Annette. My poor sister. Back then, things looked promising. She was intelligent and quick with her wits. Her school essays were brilliant and she seemed in possession of more brain cells than all her brothers put together. In my scrapbooks from those years, I've still got an essay that she wrote in her fifth year, when she was about fifteen years old, on Martin Luther King:

> Now, after 400 years of slavery, black people are still looked down upon, they are still not completely free. They are free from chains and from working in the fields from the crack of dawn until the sun goes down. White people cannot emancipate their minds to come to terms with the idea that black people are equal.

But whereas boxing was to come along and give us boys an escape, a means of venting our aggression and frustration, no such avenue opened up for Annette: she had to cope with the anger that all of us felt on her own. Eventually, in later life, this anger would boil over in public and she would be forced to accept professional help. All that rage just had nowhere to go. It must have hardly helped that insanity was clearly typed into the Christie DNA.

The youngest Christie was Simon. He didn't get off to the greatest start in life with Mum frequently announcing at a decibel-shattering level that she 'wished he had never been born.'

One sibling I haven't mentioned was the oldest – Paulette – but she wasn't an official member of the Christie family. Paulette had been born to my mum out of wedlock by another man before she'd met my dad. For years, I thought this was the reason my old man was so callous and hateful towards my mother: the knowledge that she'd given another man a child. Only when my father was dying did I ask him about it and he admitted that he'd always known about Paulette from the start, but wasn't bothered.

One day, when I was little, there was a huge commotion at home as we all got into Dad's car and bombed down to the airport to pick up a new arrival from Jamaica. This was when I first discovered the existence of my half-sister. Paulette stayed with us for a while, but she was already an adult woman. The chaotic home life in Cheveral Avenue wasn't to her taste and she soon packed her bags and left.

Her route out of Cheveral Avenue was to find a man to marry, someone who would support her. When the wedding came, we were invited, though I couldn't help feeling it was under duress. There was just this sneaking suspicion that Paulette was ashamed of us. Years later, I knocked on her door to see if her attitude had changed, but was greeted with a look of ill-disguised horror.

As small kids then, me and my brothers and sisters made a rapid impression on the neighbourhood. Most of them expressed their hostility with tightly contorted mouths, crossing to the other side of the road when they saw us coming or addressing us like simpletons, but one neighbour made it crystal-clear exactly what he thought of us.

Brooksy was ugly: exceedingly fat and very racist. Physically, he bore a passing resemblance to Yogi Bear, only not so loveable. He was a man in his mid-fifties, who wasn't in the least bit proud of his appearance. The word 'slob' wouldn't do justice to this monster.

Our first encounter came during a football game we were playing in the entries: kicking a ball round, shouting to each other to pass it. I must have been about eight or nine years old at the time:

''Ere, Mike!'

'On the head, Des!'

'Pass it, Wes!'

'Gooooaaaaal!'

The entries were supposed to give access to local residents' cars and delivery vans, but Brooksy had somehow managed to build two garages across one of those alleys. Whether or not he had planning permission remains a mystery to me. Even now, despite him pushing up daisies somewhere, his garages still live on, blocking all traffic behind Cheveral Avenue.

Confronted with this obstacle, we used those garages as the back of the goalmouth. Wes or me, or Andy would stand in front of the doors and try and block the ball. If it got through our legs or slipped out of our hands, it would smash loudly against the garage doors. At some point, Brooksy decided he could no longer stand to listen to the sound of a ball thwacking. I can imagine him indoors, his eyes bulging with rage as he heard us laughing and shouting. From his house, he emerged like a bear from its cave, his hairy gut wobbling from under a filthy T-shirt and accentuated by tight, cut-away khaki fatigues.

'Kick that fucking ball against my garage one more time, you little black cunts!'

We hardly needed a second invitation.

Thwack!

Then, from his khakis Brooksy pulled out a small shiny object. My heart began to pound. In his hand was some sort of penknife. I couldn't make it out properly. None of us had any idea what he was about to do. We just stood there, rooted to the spot. Briefly, the blade glistened in the afternoon sun, before it was plunged, deep into our football.

Brimming with indignation, I asked, 'Why did you do that?'

'What you gonna do about it, Nigger?' responded our local, joyless ogre.

It was a declaration of war: Brooksy turned a cheerful, carefree youngster into a mini-Malcolm X. To hell with our stupid, bigoted neighbours – 'The only thing that power understands is power,' as the great man once said. Our abusers couldn't be reasoned with: they hadn't started out by trying to talk to us as equals, so they'd determined their own fate. From that moment on, every racist who crossed my path would come to wish they'd walked another way.

Brooksy had bitten off more than even he could possibly chew. For the next few years, we would clamber loudly over his selfishly constructed garages, making the maximum amount of noise. Increasingly demented, the man would pound out of his house, screaming: 'Get off there, you little apes!' He'd try to run, but we could always out-run him.

'I'll 'ave you, you fucking dirty sambos!'

But the more abuse he hurled, the greater the grief that he got. Brooksy just kept upping the ante and so we responded in kind.

Generally, my parents never got directly involved. Of course, they had battles of their own to fight, but one episode forced Dad to leap to my defence. It all started with a father and son, who took to insulting us daily.

I'd be walking through the entries and hear a racial taunt, which I tried to ignore, but then the kid's father would join in. Unbelievable though this may seem, a grown man would come out of his back yard and start telling me, a small child, just what he thought of me. Of course, all the words related to my skin colour.

On one particular day, my dad – who was on the other side of the fence in our back yard – heard every word. I'd never seen him challenge another adult physically; normally, he would be far too busy beating up his own family to start fights with other people, but this incident had provoked him.

He stormed into the entries and grabbed the older racist, slamming him against Brooksy's garage door. To this day, I can only remember my father's mouth moving and loud sounds coming out, but what they were, I cannot recall. However, shortly afterwards, another white neighbour, Mrs Duckett – who was a decent woman – breathlessly informed my mother that the father and son had moved out of the area, cursing the Christies as they went.

'We're gonna live somewhere there's no niggers.'

Even Mrs Duckett seemed to think this might be a vain hope, especially on their money. The smartest areas of Britain might have been free of black faces in the 1970s, but many working-class neighbourhoods were already showing worrying signs of multiculturalism – at least for the likes of that twosome.

'They'll have to go very far away,' Mrs Duckett opined.

For a family of Jamaican extraction, religion and superstition were always close to the surface. Hell and brimstone Christianity mixed with old African beliefs. Many black people clung to this stuff, feeling it was a source of strength when the outside world was so full of hate but for me, it often seemed yet another burden.

Many Jamaicans – maybe most – believed and still do believe in 'duppies'. When your parents or other family die, they don't just stick around in the ground and rot: as poltergeists, they return to plague you, criticise what you're doing, offer advice, curse you or just make a general nuisance of themselves. As I wasn't born in Jamaica, I found myself part of a new generation of blacks in Britain that rolled our eyes at this mumbo jumbo. But Mum would frequently drone on about the duppies she'd run into. After meeting them, she'd have premonitions of things about to happen in our lives: 'Mi left eye a-jumpin', mi head a-itchin', I had a dream ... a dream.'

'Shut up, Mum,' I'd respond, very unsympathetically. This talk bugged me. 'You're supposed to be a Christian and you're going on about them things, enough of that rubbish.'

Her belief in duppies presented an extra layer of nonsense to deal with at home: the living proved enough of a problem in Cheveral Avenue without the dead joining us as well. It might have been tolerable, had Mum's premonitions had been in any way useful, like which horse would win the Grand National, but they were always over things that seemed totally useless to me.

Only on one occasion did I come anywhere near close to believing in duppies. It was the middle of the night and I was a small kid, maybe eight or nine. We had three bedrooms in the house – one for Mum and Dad, another for Annette and Paulette (when she was there), and a third, incredibly cramped space, which all the brothers shared. Two bunk beds were crammed in to accommodate us. I slept on a lower bunk and it was on the edge of this bed that I woke up in the dead of night to find a giant figure sitting by my feet.

In the shadows, this great mound squatted motionless on my bed, causing the mattress to slope slightly. Its body was hot and it breathed deeply and restlessly, like a malevolent Buddha. I said nothing, but slowly and quietly, I pulled the sheets up over my head and prayed it would go away. Fear gripped me so power-fully that I wet myself, literally soaking the mattress.

As they say in Jamaica: 'Duppy know who fi frighten an' who fi tell good night.'

Morning came and Dad walked into the bedroom, smelt the piss and went mad. In a rage I'd never seen, he grabbed my arm and dragged me to the bathroom, filled the bath with ice-cold water and threw me in.

'Dat teach you to piss di bloody bed!'

As I stood shivering with a towel round my middle, what I hadn't realised was that the big fat duppy I'd encountered had been Dad. He didn't know that, either. In some sort of schizophrenic trance, he'd wandered into our bedroom, as if sleepwalking. Of course, he couldn't remember a thing, but now I found myself punished for the terror he'd inflicted on me.

Funnily enough, Dad was convinced there was a duppy in the house. He swore he could hear it poking around the garage at night. It just so happened that my brothers and me had our bedroom above the garage. Looking back, I wonder if he'd gone into our room to listen to the duppy below, then forgot why he was there.

In a way, Dad was correct: there was indeed a presence in the garage, one that lumbered about and bumped into things. It was my oldest brother Des, sneaking back in after a night on the town. When I got older and started clubbing, my port of entry would be the living-room window, but Des was too big to squeeze his fat arse in that way and so the garage became his preferred route. That was Dad's duppy then – drunken Des staggering around.

So much for Jamaican superstition, but there was also Christianity to contend with. Hell was something our family already knew a lot about – we lived it on a daily basis. Still, it seemed we had still more to learn on a Sunday; that's the way our parents had been brought up. The longest day of the week kicked off with us kids grouped round my parents' bed, reading the Bible out loud, especially the bits about hellfire raining down on sinners, all that sort of thing. Then off to church we went, from ten in the morning until three in the afternoon.

Choosing which church to attend was a less-than-godly experience. When we first got to Coventry, the Methodists seemed like a good idea. Their church was in nearby Beake Avenue but there was only one problem – it was slap-bang in the midst of enemy territory, the natural habitat of skinheads, boot boys, National Front supporters and white people who just didn't seem to like black folk very much.

Germans to the left and Germans to the right, I used to say. By 'Germans', I meant those Nazis that the Luftwaffe appeared to have left behind in Coventry when they dropped their bombs – only they wore Union Jacks now, not swastikas. Those members of the local 'master race' coined plenty of terms for us – 'nigger', 'coon', 'sambo', 'wog' – so I felt entitled to select at least one word for them: 'Germans'.

That was my pet term for the city's racists. You must remember that the Second World War had only ended twenty-five years before and we all grew up on a diet of evil Nazis in war movies and comics. As a small child, it seemed to me that the villains who made our lives a misery must also be Germans. No offence to non-racist readers from today's Germany, I've been to that country and I know most people there are decent and tolerant.

But back to Beake Avenue, where tolerance was not on the agenda. The road ran parallel to Cheveral Avenue so we could hardly avoid it but in the 1970s, walking down Beake Avenue was more like running a gauntlet of racist abuse. As a family, we soon learnt to keep constantly vigilant as we walked down that thoroughfare, sticking to the middle of the road.

The reason for avoiding the pavement was that some folks took to setting their dogs on us. However, that could not be allowed to stop us: if we were to get to the Methodist Church and do some praising of the Lord, we'd just have to risk a mauling. So, on the day of our first and last visit to the church, we put on what passed for our Sunday Best, took a deep breath and walked down Beake Avenue, trying to look as much as possible like ordinary folk. But it wasn't long before our worst fears were realised and a snarling canine was let loose on Dad. In vain, he tried to wave away the mad mutt, his fingers perilously close to its sharp teeth.

After what seemed a very long walk, but was only ten minutes or so, we arrived at what we thought would be our new place of worship. From inside, we could hear the congregation singing like a host of angels. Truly, this must be a House of God. As we walked in, the whole place ground to a halt. As the singing ceased, faces confronted us in awkward embarrassment, an expression I'd come to know well: lacking the courage to tell us to get lost, but showing us we weren't at all welcome. These weren't angels at all, but German devils – and there were pews full of them. But we couldn't retreat. Mum and Dad acted as if everything was perfectly normal, shuffling into a pew at the back with the rest of us in tow. We were the picture of misery.

The next Sunday came around and by this time my parents had discovered a church where black people could get down to some serious praising of the Lord without feeling embarrassed. This denomination was called the Church of God. It offered everything you could expect from Caribbean Christianity: ecstatic expressions of love for Jesus, lots of singing, hell-fire preaching, speaking in tongues … and people dressed in their finest, all of them looking down scornfully on us Christie kids.

At the Methodist Church, they didn't like our colour. In the Church of God, they didn't approve of our clothes. I knew what they were calling us behind our backs:

'Ragamuffins.'

'Them kids, dressed so bad.'

Even as a little boy I found their snobbery hypocritical. From what I'd read in the Bible, we were dressed humbly, just like Jesus and his disciples – not as if we were on a catwalk, like the rest of the pious Pharisees around us. On the Christie pew, there were no sharp suits, fancy dresses or big, colourful hats: we were poor and it showed, especially to our own community. Not that my mother realised this. In our shabby Sunday best, she saw a bunch of kids who were well turned-out, worth a million dollars:

'Nobody guwine trouble you, so long unu trousers pressed, unu clothes clean. You shoes shine.'

The Church of God's five-hour 'Lawd'-praising marathon was led by the high-and-mighty Elder Nicely, the big 'I am'. Dressed in a huge cape that billowed out as it caught any gust of air, he was flamboyant with words and in love with the sound of his own voice. From an early age, he got on my nerves but he worked that congregation to a frenzy until all around us the speaking in tongues began.

Sister Kenyon would be the first touched by the spirit: her body would start to heave rhythmically – and she wasn't small, more big and strong than big and fat. We would move out of the way as this giant pressure cooker prepared to blow, her face full of sublime bliss as she sensed heaven could be that bit closer.

A cheerful, light-skinned lady, who was normally so mild-mannered, Sister Kenyon transformed once the Holy Spirit got a firm grip. Lurching to the left in spasms, she'd mutter: ''men, 'men, 'men, 'men, 'men …' Eventually, I realised this was short for 'Amen'. Then Sister Walker, a very religious woman, would be infected with the same zeal. Every week, she started to chant: 'Hipopopopopopo, hipopopopopo, hipopopopopo …' To this day, I have no idea what she meant but we never sat in her seat just in case we caught 'hipopopopopo'.

So, on one side we were hemmed in by ''men, 'men, 'men …' and on the other by 'hipopopopopo'. Just as we thought things couldn't get any crazier, Deacon Kennedy would leap into the aisle with his mouth organ and start playing like he was possessed. This got everybody around us clapping and chanting, 'Jesus, Jesus, Jesus …'

But I couldn't take any of it seriously. Where I got my cynicism from, I don't rightly know, but I soon realised I wanted no part of this. What I disliked most was the people, those snobs with their high and mighty view of themselves, the same people who gazed down on us Christies with naked contempt.

One woman I did have a soft spot for was Sister Toff. She was enormous – truly, magnificently huge, not unlike the actress Hattie Jacques that we'd see in the *Carry On* films on TV. Dad would give her a lift to church in his beaten-up Wolseley 1660 and then 'cuss afterwards about the damage her weight had done.

'When dat woman in di car, whole of car just gone down – broke up me suspension. Dat bloody woman grine broke mi car!'

The only time I heard Elder Nicely crack a joke was about Sister Toff: 'I hear that Sister Toff is going to Jamaica … I bet it's by Jumbo.'

And that was about as funny as Elder Nicely got. Here was a man who could have been a role model for the ultra-strict, often violent Jamaican fathers sitting in front of him. If he'd wanted, he could have infused those hard bastards with the milk of human kindness but the reality was he was exactly like them, capable of beating his own child as hard as the next man.

On a ledge along the front of his lectern rested a baton. This Man of God called it the 'rod of correction'. One day I saw it come into full use: his own son was messing about in the church, innocently ignoring his old man up above. Elder Nicely's eyes blazed with a godly fury – and plenty of righteousness, of course. The rod of correction was grasped and down it came towards his boy. Within seconds, he was beating the living daylights out of the kid in front of the whole hall.

The lesson that Sunday was that if it was good enough for Elder Nicely to beat his own kid, then it was good enough for everybody else. Not that my dad needed any education on the subject – he already had beating us down to a fine art.

Of course, there had to come a point when the Christies would fall foul of Elder Nicely and sweets proved our undoing. Every week, Mum used to give us a few pence to put in the collection plate but as she and Dad often attended church at a different time to get some peace from us, we'd spend the money on cheap, sugary candy instead: tooth-rotting crap packed with additives and E-numbers that any 1970s' British sweet shop sold for next to nothing; sherbet dips and flying saucers, stuff that fizzed and dissolved in your mouth.

During one of Elder Nicely's never-ending sermons, Simon and Annette sneaked off to buy some sweets from a nearby shop. With the church packed to the rafters, he didn't notice them go, but it was a hot day and the main doors were swung open, allowing a clear view from the lectern to the road outside. So, while he hadn't seem them leave, Elder Nicely certainly saw them sneak back, clambering through the fence that ringed the church outside. He was in the middle of a Bible passage at the time.

'And then the Lord said ... A-who dat a gu through the fence?'

The congregation looked up, confused by this deviation from the words of the Good Book, but Nicely was no longer reading from the Holy Scripture: he was pointing angrily at the two little devils outside. Sister Garvey was always eager to please the Elder and do his bidding. A short woman with a chubby face, who definitely felt she was a cut above the Christies, she waddled rapidly out of the church, shouting behind her to the big man.

'I'll get them, Elder ... I'll get them, Elder ...'

Moments later, she returned and marched down the aisle with a lollipop held high like it was a trophy.

'I got it, Elder ... I got it!'

Behind her, nervously sucking on his thumb, walked my brother Simon and sister Annette, about to feel her spirit crushed a little further by these oh-so righteous people. They were made to stand in front of a very disapproving throng and received a sound telling-off from Elder Nicely. During this humiliation, my youngest brother just concentrated on his thumb, but Annette reacted with a vacant stare as she desperately tried to screen out what was happening. Meanwhile, all those finely dressed Christians just stared, their hate-filled eyes boring into the two young children.

'It's them Christies again.'

Us Christies – the ragamuffins.

Needless to say, those same Christians made sure my parents, who were both working that day, found out about Simon and Annette's 'terrible' crime of buying sweets instead of speaking in tongues. Mum and Dad would have been crushed by the weight of disapproval from the high and mighty types at the Church: that night, there was even more hollering than usual from the house in Cheveral Avenue.

Anybody who truly turns their back on religion will always remember the moment when they stopped believing, the fateful day when they and their church parted company. For me, the last straw was the incident with the grass snake.

We were only halfway through another five hours of torture when an unwelcome guest slithered into the church from the garden outside. At first, the finely dressed ladies and the big 'I am' at the front didn't notice the small (and very foolish) grass snake. A crescendo of 'Praise the Lawd!' was building and they'd started speaking in tongues. Then one of the ladies spotted the creature and let out an ear-splitting scream. Like Moses with a mission, Elder Nicely descended from his lectern. Down the aisle his big form thundered until he confronted the dumb creature. Without a second's thought, he crashed his foot down on the snake's head, killing it instantly. Turning triumphantly to the congregation, he boomed: 'Today, yes, today ... we have killed Satan!'

It's difficult to express what I felt. As Elder Nicely removed his well-polished boot, I gazed down at the dead snake, its tongue pathetically hanging out. If this was the Lord of Darkness, I couldn't imagine what all the fuss was about. Satan, it seemed, could be defeated with a big foot.

'Amen!'

'We have killed Satan!'

'Amen!'

My jaw dropped in disbelief. Truly, this had been a snake in the wrong place at the wrong time – minding its own business only to be brutally killed in a place of love. Those big people who bored holes in my siblings and me over our ragamuffin clothes were completely, barking mad, I concluded.

Of course, the fate of the snake should have been enough to convince me that the milk of human kindness did not flow through the Church of God, but somehow I needed one more proof and this I got closer to home. Like many black Christian families, we regularly trooped off to religious conventions to be yelled at in a huge auditorium. Every year, a big meeting took place at an enormous venue in Birmingham that had been bought by the Church of God. All the ministries from the Midlands would pour in and there would be the usual singing, with every minister taking their turn to preach. People would get up on stage and be touched to be cured, too.

With all the screaming and shouting going on, I often wondered what any white people wandering past would have thought was going on inside – a voodoo ceremony, perhaps? But this was Christianity, our style: a little bit of Africa and Jamaica in a British street.

Eventually, the founder of the church – Bishop Dunne – would take to the stage amid massive cheers like a second coming. His would be the set-piece session of preaching, whipping up the crowd to maximum frenzy, after which he got round to the subject of money. He wasn't going to save our souls free of charge: like the rest of us, the Church had their own bills to pay.

But no spirit was going to take me over: I hated the whole

experience and counted the hours until the ordeal was over. It wasn't just the event itself, but the journey there and back in Dad's Wolseley, all of us crammed inside and getting progressively grouchier. On one trip back to Coventry, it became clear that the old man had no idea where he was going; his mind was in its usual state of confusion and unrest. To add to Dad's already irritable mood, my older brother Des was attempting to give him directions by making gestures with his hands. Pointing and waving mainly, he was trying as hard as he could to get through to him that he was on the wrong road.

I noticed my dad's increasingly furious eyes focus on my brother's hands. I'm not sure what he was seeing, inside that crazy head of his: something obscene, maybe? Perhaps he thought Des was mocking him. Whatever it was, he suddenly rounded on Des and hit him very hard. That shut my brother up and his hands fell to his lap. We drove on, but it soon became clear we were still hopelessly lost.

Now my mother chirped up: 'Lawd Jesus, Ralph! Me tell you which way fi [to] gu … Me tell you already which way fi gu … Lawd Jesus!'

The 'Lawd Jesus' routine went on for quite some time and now it was Mum's turn to get Dad's evil eye. Ramming his foot on the brake and breathing very heavily, he gave his wife her marching orders: 'Git out of the bloody car, birdie!' That was his nickname for her. It was never a particularly affectionate one, just a word he used for Mum. For a few seconds, she sat paralysed and then he repeated himself. Meekly, she stepped out of the Wolseley … and then he drove off.

I gazed back at my mother on the pavement of a street somewhere outside Birmingham, but was helpless to make Dad stop. He just snarled at the wheel: 'Dat bloody woman!' Somehow, Mum made her way back to Coventry. We'd already been back for hours and were sitting in the living room when the key announcing her return rattled in the front door. She walked into the living room, sat down and said nothing.

The tension was too much for me to bear and so I crept upstairs to my bedroom, wondering if this was any way for Christians to behave. On the way upstairs, I caught sight of that blond Jesus yet again, the one who never seemed to help us out: a Jesus who seemed curiously out of place hanging on a wall in Cheveral Avenue.

Like all kids, I had to attend school from the age of five. Up the road from our house was Hill Farm Junior School, my first experience of education. If we hadn't fully grasped how racist Coventry was before we entered those school gates, it didn't take long afterwards.

On my first day, I walked into the playground with my younger brother, Andy. Even at five years old, I knew the silence didn't bode well for us. As we walked through the sea of staring white faces, I wondered what would happen next. The bell rang and off we went to our first class, but it was when the mid-morning playground break came that all hell broke loose.

'Nigger!'

I found myself scrapping on the ground with the kid who'd let the insult loose from his lips. He turned out to be the son of one of my teachers, which meant I got the biggest telling-off while he received a slap on the wrist. By the end of the first week, my own age group had backed off, realising I was no pacifist. Now it was the turn of the older kids, who decided to kick the back of Andy's and my shins every 'play' break.

Andy didn't want to go back. Years later, Mum told me he cried bitterly whenever he got back home whereas I was much braver. From the name-calling to the kicking, he couldn't stand the treatment we faced in that playground. Even as a five-year-old, I wanted retribution, though.

The next morning, neither Mum nor me could persuade Andy to leave the house. He whined and groaned from the moment he clambered out of his bunk bed. I suppose I understood what he was going through: in that grim little playground, Andy and me couldn't hide what we were, so blending in wasn't an option. There was no corner to hide, nowhere we'd go unnoticed – our identity was there for all to see.

I looked down at my brother: 'It's not good, we gotta face them.'

But he wasn't convinced and so I resorted to some heavy persuasion. Grabbing him, I hauled his little body down to the school gates as he cried and complained all the way: 'Leave me alone, Errol – I don't wanna go!'

Our lives would have become completely unbearable if we hadn't faced up to our new enemies, the little white kids, who brought their parents' prejudices and nasty turns of phrase with them into the playground. Their noses would have to be bloodied, all of them, if need be.

'Nig-nog!' chuckled one kid, as I came through the gates and I marked him down for a date with my fists.

After a few days and several altercations of varying degrees of violence, I got some respect from a surprising quarter. Outside the school, an old white lady approached me with a pasty specimen of a kid. Hopelessly weedy, he had 'bully me' written all over his face. Unexpectedly, she smiled at me and pushed the boy forward: 'Please look after my grandson.'

So, I wasn't just a mini version of Malcolm X fighting a playground battle for civil rights, now I was the defender of downtrodden white kids. This was quite a turn-up for the books. As I took Andy in on one side and the skinny white kid on the other, I beamed with pride: Errol Christie had arrived at junior school.

Meanwhile, Mum was trying to get Simon into Hill Farm Nursery. None of us had been accepted; they had always nodded their heads and claimed there were no vacancies. We didn't hold out much hope until something very significant happened to me at school: I was given some money.

It was a big blue bank note with the Queen beaming out from it – a fiver, to be exact. In 1970, this was a king's ransom for a kid like me. One of the kids had found a wallet stuffed with cash lying in the road. He'd brought it into school and handed out the notes between us. Most of the other kids bolted down the sweet shop, but something about this troubled me: I was no thief. My mother had always told us that if we found any money, we should hand it over to somebody in authority, the reason being that a family poorer than us might have lost it. Imagine how they'd be feeling, she'd say. Sometimes I had the suspicion she really meant us.

And there was another good reason for handing over the money: it was bad enough for the average Briton to be accused of stealing, but in those days most folks just assumed that a black kid was a criminal waiting to happen. We had to operate much higher standards, if we wanted to prove our critics wrong.

Back home, I offered up the lovely blue note: 'Mummy, I got some money.' As my hand uncurled to reveal the booty, she was gob-smacked, truly terrified by what she now saw in front of her.

'Where did you get all that money?'

So, I told her the truth. She hardly slept that night and neither did I. The next morning, Mum strode up to the school with me and asked to see the head teacher. She then handed over the five-pound note and explained what had happened. The Head was speechless and straightaway organised an identity parade of sorts in the playground.

With my entire year standing in a silent and sullen row, I walked past their worried faces and one by one, pointed out the villains. This didn't faze me in the least – I'd made no great friendships in my first few weeks there and shopping the culprits gave me no qualms. My little finger jutted accusingly at the wrongdoers. Then I got to the boy who had found the wallet. My mum's words about the misery that we would have caused to the person who lost all that cash came back to me and so I grabbed the kid's collar.

'It's you, it's you that gave me the money!'

The head teacher was overwhelmed, to put it mildly, by this performance of mine. Gasping for breath, he turned to Mum.

'Oh my God, Mrs Christie – I've never seen a braver boy!'

With that, Simon miraculously gained a place in nursery. The Christies got their reward not in Heaven, but here on Earth. For the briefest of periods, we almost won ourselves some respect in the community, though it wouldn't last long. The biggest satisfaction was being able to return a big chunk of the money to the woman who had lost it. As Mum predicted, it turned out she was poor as a church mouse and carried what little cash she had in the world on her person.

For a while, I dwelt on the moral high ground but it didn't take long for me to screw up. My downfall came through my love of sports. From day one, I'd come to realise that I was an academic disaster area, at least in the eyes of my teachers. At both junior and secondary school, I suspected – as did most black kids in those days – that I'd been written off from the word go as dole fodder or at best, a petrol-pump attendant, so there seemed little point in sweating over my times tables or sticking my nose in a dictionary. Besides, at home there was none of the peace and quiet that would have allowed me to spend hours doing homework. Basically, there was no obvious goal for me to aim for that would have made academic study seem in any way worthwhile.

But where I did excel, and nobody could fault me, was in sports. By the age of seven, I was already making my mark, whether on the hard track and field or on the football pitch. It has to be said, my kit was a bit out of the ordinary, though – there were no cricket whites or football boots with shiny studs for me. Everything, from rugby to the hundred-metre dash, was pretty much done in the same clothes that I wore to walk through the school gates.

On my feet was a pair of completely knackered plimsolls, handed down from one Christie brother to the next. Underneath were some nasty nylon socks that helped the fungus grow between my toes. Often those socks would be one of the lurid numbers that kids wore in the 1970s, a tartan design or chequered. As they were the same socks that I wore all day, my feet must have given off some interesting odours, come home time.

Instead of rugby or football shorts, I'd just wear the knee-high school trousers that I'd arrived in that morning. Covering my top half would be a cheap school shirt with grease marks round the collar, which hung out scruffily after I'd been running about for a while.

During sports, I'd stick around with another black kid called David Nelson and ended up going to his house after school all the time. It was a welcome relief from the atmosphere at Cheveral Avenue. His mum would feed me and I was always made to feel very welcome. Unlike me, he had lots of toys and it was such an escape to play like other kids for a while. It's a pity that I repaid his friendship with dishonesty.

One day, we were both getting changed to play football. For me this meant taking off my shoes and putting on the pair of well-scuffed plimsolls. While sitting next to David, I couldn't take my eyes off some brand-new football boots nearby; the smell of their newness filled my nostrils, the studs gleamed and the laces were undone, almost inviting my feet to step into them. For once,

I thought, I'm going to play football in the right gear.

They were a bit on the small side and a slight squeeze but once on, they were a huge improvement. I stepped onto the pitch feeling like a professional. Instead of slipping around in my usual shabby footwear and struggling to direct the ball to the goal, I now found myself sprinting from one end of the pitch to the other, scoring time after time. Back in the changing room, I decided me and the new boots couldn't part company, not yet, so I took them home. Not just that, but off came the studs and I wore them like shoes all weekend. Little did I know what lay in store for me when I returned to Hill Farm on Monday morning.

As I arrived at the school gates for another week of hell, a group of hysterical white girls gesticulated wildly at me: 'You took them football boots, *you* took them!' Now I was in a blind panic. Fortunately, I hadn't been dumb enough to wear the boots into the playground, but I would have to convince my accusers that I had nothing to do with their disappearance and so I said the first thing that came into my head: 'David Nelson took them.'

And that was that. I'd eaten his food, played with his toys, been treated like a member of his family and the Nelson house had been a place where I could escape after lessons and avoid the hell of home. With one idiotic remark, I'd closed that door for ever. Now David faced the playground inquisition and although he didn't finger me, nor did he forgive me. Being also a black kid, the accusation of theft made his existence a nightmare for a very long time. When his mother found out what I'd done, I was duly banned from ever setting foot in their home again. To this day, I regret that childish act of betrayal, which led to me being denied a little bit of paradise that might have made my childhood more bearable.

With no David to hang out with, I had to find new friends elsewhere in a place that would also appeal to my quest for some order and discipline in life. Which was how I ended up joining the Cub Scouts.

Already I'd seen the Cub Scout badges, recognition for different activities, on kids' uniforms and I suppose this appealed to me because I too wanted to be recognised for something. In the same way that trophies and boxing belts would give me a sense of self-worth later on, those sew-on badges became objects I had to have.

The 8th Pack was based round the corner from our house in a pre-fabricated Nissen hut with the '8th Pack' painted sign hanging over the door. All the other kids had well-laundered green sweaters, crisp neckerchiefs and nicely washed grey woollen socks. As usual, I turned up in my ragamuffin clobber. If this had been the Army, I'd have been a one-man Dirty Dozen.

From the start, the terrible truth began to dawn: me and the 8th Pack would not see eye to eye, even though I gave it my best shot. And the alternative of going back home was too grim to contemplate. One weekend, me and the other Scouts went off to camp in Rough Close, a big stretch of open ground just outside Coventry. Despite its forbidding name, this was a nice area of ancient woodland and so far away from the humdrum streets of Radford that I began to feel that I was finally getting away from the hell of everyday life.

The scout leader gathered us all round. I shouldn't have to say that I was the only black kid in the group and so I stuck out like the sorest of thumbs.

'OK, everybody,' boomed the middle-class man, 'I'd like you to go and find something beginning with the letter "B", anything you can find starting with that letter. But don't stray too far off, back here in thirty minutes.'

I ran off on my own, already taking the challenge seriously and competitively. But I wasn't just hunting an object: I was looking for a bit of glory and acceptance. And then I saw it – a bee, sitting on a flower minding its own business, collecting pollen in its little black legs. A bee, that starts with 'B': my first sew-on badge was in sight.

What I had to do was quickly stun the bee. With a quick-fire flick of my hand, I knocked it out and the bee fell to the ground. Now I incarcerated my victim in a ragged piece of paper and headed back to the scout leader, bursting with pride. All the other kids had returned with bark from trees or a brown leaf. I rolled my eyes at their lack of imagination.

Out came the bee. I held it up, smiling triumphantly, but looking round all I could see were disgust-filled faces. 'Urgh!' said one kid. 'Has he killed it?'

'Thank you, Errol,' the scout leader sneered, before congratulating another kid as he produced yet another piece of tree bark. So, I chucked the bee away.

Sarcasm was a standard weapon of adults in authority over kids in the 1970s. It seemed teachers thought they could retain whatever fragile popularity they might have by singling out a victim for hateful remarks in a way that wouldn't be tolerated today. And so it was with this scout leader, who was about to hand out the money our parents had given us for the weekend. He'd been entrusted with the cash while we went off and played games.

'Darren Smith, five pounds from your mother.' I gulped. Why did a kid need five pounds in the middle of a field? 'Paul Edgar, one pound fifty for you.' And so on, until finally, with a thin-lipped smile, he turned to me and opened out his hand.

'Errol Christie, I've got fifteen pence from your mother.'

Malicious giggles all round. A week later, I defected to the 32nd Pack. In my humble opinion, the 8th Pack could go screw itself. For the 32nd Pack, I was kitted out with a neckerchief and green sweater. I still had my own dodgy shorts and socks, but the top half was pure Cub Scout – even topped off with a cap. If I caught my own reflection from the waist up in a shop window, I could almost delude myself that I was as well dressed as the other kids.

Only having fifteen pence for that weekend with the 8th Pack made me determined to go out and make my own way in the world, to earn some money whatever way I could, and so I got a newspaper round. The shop was in Kersley Village, close to the school, which was near a coalmine and about two miles from Cheveral Avenue. It meant that I could leave school, pick up the huge paper bag – it was nearly as big as me – and start delivering in the direction of my house. The paper round was every weekday, plus weekends. Hulking that huge sack of newspapers around was yet another physical ordeal that toughened up my young body.

It didn't take long for my family to mess things up for me, though. One Saturday, Mum insisted I help her with the shopping and saying 'no' was not an option. Her chores took way too long and I knew I'd be late to pick up the newspaper bag. I needed to get a bus, but found I was half a pence short of the 3p fare. As we came through the door, lugging our shopping, I turned to Dad:

'Daddy, you got half-pee?'

'A-wah you wan half-pee for?'

'Need it for my paper round.'

'Don't be stupid, bloody boy!'

Needless to say, I was fired from my paper round. Now penniless, I was once more completely at the mercy of my parents. Christmas was coming and I wouldn't be buying cards or presents, but that was OK as there would be little in the way of seasonal cheer. As a family we'd sit around wondering which one of us Dad would beat first: our Christmas Day walloping. Which of us brothers would end up hiding under the stairs while a deranged maniac thumped up and down, looking for someone to plant his fists into?

We did get presents of a sort, usually a pair of nylon socks or cheap underpants. But one year Mum produced almost a proper Christmas present, the sort of thing other kids at Hill Farm School would have been getting: a plastic rifle. It came with a set of little plastic rabbits to shoot at. Regrettably, all Dad saw was a new object to hit us with. For whatever reason, he ended up wielding the plastic rifle towards us while we fled in all directions.

'You bloody boy, come here!'

While he was raving downstairs, I went into my sister's room – I figured he wouldn't find me there. I walked over to the window and stared out onto the street. Outside, white kids were playing on their brand new Chopper bikes, doing wheelies and zooming around. Some had new scooters or roller skates, on which they balanced awkwardly, holding onto each other. I was spellbound: this was a different world, one of unlimited consumer goods and endless happiness.

'No, Daddy, nooooooo!'

He'd caught up with Andy or Simon. Pressing my hands and nose to the window, I gazed out at the lucky creatures in a parallel universe to ours and wondered whether I'd ever experience that same carefree joy.

Mum knew our lives were odd, different from our neighbours. She was aware we had all sorts of pressures heaped on us that white families didn't have to endure. We'd walk into a shop and the owner would be on red alert, monitoring our every move, looking forward to the moment we left. I'd go home on a bus and realise the person next to me had edged away as if they might catch 'blackness' by making physical contact. Or I'd stroll into a café – or later in my life, a pub – and an old dear would suddenly pull her handbag closer to her. Our eyes were sensitive to all these things and although we did our best to appear nonplussed, we took offence every time.

The chips on our shoulders grew larger and larger; our tempers became worse and worse. To try and relieve the pressure, one summer Mum decided to take us all to the seaside. This was what ordinary families did, so we should give it a go. From the moment we climbed into the Wolseley and set off, packed in like sardines, I knew it wouldn't end well.

Our destination was Weston-super-Mare: one of those British resorts that was once classy in Victorian times but now it was long past its sell-by date, even in the 1970s. As we drove erratically down the motorway, the heat and smell in the car became too much; I had to throw up by the roadside. Dad hit me for throwing up and then we all got back in and continued our journey, arguing all the way.

Once in Weston-super-Mare, our poverty was made only more obvious. While other kids were enjoying donkey rides and eating ice creams, Dad turned down even the smallest request for money – no rides or ices for us. Instead, we walked aimlessly up and down the Grand Pier and watched the brown sea crash against the rusty iron girders below. Meanwhile, the scent of fish and chips made my tummy grumble – a form of torture I'd never known before.

As the sun grew low in the sky and our day came to a thankful end, my folks wandered off, leaving us siblings to argue among ourselves. It was the usual ding-dongs over nothing important; kicks, shoves and nasty words. But as we got down to our well-rehearsed pattern of bad behaviour, I caught something out of the corner of my eye, something I'd never witnessed before and would never see again. In front of the sea, Mum and Dad stood motionless. Maybe they were wondering why they'd ever come to the mother country. The sun sank a little lower and a cold, sharp breeze was picking up. Without looking at each other, my totally worn-out parents suddenly held hands. For just a couple of seconds, Dad's big round hand clasped Mum's before they fell apart again. My mother stared down gloomily at the wooden pier planks.

'Time to gu back.'

Once more, we climbed into the creaking old jalopy and resumed our family arguments; every so often Dad's fist would sail into the back seat to try and catch one of us. My mother's face was far away, her eyes lifeless: for just one single day, she'd tried to make us a regular family and failed completely.

2

STREET FIGHTING

'I have to carry a knife
Because there's people threatening my life
I can't dress just the way I want
I'm being chased by the National Front ...'

'Concrete Jungle' – The Specials

'Run!'

We'd hardly left the school gates. I grabbed Andy and pulled him along as fast his feet would take him.

'Oi, nig-nogs!'

Some of the skinheads chasing us weren't even our own age or just a couple of years older – they were grown men, out to batter two little kids on account of their skin colour. Heart pumping and my body exploding with adrenalin, I took a quick look back. All I could see was a mass of bomber jackets, tight bleached jeans, big white lace-up ox-blood coloured Doc Martens and skinhead haircuts. Piggy little eyes and pasty skins, some of them were covered in acne – none of the boot boys were what you might call a pretty sight.

This was no joke, no pretence. If they caught up with us, I knew their fists and boots would fly without restraint, there would be no mercy or reasoning with them. Their hatred of us, even at eight years of age, was total. In their pubs and in their homes, they ranted about how we were taking their jobs, bringing their property prices down; that we were fucking their sisters and littering their city with coffee-coloured babies. But more than anything else, like a Stone Age tribe they saw us as outsiders who must be beaten down, sent back to wherever we'd come from.

'Run, you fucking sambos!'

Past the familiar houses we panted. Andy always wanted to stop, somehow hoping they wouldn't really smash us up, but I knew better: we had to keep on moving. It wasn't far to Cheveral Avenue now. I was panting so hard my throat was burning. Andy was close to tears, his skinny legs buckling. Only when we got through the front door could we hope to be safe.

The Radford Boot Boys were cowards who operated in packs and terrorised us every day. The only good thing they ever did was to erode my fear of fighting bigger men. When I was older and strong enough to stand my ground and take them on, I was thumping skinheads five or ten years older than me but, as a small boy in shorts, I had to keep running.

For Des, it was different. My oldest brother was able to tackle them but he had height, stamina and age on his side. One day, when I was about eight years old and he was fifteen, we were walking along the entries behind our house. The weeds had grown ridiculously tall. With my shorts on, I needed to avoid the stinging nettles that had sprung up everywhere. Some locals had dumped their rubbish nearby and I briefly spied a rat scurrying off, but then a much larger rodent appeared: a Radford boot boy on his own, hands in his pockets, looking cocky as hell. Even though he was without his mates, he clearly believed he was untouchable. As he approached, his swagger became more pronounced as if to make it crystal clear that he was the boss, not us. Then his mouth snarled open: 'Black cunts!'

Like he was saying good afternoon. This was coupled with a shoulder barge, which briefly tipped Des sideways. My brother didn't need further provocation. Soon the two of them were trading punches while I aimed a few kicks at the boot boy with my little legs. I wasn't doing him much damage, as I recall.

Desmond was very strong. Gripping the teenage racist in a headlock, he began to squeeze till a strange gurgling sound was emitted. Then he let go and the skinhead spewed up over the nettles. Crimson in the face, his veins bulged and he was shaking like a leaf. Looking up from his vomit, he tried to make sense of what had happened: a black kid lashed back instead of meekly accepting the insult. I could tell by the look on his face, even at that young age, just how horrified he was that we Christies didn't seem to know our place. Des gestured to me to leave him among the nettles and the mess that he'd made.

We saw this creature many times over the years, him and all the other thugs who infested the area around Radford's Jubilee Crescent, their base of operations. As a black kid, you knew that if you walked down Jubilee Crescent, you were courting danger, big time. One of the ringleaders was a bloke I'm going to call 'Dennis'. He was at least ten years older than me, though mentally, probably younger.

Dennis and his gang soon found a new way to strike fear into us. Walking through the entries with Andy another afternoon, I suddenly became aware of a buzzing sound, like a load of electric sewing machines. It was getting closer. Darting round, I saw six or seven 50cc motorbikes heading towards us, a snarling boot boy astride each one. They were chanting their usual war cries:

'We're gonna fuckin' kill the coons!'

'Look at them black bastards leggin' it.'

'Go on, Dennis – run 'im over.'

Andy and I bolted into our back yard and then the house, thinking this would be the end of it. But on that day, we were very wrong – they were getting bolder. The gate from the entries to the back yard burst open and in they came on their bikes, whizzing round the small garden, tearing down my mum's washing. Knickers, socks and a couple of bed sheets ended up covered in dirt on the ground. Even to a battle-scarred kid like myself, it felt like the end of the world.

Having come into our back yard, I wondered if the house might be next. Would I find myself barricaded in our cramped bedroom while a gang of skins tried to smash the door down? For the next few days, sleep was impossible as I struggled with images that became progressively worse. The skinheads, I concluded, were going to lynch us.

A little while later, Mum and Dad had some relatives round from Birmingham. The adults were having tea and some Jamaican food, as well as rum punch. For once, they seemed to be enjoying themselves. Bored by the adults' conversation, Andy and me retreated to the back yard to kick a ball about. I then became aware of a threatening presence which announced itself in the form of four or five boot boys storming through the back yard gate towards us. The two of us were trapped and encircled.

I just accepted that at last the boot boys were going to do whatever it was they'd been longing to do; all the frantic running we'd done from the school gates back to Cheveral Avenue had been futile. Now they'd well and truly caught up with us. Boot-boy justice was about to be meted out on us niggers. That was until the rescue squad appeared. Maybe Mum had seen what was going on outside and raised the alarm, I don't know, but the kitchen door burst open and several middle-aged, pot-bellied black men marched out. For a brief second, the skinheads laughed, convinced they posed no threat but they didn't laugh for long.

Dennis squared up to my dad without realising he was dealing with an enraged, undiagnosed schizophrenic with the worst temper of any black man who ever lived. Before the hooligan knew what hit him, Dad grabbed him by the throat and then threw him to the ground like a bag of rubbish. Seeing their leader manhandled was enough to send the others scooting off back to the entries on their bikes.

It wasn't often that I regarded my father in a heroic light, but right then it felt as if he had finally earned the right to lord it over us like a tyrant. Not only had Dad cleared our property of fascists, he'd also earned the Christie name a little more respect among the low life. His actions were to give us the briefest of reprieves as they licked their wounds.

A few weeks later one of the skins who had invaded our back yard was killed in a hit-and-run almost right outside our house. Years later, Mum heard that some of the locals believed we had cast a few spells. The word went round that the Christie family had summoned up the voodoo curse, black magic or whatever you want to call it. As a result, one of the skins was flattened underneath the wheels of a passing car. If only all our problems could have been solved so easily.

Meanwhile, the torment at Hill Farm was coming to an end and the next place to fail me educationally was to be President Kennedy Secondary School. My older brothers had attended Coundon Court School and bloodied so many faces that the family name was to become a byword for psychotic violence. No doubt the boys were duly provoked but Mum was naturally keen to send me to a place where the name 'Christie' might not inspire blind fear or hatred.

She was to be disappointed, of course. Things had changed since that first day at Hill Farm. Not only had I notched up a string of fights in the playground and even some on the streets but I'd started my boxing as well. From the age of eight, I was wearing wraps and gloves at a local factory gym – any kid at my new school who fancied taking me on was in for a nasty surprise.

Once the word went round that I was a boxer, my peers kept well away. At thirteen years of age, the playground buzzed with the news that I had become Schoolboy Champion of England. Of course this was an invite to every kid older than me to try their luck so the years at President Kennedy became one long scrap.

Looking down at my hands now, I still proudly sport a small scar in one of my knuckles, where I removed one older kid's tooth. My fist went into his mouth and when it re-emerged, one of his teeth was standing upright, embedded in my hand. I pulled it out and handed it back. He could explain to the tooth fairy what had happened.

The main cause for these fights was the explicitly racial taunts. There was no reason to be subtle: the TV programmes at the time were full of comedians making jokes about people like me. 'There was this nigger, right …' Or they could go to a working men's club and hear the same gags, this time undiluted: 'Bloody coons, right … I tell ya …' 'What do you call a black man who laughs – a snigger!'

One of the most-watched sitcoms on the box was *Love Thy Neighbour*. In theory, it was a parody of a thick white lump living next to a bright black guy who outfoxes him every time. But the dialogue given to the white character included liberal use of the word 'sambo' and just got mimicked around the playground. None of the junior school appreciated the irony of the situation or that the sitcom writers' intentions might not have been racist. Instead, they saw it as yet another licence to come into the play-ground the next day and call me all sorts: 'You randy nig-nog!', 'Ignorant sambo!' and even 'Black troublemaker!'

Always, there was one quote from *Love Thy Neighbour* that stuck in my head: 'Look at Tarzan, took a white man to swing through those trees: King of the Jungle! Not a sambo, a white man.' Throughout my life, I'd hear it in different forms: 'We taught you how to read, we taught you how to write, gave you religion …' And so on.

The 1970s' TV series based on *Planet of the Apes* was another unwelcome development. I can almost laugh about it now but when it first started on Saturday mornings, I sat at home knowing it could only mean trouble for me. Sure enough, I earned the nickname of 'Urko' for a while. General Urko was the baddie ape charged with rounding up the humans – a short-tempered gorilla who meted out violent punishments. Somehow it never occurred to the white boys at President Kennedy that the apes on TV were in control of society while the humans were their slaves: they actually named me after a slave master.

But no such mistake was made when it came to *Roots*. The groundbreaking TV series of the 1970s chronicled the struggles of an African slave family through the generations. Black people loved this programme and in America some black kids beat up their white classmates in revenge for the actions of their ancestors. Back home in Coventry, that wasn't an option open to me – I was too heavily outnumbered.

Instead, I earned a new nickname: Urko was dropped and now I was 'Kunta Kinte'. This character gets whipped for refusing to accept his new slave name of Toby. His owners even chop off half his foot to stop him running away. If I entertained the idea that anybody at President Kennedy might feel guilty or enlightened after watching *Roots*, I'd soon get a rude awakening. The day after the whipping and mutilation episode aired, I walked through the school gates.

A kid yelled threateningly at me: 'Your slave name is Toby – we'll chop your fucking foot off!'

I sighed, but then another idiot fired up: 'You gonna get a whipping, Kunta Kinte!'

Had the black-American author Alex Haley who penned *Roots* known that in Coventry, England, this would be the end result of his labours, he might have snapped his pen in two and not bothered. His celebration of black civil rights had been turned into yet another weapon of ridicule.

'We chop your foot or your balls off, Kunta Kinte – which is it to be?'

Some white kids addressed me in a way that they believed black people talked, even though the evidence from my own gob proved otherwise. Either they tried to talk some kind of jive – much as white kids doing Jamaican gang slang today – or worse still, some sort of brain-dead simpleton speak that was supposed to resemble all black people. For the latter, they took their inspiration from a character called 'Chalky White', who was created by the so-called comedian Jim Davidson. This involved a 'Chicken Walk' and a squawking, dumb-ass nigger voice. One kid kindly did the Chalky White routine for me:

'Hello der man – wot you doin' tonight?'

Revealing my growing strength as a young amateur boxer, I gripped his forearm in a pincer. As he hollered and I moved him towards the ground, a frank warning was issued: 'Behave yourself, son – or I'm gonna hurt ya.' All this delivered in the 'hard cockney' voice I was developing, like the detectives on *The Sweeney* – a very popular cop show on the TV back then. I'd decided the lilting Midlands accent of Coventry conveyed neither menace to my enemies nor charm to the girls and so, at around thirteen years of age, I started to go cockney. Even then, London seemed such a cool and trendy place. Deep down, I started to realise this was where I wanted to end up – far from the maddening stupidity and closed minds that I'd grown up with on the streets of Radford.

By that point, all too often the name-calling ended in blows. My fists were getting used to what they'd be doing for the rest of my life. Urko – bloody mouth; Kunta Kinte – bloody mouth; go back to your own country – bloody mouth. Dentists all over Coventry must have been wondering why so many children turned up in their surgeries needing cracks and fillings repaired. Then one kid made a remark that knocked me for six: 'What colour was Jesus, Errol? He was white!'

Of course, he was nothing of the sort. A short Palestinian with Arabic features might have been closer to the mark. This did hit home, though – the Jesus in our hallway was exactly the man this boy had described: a Hollywood pin-up Lord Jesus with blue eyes, long blond hair, an angular chin and perfect teeth. An Anglo-Saxon Messiah, who had been singularly lax about protecting me from evil and who I'd begun to suspect was secretly working for the boot boys.

With all the insults and fights I faced on a daily basis, it was clear that I wouldn't survive President Kennedy without a gang around me. Many will moralise about youths and their gangs, but in the dog-eat-dog world of an inner-city comprehensive in the 1970s, you needed a gang to look cool, to defend yourself, to attract the opposite sex: end of story.

Maybe we looked naff in retrospect, but the Mighty Seven thought they oozed charisma in 1977. Slouched up against a school wall and up to no good in our Bob Marley red, gold and green hats, we were sure nobody would dare touch us. But we were wrong: there was always somebody stupid enough to take us on.

The Mighty Seven was made up of David Dennis, David Carty, Tony Burchill, Eddie Myrie, Clive Deslandes, Ian Plastow and myself, of course. David Dennis shared my passion for sport. He was a fast runner, good at rugby and could handle himself well in a fight. David Carty was the tallest of us. Slim, black and good-looking, he was always babbling on about what the world would be like in the future, what we'd be doing in the year 2000. It was all a bit Buck Rogers meets *Tomorrow's World* – a mix of hi-tech gadgets and cars that hovered off the ground.

Tony Burchill talked us into wearing the red, gold and green hats – his dad was a Rastafarian. In our later teens, he and I would become clubbing buddies, forced to deal with bouncers who tried to block our way into discos, who would come to regret their heavy-handedness.

Eddie Myrie was a tough black kid, hard and uncompromising. On one occasion a white bloke bottled out of fighting and instead offered him a hand: 'Let's shake hands and forget about it. Ay, mate.' But Eddie couldn't bring himself to forgive that easily or quickly. He took a firm grip of the bloke's hand so that he couldn't get away and then decisively kicked him in the bollocks. That's the sort of person Eddie was: only when you were on your knees was the battle over.

Clive Deslandes was light-skinned, a bit of a loudmouth and spoilt. When the gang first formed, he fancied himself as the leader of the pack, but I had different ideas. The Mighty Seven was going to be my empire, not his, and so we had to resolve this in a brutal manner with an all-fists flying, playground tear-up. Clive saw sense and recognised me as number one though there was still a bit of tension between us. You might say we hadn't got off to the best of starts.

Last of all came Ian Plastow, the only white member of the

gang and a good kid that I still know. He nailed his colours to the Mighty Seven's mast and we welcomed him with open arms. Any white schoolboy who didn't throw names like 'coon' or 'sambo' about could be part of Errol Christie's gang. Having got my posse together, it was time to put the world to rights. We were to be champions of the underdog and scourge of the boot boys.

The first opportunity to build a better society with our bare knuckles came around pretty quickly. At the end of school one day, we were all horsing about by the gates, chatting up girls and messing generally. An Asian kid on the sort of Chopper bike my dad was never going to buy me cycled past, but then came rapidly to grief. From round the corner sped a Hillman Imp – a beaten-up old car like the Christie family's Wolseley – and knocked this kid off his bike. Furious, the Asian yelled: 'Look what you done to my bike!'

The Chopper was a write-off. At this time, Asian kids were thought of as quiet and non-aggressive whereas blacks were increasingly seen as being able to handle themselves in a fight, as I had done my bit to prove. Noted by the boot boys, they began to shift their violence from us and increasingly engage in what they called 'Paki-bashing'. When the Asian kid's bike was mangled under the wheels of the Hillman Imp, the teenage thug driver wasn't too bothered – he certainly had no intention of paying for the damage he'd done.

Still incensed, the Asian boy went over to the Hillman Imp and kicked the bumper, pretty weakly as it turned out. But this took us all by surprise: an Asian kid standing up for himself, now that was a turn for the books. The driver couldn't believe his eyes either. Climbing out of his car, he hitched up his jeans and clenched his fists.

'What d'you just do, Paki?'

I nodded to the Mighty Seven. It was time to get involved – a victim of racism needed our help.

'What d'you call 'im?' I asked in my newly acquired cockney accent.

'Paki – what's it to you?'

'That's what I thought you said,' I continued, 'Well, don't say it again, if you know what's good for you.' I was enjoying this

Sweeney-style dialogue. 'You knocked 'im down – now say yer sorry and fuck off, there's a good lad.'

The thug was trying to compute what was going on around him: an Afro-Caribbean boy standing up for an Asian boy. Well, that was confusing enough. By and large, our two communities didn't mix a lot. In my own experience, only at the newsagent when the Asian owner would continuously stare at me, watching to see if my black hands were about to pocket any of his sweets or magazines without paying; that was the normal extent of our interaction.

'Mind your fucking business, you black bastard!'

With those ill-chosen words, he flicked the switch in my head. Now I was in fighter mode and he was about to get the full benefit of my training. I would give him a personalised demonstration of what my father had meted out to my brothers and me ever since we could walk and talk.

'What d'you say?'

'I said, what the fuck's it gotta do with you, sambo? This is between me and the Paki, right?'

Even at a young age, I'd worked out how to stun my prey before killing it. I'd fix the soon-to-be bloodied individual with a hypnotic stare. Not looking at any other part of them other than their eyes, already I'd rapidly scanned their body shape, arm length and the likelihood of their being able to strike back with much effect. Now all I had to do was take in their facial expressions to know how they were likely to react, so I duly stared at this thug and prepared my first move.

'I told you to fuck off, you stupid coon. Go on, piss off!'

I was smaller than him. He waded threateningly towards me, underestimating my power. Then he made the dumbest of mistakes: he shoved my left shoulder – hard. I swung around, which allowed me to come back with my fist fully charged, pivoting on the balls of my feet as I did so. My fist and forearm, straight and true, smashed into his face. It seemed to me as if this happened in slow motion, though for him it was probably a bolt of lightning. This proficient cross was followed by a couple of upper cuts and then a mean hook into his flabby cheeks.

Dazed, he couldn't land a single punch on me. In spite of his larger size. He was like the man that Michael Caine sneers at in the film *Get Carter*: 'You're a big man – but you're out of shape.' The thug lifted his head, his eyes bloodshot, and tried to say something – possibly the word 'stop'. Instead, his front teeth slid downwards, completely dislodged from his gums. I pulled my fists back in the same way as a gunslinger would put his shooter away after gunning down the sheriff – they'd done their work well and now I could retract them.

I looked to the Mighty Seven for approval, but instead became aware of the voice of our geography teacher, who was shrieking from somewhere nearby: 'Oh Errol, *no*! Errol, *no*, *stop*! What are you doing?'

Next morning, I found myself gazing at the sunlight streaming through the windows outside the deputy headmaster's office. The geography teacher had shopped me and I now had a date with the bamboo cane. Nearby, the parents of the thug I'd beaten were seated and scowling at me. I never spoke to them directly but saw them talking to the deputy headmaster on their son's behalf – making sure that I got the worst possible press. I'd stood up for an Asian kid being bullied but now I was cast as the vicious hooligan. The only reason I was being punished, I thought, was because I'd won the fight.

I walked into the deputy headmaster's office and listened to the usual homilies: 'We do not tolerate this sort of behaviour on school premises ...' Etc., etc., etc. I'd brought this magnificent centre of learning into disrepute, I'd let the side down; violence was never the answer. He didn't want to see me in his office again.

It all went in one ear and spilt out of the other. Already bored, I just stuck out my hands. Nothing he could inflict would be worse than my father's beatings. The cane made a whooshing sound as it reddened my palms and I left, rubbing my hands on my trousers to get rid of the stinging. I knew soon enough I'd be back for more.

After a few hours of staring out the window and daydreaming my way through lessons, I teamed back up with the Mighty Seven and we soon found ourselves strutting down Beake Avenue for no reason other than we had nothing else to do. As ever, we occupied the middle of the road to avoid the residents and their dogs: Germans to the right, Germans to the left.

My brother Andy was with us as well, sporting his new Doc Martens. They had been blue with steel toecaps but this was a bit too glam rock for us and so we'd painted them black all over. Oxblood was the favoured colour of the boot boys, so we went for black, appropriately enough.

Grouped together, I felt we were safe – until a red car screeched round the corner. Red with a white swoosh down one side in the style of the motor driven by seventies' TV detectives Starsky and Hutch. I didn't have time to chuckle, though: the car hurtled its way towards us and we flung ourselves at the kerb to avoid being flattened.

'Wanker!' I yelled as the car screeched to a halt, its brake lights blazing red.

'He's stopped,' said Tony Burchill.

There was an odd pause until the car door swung open and out stepped a white bloke dressed almost identically to Starsky. For those unfamiliar with the American TV series, this involved a thick woolly cardigan with a wide belt, duck-shaped shoes with big laces and permed, wavy hair. No Hutch, just Starsky – and this Starsky was making aggressive, beckoning motions with his hands.

'Come on, then. Reckon you're hard? C'mon, I'll 'ave ya.'

We all took a step forward.

'No, no, one at a time! Too cowardly to take me on man-to-man are ya, eh?'

The Mighty Seven could see I was ready to answer this charge of cowardice but Clive Deslandes decided to throw his weight around to prove that he hadn't completely surrendered leadership of the Mighty Seven.

'You had the fight with that other bloke, Errol. Our turn now.' He was referring to the thug in the Hillman Imp. 'You gotta let one of us kick his head in.'

'No, I don't – I'll take this geezer on,' I insisted.

'He's gotta point, Errol. You can't have all the fights,' Tony butted in on Clive's side.

'Maybe we should toss a coin, see who's gonna punch him

first,' Eddie chipped in.

But this wasn't my way of operating; I didn't take well to the idea of democracy in the gang. I decided to abide by the majority decision just this once, though. We began to toss a penny coin and eliminate each gang member, one by one. This riled Starsky, who was waiting for his fight.

'What you lot up to? Lost your bottle? Who's gonna come and get it?'

To everybody's dismay, I won the coin toss, but sensing the bad blood I stepped aside for David Carty.

'Go on, mate – show him what you're worth.'

The tall and imposing David moved towards Starsky, who was still standing, talking tough, in front of his red and white Alpine.

'What you gonna do, eh?'

That question was answered with a devastating blow to Starsky's midriff, which brought him to the ground. Abandoning all pretence of the Queensberry rules, David then stamped on his manhood. A little unsporting, perhaps. But so too was our next move – we all joined in, with Andy giving his new DMs a much-needed scuffing-up.

As we tenderised the wannabe TV detective, ignoring his squeals for mercy, one of my teachers drove by slowly, pretending not to look but registering everything. No doubt he was trying to work out whether this crime of ours merited a caning or a detention. It never ceased to intrigue me how teachers had a knack of knowing when trouble was about to occur and would turn up at just at the wrong moment. No doubt this latest incident would be the talk of the staffroom the next morning.

Blood-splattered, Starsky staggered back to his car and somehow managed to drive off. We continued our early-evening stroll, convinced we'd seen the last of him, but as we neared Cheveral Avenue the idiot reappeared, parked his car and clambered out. This time, he was a little unsteady on his bruised pins, his cardigan hung loosely around him, the belt broken.

'What *now*?' I asked.

'Who kicked me up the arse? That fucking well hurt!' he demanded, scratching his head.

Proudly, I pointed to Andy. It was his handiwork, not mine

– the DMs had done their work well. A few days later, on a Saturday afternoon in town, I bumped into Starsky yet again. He'd somehow learned of my boxing prowess. By then, I was Schoolboy and County Champion and there had been some coverage of my fights in the *Coventry Evening Telegraph*, though the school couldn't have been less interested, had they tried.

'Didn't know you were a fighter, like.'

'Well, you do now,' I grinned back at him. At least he was giving me some recognition.

After beating up Starsky good and proper, the Mighty Seven had worked up an appetite and so we stopped off at the chippie on Beake Avenue only to be confronted by a hostile gang from our rival school, Cardinal Newman. The rivalry had been steadily building as boys from both schools attended the same weekly Sunday evening disco at Christ the King, another Catholic school in Coventry.

Those discos started off innocently enough, but the skinheads – some of them from Cardinal Newman – would always insist on having their choice for the final record. A red rag was duly hoisted and we went for it: the evening would end up with a mass of teenagers taking swipes at each other. Meanwhile, a large figure of the Son of God, arms outstretched, looked on helplessly as we pummelled his disciples.

Those Catholic schoolboys from Cardinal Newman deluded themselves that they were harder than us. As we entered the chippie, they stood around, jeering and muttering insults, while we ordered our saveloy and soggy chips. The rigours of beating up Starsky had taken it out of us, so we didn't react there and then but we couldn't ignore their jeers. Insults always needed a response.

Next day at President Kennedy, I made it clear to the Mighty Seven that we were now on a mission to crucify the Catholics at Cardinal Newman, but first I had to get through another morning of daydreams. The lunch break seemed to take for ever to come round but when the bell rang, we marshalled our forces and made our way towards the enemy.

Between us and Cardinal Newman was a big muddy field: the rain had done its work and turned what should have been a pleasant green space into a bog with the odd clump of grass. In our platforms and flares, we stomped across the wet earth, making a complete mess of what passed for our school uniforms. But as we came in sight of our target, an unexpected group was there to greet us: our teachers from President Kennedy. Not only had they been tipped off that we were on our way over, they'd gone to the trouble of taking the minibus and driving over in time to head us off.

Eddie's jaw dropped: 'Shit, we're done for!'

Wheeling round on our platforms, flares flapping in the wind, we squelched our way back across the muddy morass, somehow hoping this would save us from the inevitable punishment in store. Within hours, of course, the Mighty Seven was outside the deputy headmaster's office. His head poked out, with the sternest of expressions.

'You lot – *in*!'

Standing in a row at the front of his desk, our palms were stretched out, ready to be rendered red-raw by his cane. Whereas I was resigned to my fate, even bored by this ritual, I was appalled to see fear on the faces of my fellow gang members. This wasn't supposed to happen. Surely the Mighty Seven was made of finer stuff? But as the stick of bamboo swished down, I saw hands draw back slightly.

If anything, to be caught on the fingertips instead of the fleshy palms of your hands made the pain far worse. As the cane repeatedly struck, faces flinched and eyes watered. In turn, I was horrified by this girly performance from my comrades and decided to show the Mighty Seven how a real man gets caned.

When it came to my turn, I stuck my palms out defiantly. The deputy head didn't take too well to this display of cockiness and raised the cane higher, bringing it down with his full body force. It hurt, but I boldly feigned indifference. Pain was an old acquaintance of mine.

'Wherever there's trouble, there's you – isn't there, Errol?'

Sport was my only consolation at school and the only subject the teachers could be bothered to spend any time drilling into me. Every weekend, I gave up my spare time to run round tracks, kick footballs, throw javelins, shot put, throw the odd discus and swim endless lengths. Whatever the school wanted me to do, with whatever type of ball – from hockey to rugby and something called shinty – in my ragamuffin sports clothes, I was ready and willing.

I didn't expect to be mollycoddled or patted on the head – and I'd have waited a long time for that to happen. The child singled out for huge dollops of kindness and attention from the PE staff was a weedy white kid called David Gibbs. While I thundered along, doing the four hundred metres, high jump and scoring goal after goal, a curious little figure at the other end of the field was doing something completely different.

Gibbsy had been told that to develop some – *any* – sporting ability, he could bring in a bow and arrow to fire at a target. As my lungs burst against my ribcage, giving every sport maximum effort, there was Gibbsy trying to get a bulls'-eye. Not that I had a problem with that, but it was what happened next that got my goat.

When my school report arrived at the end of term, I was more than a bit disheartened to find a BB against sports. They'd grudgingly given second-class marks to a Schoolboy Boxing Champion for the whole of England, who gave up all his weekends for President Kennedy. But then Tony Burchill shipped up to give me the real bad news.

'Hear they gave Gibbs a double A for sports – what d'you make of that, then?'

So, Gibbs had got an AA – a vote of pity. A hot tide of anger swept through me. It wasn't Gibbsy's fault that the teachers drooled over him but, as a teenager bursting to get some recognition from the school system, this was the final straw. If I couldn't get a top grade in sports, then I wasn't going to achieve one in anything. Deep down, I wanted one small part of my report book to have an A grade amid all those Ds and Es. Maybe all those black kids who said there was no point in trying to play the white man's game were right.

'Woz the point, Errol – they ain't gonna give us no jobs.'

'Don't matter how hard we try …'

'All we're gonna get is some lousy fucking job in a chip shop.'

I'd even struggled to get my sister a job in the local chippie. The owner had been moaning about how much he needed a pair of extra hands and so I piped up to him one day: 'My sister'd work here – she'd peel the spuds and cook 'em, and all that.'

He wasn't unsympathetic, but he gave me a weird look: 'Nah, Errol! People don't like ... you know ... Wot I'm getting at is ... Well, they wouldn't buy my chips, see. 'Ere what I'm saying?'

After the Gibbsy incident, I went on a work to rule. From now on, it would be minimum effort. When the sports teacher came up to ask if I'd be running for the school the next weekend, I snarled: 'Get your hands off me – I'm not doing your sports no more!'

Despite my decision to embark on a go-slow, I did manage to earn one merit point, though in a rather unorthodox and typically Errol Christie manner. Mooching around on the stairs at President Kennedy one day as part of my extended sulk, a teacher called Mr Erskine rounded on me, bringing to bear his full authority.

'What are you doing here, Christie?'

But I was in no mood to be addressed like a fleck of mud on his boot. My face must have brimmed with that sullen resentment that whites always find threatening in blacks, without comprehending where it comes from. Then he jabbed me in the gut.

'I asked you – what are you doing here?'

The letters 'B' and 'B' went through my mind. I visualised that report card, then Gibbsy's with his glowing AA for sports. Unable to control myself, I stepped forward, determined to treat Mr Erskine in the same way that I now handled other adults on the streets. He was about to feel the benefit of my boxing training and he knew it. Very quickly, he changed his tone to one of grovelling friendship.

'Come on now, lad – no need to be like that. Look, I'll ... I'll give you a merit. What do you say to that?'

And that was the only merit I earned in my whole time at President Kennedy. By the end of my studies there, I walked away with seven CSE passes: Art and Craft (grade four), Elementary Mathematics (grade five), Physics (grade five), Community Service (Handicrafts) (grade four), English (grade five), Geography (grade three) and Social Studies (grade four). It was the academic profile of the average person on the dole in 1979.

Meanwhile, the unemployment level at the time was rising rapidly. Coventry's factories were closing: the jobs-for-life in the car industry that locals always expected were now coming to an end. Production lines were halting, properties being boarded up. The next few years would see many of my fellow classmates struggle to find work at all. And the lack of jobs only further fuelled the hatred of the boot boys and the skinheads towards us. The extreme right was more visible, more confident than I'd ever seen it before.

On the streets, I wasn't just coming up against short-haired morons fighting blacks out of gut instinct. Now, some of them were reading pamphlets dripping with poison that set out to justify their racism. This gave their violence a new intensity and purpose: everything they'd ever thought about us was given a new structure in their heads. They were the true Britons, the owners of these islands, and we were interlopers come from the Caribbean, arriving on our 'banana boats' to take away their livelihoods.

The skinhead Des had made puke – Dennis – had made himself scarce but my new boot-boy nemesis was a young hooligan; the new breed of skinhead, from his oxblood DMs to his green bomber jacket. Determined to defend the honour of white girls from black boys, he was someone who believed our faces should not be visible in the local pubs and clubs, particularly those on his turf: namely, Jubilee Crescent.

For me, it was difficult to stay away from Jubilee Crescent, though. It was at the top of our road and, as I got older, the lure of the discos at the local community centre proved too much. My teenage hormones were raging, I badly needed to get down and dirty with the opposite sex. Between my desire stood Russell, Guardian of the White Anglo-Saxon race. On no account was I to get anywhere near the local female talent to defile them. Naturally, I thought differently. One of us would have to back down.

For my Jubilee Crescent clubbing excursions, I hung out with two new Asian mates, Suki and Pups. They were nice mellow Indian kids with a great sense of fun and humour. Their old man was also a bit off the rails, temperament-wise, though no father could equal mine for general insanity.

Brothers, they owned a garage with a blue Cortina MK 1 parked inside, which we sometimes slept in overnight. We'd sit in that car until late, chatting and listening to music: the *Radio 1 Chart Show* on a Sunday afternoon with Tony Blackburn, counting down from number 40 to number one. Or we'd play some reggae and ska tapes on a hand-held tape recorder. After slotting in the cassette, there was a clunking sound when you pressed the big 'Play' button down. Soon, we'd all doze off.

The three of us decided no army of skins was going to stop us getting to the girls at the Jubilee Crescent Community Centre. One weekend, we sauntered down there, passing The Pilot pub – skinhead central – as we did so. These days, it's completely multi-cultural, but in the late 1970s the place was wrapped in the Union Jack and crawling with boot boys. Inside, Russell and his mates would have been beering themselves up before heading down to the disco as well, but I didn't give this a second thought: my mission was to find a girl and satisfy my lust.

We got to the Community Centre and pretty soon, we were inside dancing and chatting to the girls. They liked taking to the dance floor with black guys because we could dance. At that time, there weren't too many white blokes who could follow a rhythm – and that applied to the boxing ring as much as the disco. They could be rigid and wooden whereas we were grinding and pumping to the sound from the speakers.

One of the weird ironies of the boot boys' versus black kids' war was that often both sides liked the same music. The early skinhead scene was rooted in Jamaican music and fashion, but the current wave of late 1970s' skins had lost the style of the decade before. Now, they just wore a thuggish uniform and refused to acknowledge their debt to our culture.

Many nights out would start with both sides dancing to Bob Marley or 2 Tone bands like The Specials, but then something would provoke a fight. The same guys who'd been dancing next to each other moments before would be cracking open each others' skulls open the next. And the only reason was race.

Dominating the dance floor with my moves, I made the girls laugh with some corny jokes and taught one of them how to move her ass to the music. As I did so, I was totally unaware of the menacing horde that was coming through the door. Russell and his cohorts had left The Pilot and were now inside the Community Centre. Suddenly I felt a tap on my shoulder.

'What you doing here?'

I ignored him. Another tap.

'We don't like that, see.'

Russell seemed to be under the impression that I had to apply for a licence to dance with white girls. I carried on ignoring him until yet another tap.

'I said, what you doing here, nigger?'

I stopped dancing. For a few moments we were eyeball to eyeball. Hanging out of my mouth was a match I'd been chewing, which I now spat into Russell's face. It bounced off his cheek. For some reason, we didn't fight there and then. Maybe he didn't reckon his chances one to one – they never did. Those boot boys were only happy when they hopelessly outnumbered their victims. His mates hung back and he walked away but I knew the situation would have to be resolved at some point in the traditional manner.

A confrontation like this could never be left hanging. Russell had put down a very public marker: in this brutal environment, there was no option but to retaliate. If I didn't do something, I'd have to obey his rules; that would include staying away from the Jubilee Crescent discos and generally becoming invisible. I had no intention of letting this happen: Russell might have been older, but I was stronger. On the right terrain, I would defeat my enemy and duly send him packing.

And the opportunity presented itself sooner than I could ever have imagined. The very next day I was at Coventry station, waiting for a train to London. I'd just won the NABC Boxing Champion trophy and part of my prize was to be sent to a boxing training camp in Sweden. I was over the moon at this opportunity, not only to get out of Radford and Coventry but also to leave Britain behind for a few days, even though the transport arranged for us young boxers was a creaking ferry across rough seas. No air flight for us.

As I sat with my dishevelled excuse for a sports bag, wondering if the train would ever arrive, I caught sight of a familiar figure. Standing up, I went over to him.

'Listen, Russell,' I told the startled skinhead. 'When I get back, I'm gonna finish this off.'

Then I strode off like John Wayne. This town sure wasn't big enough for the both of us. A week later, I returned to Coventry, having spent a period in intensive training, perfecting my jabs and crosses, so the fighter inside me was primed and ready for action. And then Fate decided to deal me a good hand: as my train pulled in, there by the No. 15 bus stop was Russell, right in front of the Nickelby's clothes shop (where in my later teens, I would buy tank-tops and flares to go clubbing).

I felt no fear, no apprehension and certainly no respect for my opponent. It helps to get a little anger pumping round your system before you demolish another human being. On this occasion, that little injection of fury was provided by the meathead that Russell was chatting away to. Neither saw me emerge from the train station.

Russell's mate was no stranger to me. To my horror and regret, he'd been seeing my sister Annette. She often went with white guys and I believed this skinhead deliberately made a beeline for her. Why? Because in the weeks that followed, he took a particular delight in pointing out to the Christie brothers what he'd done to Annette.

'I've been fucking your sister – what do you think about that?'

We told him what he thought with our fists. First, I hit him and then Andy and, finally, Simon. Still, he hadn't learnt his lesson. There he was with Russell and a stupid smirk on his face.

'You didn't mind me seeing yer sister then, eh?'

Both cackled in the way that boot boys did – a dirty rasping laugh. He'd just booked himself another session with the Christie brothers.

'Tell ya, Russell mate, she *loves* it!'

I pictured the two of them as punchbags: soon they'd find out how tirelessly I worked over those inanimate objects in the gym – fists flying, pummelling the bag, from top to bottom with sweat always poring in rivulets down my face and torso. Beating those two up would be no more than a sparring session on the street. My life, it often seemed to me in those days, was just one long fight – sometimes in the ring, sometimes out of it.

'Funny, aren't ya?' I whispered.

'Yeah, reckon we are.' Russell moved forward. 'I'm feeling peckish. Got a banana on ya, nigger? That's what you lot eat, innit?'

He needed his mouth filling all right. At that moment, the difference between us was that I was scientifically sizing him up to gauge how far he could reach: height, weight, length of arms – also, the position of his feet to judge his ability to balance. Most importantly, though, his attitude: everything pointed in my favour. So arrogant was Russell, he thought the black boy wouldn't dare touch him. Time to disabuse him of that belief. His thin-lipped mouth opened again, but I'd heard enough.

A mighty cross was unleashed, like a piston hammer to his gob. The power jolted from my right foot through my body and down my arm like an electric charge. A good boxer knows how to pivot and uses his entire frame to deliver the strongest punch. Russell fell like a tower block or a factory chimney that had been dynamited. In one swift movement, he collapsed to the ground, speechless.

The skinhead who'd been seeing Annette now held the groaning body of his buddy in his arms: 'Russ, Russ! You all right, mate? Speak to me!'

'And *you*,' I gestured to the boot boy, 'shut the fuck up about my sister, right?'

Proper balance restored, the world had been put right. Now I could walk in Jubilee Crescent and chat up any white girl I wanted. No knucklehead or racist would tell Errol Christie where he could go, or who he could speak to. I strolled back towards Cheveral Avenue, uncharacteristically at peace with the city of Coventry and myself.

Of course, it wouldn't last: I now had my first run-in with the West Midlands Constabulary. In the 1970s, little love was lost between Britain's black population and the police, especially in Coventry. Young black men like me always viewed the cops as another form of boot boy, only this time with the full support of the State behind them. Surrendering to a copper was a one-way ticket to having your head stuck down the loo at the police station, or so we believed.

It wasn't just us kids who had a bad view of the police, either. Even my law-abiding, Jesus-praising mother told horror stories about what the boys in blue had done – and nearly always to black people.

'Lawd Jesus, dem beat that disabled man! Dem beat him bad, sweet Jesus, for the mercy of the Lawd! Dragged him out of his car, dem beat him with truncheons. He scream out – till now mi can hear him screaming – dem fling him on the floor. Lawd Jesus, could feel it myself.'

So, now it was my turn to have my collar felt. I was fourteen years old and sitting at home when a fist banged so loudly on the front door that the picture of blond Jesus jumped about on the wall. Mum answered and there was an exchange of words in the corridor that became more and more heated and fraught; I could tell she was getting upset. Looking round at my brothers, I wondered if one of them had done something stupid – robbed a house, stolen something from a shop. No doubt the police at our door were on a mission.

Mum walked into the living room: 'Errol ...'

Dumbstruck, I gazed up: 'What?'

'Best if you come with us, son – alright?'

For once, a feeling of fear gripped me but then righteous anger took hold: 'I haven't done anything.'

The look on the copper's face spoke volumes. Yeah, he was thinking, another black kid whinging his innocence but they're all the same: guilty as hell, the little bastards. I knew from that malicious stare that no good would come of appealing to his better nature and so off I went, complaining constantly as I was manhandled into the waiting police car.

The police station was my first taste of the whole rigmarole of being processed as a criminal. By now, I didn't know whether to find the whole episode amusing or tragic. It turned out that somebody called Errol had indeed committed a crime – burglary or some such. Indignant, I kept repeating that just because I was black and also called Errol, it didn't mean they had the right man.

To Mum's credit, she never got off the phone to the station. Her harsh words wore me down and I think they finally began to have the same effect on the coppers. After a few hours, they eventually admitted I wasn't their man but, in one last act of spite, they pushed me out of the cop car on the drive back home, miles away from our house in the dead of night. Presumably, they were revolted by the idea of playing chauffeur to a black kid.

Mum has a different theory, though. She thinks they didn't want to face her because she'd have torn several strips off them. To this day, the memory of that incident still makes her shake with rage.

The weekend after that unpleasant encounter saw me helping Dad in our back yard. He was giving his van its annual service – at least, that's what he *thought* he was doing. This ritual involved him revving up the motor for hours on end in the insane belief that it would do his van some good.

Bored out of my wits by his lunacy, I heard the tinkling chimes of an ice-cream van in the road outside. For once, I had some loose change in my pocket and, with Dad cussing behind me, ran off to get myself a lolly. The van was parked in the middle of the road and I stared at the familiar images of cones with whipped vanilla ice cream and chocolate flakes stuck in them, as well as lurid lollies with names like 'Rocket'.

Having made my choice, I looked up to give the order. Gazing down at me was none other than Dennis, the nigger-hating skinhead who my brother reduced to a vomiting wreck, about eight years before.

'Which ice cream?'

'99 – two flakes, if you don't mind.'

So the hard man of Radford – one of those vicious lads who had terrorised us in the entries – was now our local ice-cream van man. Not that there's anything wrong with being a lolly vendor but seeing him made me more determined than ever to show all those boot boys, skinheads and fascists that I would amount to a whole lot more than any of them.

3

BOXING: MY SALVATION

'I hated every minute of training, but I said, "Don't quit. Suffer now and live the rest of your life as a champion."'

Muhammad Ali

My brother Michael *(front)* and me *(right)* as we join the England boxing team.
Mirrorpix

Warwickshire's top amateur boxing talents and their trainers, 10 June 1975.

Mirrorpix

The schools ABA finalists from my home county – the black kid knows he's going to win, 11 March 1976.

Mirrorpix

Bringing back more boxing prizes, me *(in the middle)*, Andy, my brother *(to my right)* and Raymond Setchell *(far right)*.

Errol Christie, personal collection

The boys from the Standard Triumph: Des, Michael and Andy at the back, me *(second from left in the middle row)* with Wesley, and Simon *(front)*.

Allsport Photographic/Getty Images

Super Christie nine minutes away from glory

By ROGER DRAPER

Smile, charm, talent — he has it all

With my workmates at the Coventry Clutch Centre.

Mirrorpix

Bringing home another amateur trophy, 1981.

Mirrorpix

Sitting with Henry Cooper at a live TV screening.

Errol Christie, personal collection

'm Tom McGarry. I'm the gaffer, the boss. Come in, get some gloves on.'

I stood wide-eyed in wonderment at this giant of a man. A trade union shop steward from a local Coventry car factory with a booming Lanarkshire voice. Men like him would soon become relics of a bygone age: in the Thatcherite eighties, they disappeared, along with the factories that they could once bring to a standstill simply by yelling, 'All out!' They were part of the old style of working class that doesn't seem to exist anymore.

In 1972, Tom stood before me, offering a path out of the ghetto, a route to salvation. From that day on, he would be like a second father to me because, as well as knowing his trade union rule book inside out, he'd also memorised every word of the Amateur Boxing Association Rules & Regulations.

By day, Tom was a leader of car workers and, in the evening, he ran the Standard Triumph ABC – a basic, old-style, no-nonsense, no-frills gym that was linked to the car factory of the same name. Back then it was only sports facilities such as this, something that's now missing in Britain, that gave kids like me a chance: you don't get boxing gyms and social clubs linked to call centres and estate agents.

It was Des who first heard about Tom's gym and he announced it breathlessly to us at home one day. We'd been under a sort of curfew for months. Mum was terrified that the skinheads were going to kill one of her boys or a speeding car would mysteriously mow us down while we played in the street. She'd ordered us indoors, but this only added to the pressure-cooker atmosphere in Cheveral Avenue. So, when Des told us what he'd found, we sped out the front door with Mum shouting helplessly behind us.

From outside the Standard Triumph, we could hear shouting and laughing; kids were sparring or training on bags. Then the Christie brothers went in. That day, there were four of us – Andy and Simon were still way too young to don the gloves and wraps. I was only eight years of age, but ready to fight.

As we appeared at the door, everything stopped. The sight of us black ragamuffins, with a lean and hungry look about us, brought the whole joint to a halt. Yet again, faces stared, unsubtly, as if to say what are you doing here? That was when Tom, a grinning Scot, stepped forward to break the ice. Straight off, we decided that he and the Christies would be joined at the hip; he'd take us rough diamonds and transform us into top fighting material.

Inside, the Standard Triumph resembled an aircraft hanger. It was a huge Nissen hut with curvy walls and ceilings of corrugated iron; the sort of building thrown up after the war because it was cheap and sturdy. The gym was also freezing: there was no heater or, if there was, it certainly never worked – the only way to get over the bitter cold was to pick up a skipping rope and start moving from the moment you got in there.

In one corner was an empty trophy cabinet; it was bereft of silver and a monument to the gym's mediocre achievements in the various ABA championships that took place around the country. This was no good for Tom McGarry: he needed to notch up some successes to bolster the Standard Triumph's reputation, to make the gym's blue and white colours a sporting emblem that any young boxer would be proud to wear. Looking back, I think he took one look at the ragamuffin mob coming through the door of his gym and thought: 'There's my winners.' We had nowhere else in the world to go but up – we certainly couldn't slip much further down.

None of us had boxing kit: we came in wearing what we'd usually have on our backs any day of the week. Dad wasn't going to dip into his pocket to pay for boxing boots, shorts or sweatshirts and so Tom got us the clothes we needed, bit by bit. He handed us over to an old boy of a trainer, who forbade us to climb into the ring or even go anywhere near the bags. Instead, we had to master each boxing move by jabbing, crossing and letting loose hooks and upper cuts into thin air. He'd go round each of us, correcting our hand position, getting us to twist our torsos for maximum impact with the cross, stepping forward correctly with a jab, and so on.

We had been raw street fighters, but now we were being taught to fight with finesse, elegance even. In that sweaty factory gym, I began to realise that boxing wasn't just about punching your opponent in the head till they dropped, but putting on a display of well-rehearsed moves: dancing round the other boxer and working over his body, bit by bit. A hammer blow of a jab, then a cross to the solar plexus followed by a rapid pivot that allowed a sharp right upper cut aimed low into the kidneys; returning to the opponent's front to deliver a series of punches before swooping to the left to power a hook into the rib cage and liver. And finally, when the other man showed signs of wilting, a devastating jab and hook into his unsuspecting head.

All this we practised into thin air with an imaginary opposing fighter in front of us. My mind didn't have to work too hard on that score – already I had plenty of people on whom I liked to imagine myself landing deadly punches. All the Christies pictured a local boot boy they detested and it was noted by others at the gym our shadow boxing had a certain intensity: the eyes of the Christie brothers were fierce and focused on the invisible skinhead before us.

Of course, our role model was Muhammad Ali. To us, he was a living god – a black man with unbeatable fists, a clever mind, a mouth he didn't fear to use, strong opinions and a refusal to be cowed by the Establishment. His dancer-fighter moves were a complete inspiration to my brothers and me, and we all tried to mimic the legendary 'Ali shuffle'. This was a move that I would often repeat over a knocked-out opponent, much to the disgust of many future ringside onlookers.

Day after day, I ran down to the Standard Triumph. This was my real home now. From that young age, I knew I'd finally found my purpose, something I could totally immerse myself in. As I raced in and stuck my gloves on, Tom McGarry would slap me on the back – I'd never been happier.

McGarry was keen to see us progress. Every day he would walk past the empty trophy cabinet and it quickly dawned on him that the tough black brood who had walked into his gym might well bring some glory to the Standard Triumph. He urged us into the ring. We'd perfected our moves – now it was time to get sparring. A queue of white kids quickly formed to take us on: they wanted to put us in our place, to teach us a lesson and send us packing. What should have been sparring became all-out fights to the finish and, much to the horror of the little white fighters, we were coming out on top every time.

For my brothers and me, this was a legal way for us to beat up white kids without getting arrested and so we took full advantage. The anger and frustration that we felt with life in general was channelled through our gloved fists. At home and on the streets, we had known nothing but violence and now it all came flooding out. The queues of kids waiting to fight us soon shortened dramatically until nobody wanted to climb into the ring with a Christie.

Meanwhile, McGarry looked on and was pleased with what he saw. Very soon, I was winning the gym's annual prize for Best Newcomer, Best Technical Boxer, and so on. The reward was in the form of brand new trainers, gloves, socks, shorts and all the items that Tom knew I badly needed. His son, Eddie McGarry, started training me with a view to taking me on the road to the ABA Championships that were held around the country. I'd earned my spurs at the Standard Triumph and now it was time to unveil this new talent to towns and cities round Britain.

The mid-1970s were glory years for boxing. Giants like Muhammad Ali, George Foreman and Joe Frazier dominated the international stage. When I was eleven years old, Ali and Foreman fought the so-called 'Rumble in the Jungle', one of the all-time great boxing events that was held in Zaire. Throughout Britain, amateur boxing nights in working men's clubs and sports halls would attract capacity audiences. Every kid wanted to wear a coveted Boxing Championship belt; to one day find themselves at Wembley, holding their arms aloft to receive the adulation of the crowd. It was the dream of thousands of working-class kids who wanted their lives to amount to something.

For a black boy, that dream burned even brighter.

Tom and I formed a special bond: man and boy with a shared passion for boxing. 'Errol, any time you want to train, just take the keys to the gym,' he told me. From a very young age, early in the morning I'd go on my own to the Standard Triumph and start working over the bags. I think my parents were just relieved that I wasn't getting into trouble. 'First in and last out,' Tom used to say approvingly. Soon this place became my home, far more than Cheveral Avenue ever was.

Without realising it, Tom and that big Nissen hut became the centre of my life – 'my temple', as I called it later on. All our exchanges were about the sport; we didn't have big intellectual conversations. In return for the gym keys, I never abused his trust. I could have taken mates there and horsed around or even brought girls back in my teens, but I never did. Tom had opened the door to my future and I owed him something.

My first proper fight was when I was ten years old – below today's official age limit for amateur boxing. Strangely, I can't remember anything about it now. Amid countless bust-ups in boxing rings, it became a blur but, from the age of twelve, I spent a lot of time in the Standard Triumph transit van. With Tom and Eddie, we hit the road for boxing clubs all over Britain.

Out of Coventry, we travelled to places I'd never heard of. We visited an England that still had mile after mile of factories and mines. There were men with long hair, flared trousers and platform shoes, and the women had mini-skirts and tank tops. In the shopping arcades, Dolcis and Ravel still reigned supreme. This was an England with no McDonald's – just Wimpy Bars or local bakers serving heated-up sausage rolls. Back then, the chippie was still more popular than the curry house and an English pound was a note, not a coin.

Those trips in the transit van were almost as harrowing as family journeys in Dad's old Wolseley. Rides were never smooth, the seating basic and Eddie McGarry – my trainer – smoked all the way from Coventry to wherever our destination happened to be. One fag after another was lit up till we were enveloped in a nicotine fog. I hated the sense that my lungs were filling up with tar and smoke, but this was a time when no one was railing against passive smoking – you could even have a puff on an aeroplane! By the time we arrived at the venue, I practically fell out of the van's back door, I was coughing my guts up so much.

Sometimes, I'd stay in a council house or flat belonging to somebody linked to a local ABA, in a place like Whitby or

Plymouth. Initially, I was a bit scared to find myself in a strange white family's house. Like a dog repeatedly kicked, I expected to be an unwelcome guest, owing to the colour of my skin. But to my amazement, these white working-class families couldn't have been nicer. Growing up in Coventry in the 1970s had convinced me that virtually all white people hated ethnic minorities. Now I started to meet ordinary folk, who thought we were OK.

Plymouth, like many parts of the UK, still seemed to be shaking off the Second World War. In this port town, you could still see army surplus gear being sold, old ships in the dock, even a rusting tank. I seem to recall buildings that still had camouflage on them from the 1940s. It was as if Hitler had surrendered the previous week.

Hardly had I set foot in Plymouth than us boys from Coventry were told to get down to the bout. There was no time to put our feet up, have a soft drink or watch a bit of telly – it was straight into the war zone to meet our enemies. Often I went to those fights with one or more of my other brothers as a 'spare' if I wasn't already on the ticket, but on this particular occasion I was on my own – Mum and Dad had met Tom and trusted him to look after me.

We arrived at the venue and, one by one, climbed onto the scales. I weighed in at 60kg, which put me in the light welter-weight class. Later, I'd go welterweight, then light middleweight and, finally, middleweight. The crowd that night seemed huge, and still does in my memory. Pint glasses clinked and ABA offi-cials with badges on their lapels marched about self-importantly. An hour after the weigh-in the fights started.

All of us – pre-teen and teenage boxers from around the UK – went into a changing area to get into our vests, shorts and boots. We were like gladiators kitting ourselves out before striding into the arena. Most of the other kids were nervous now: I could see the fear etched into their faces but I just didn't understand it. For me, this was a great day out, a Saturday night far from Cheveral Avenue and my dad's fists, which I could never respond to. Here in Plymouth, I could put on some gloves and punch away to my heart's content.

Quite possibly, I was the most irritating person to share a

changing area. Like Tigger in *The House at Pooh Corner*, I couldn't sit still but bounced around enthusiastically, cracking bad jokes and trying to be an all-round icebreaker. I'd introduce myself to the other kids and then ask their names, all the time smiling and laughing. But this wasn't me masking any fears about the fight ahead because I wasn't afraid: I was genuinely happy. Life had taken a decided turn for the better, I was enjoying every moment of it and it was all thanks to boxing.

Eventually, my turn came to enter the ring and I was handed a pair of smelly gloves. Sticking my hands into them, I could feel the sweat of three or four previous young fighters. There were only two pairs of gloves and we all had to share them. Emerging through the crowd, I had all the cocksureness of a young Muhammad Ali.

'You know what you gotta do, son' – Tom McGarry's words in my ear as I climbed through the ropes.

I was almost disappointed to find myself facing a rather puny specimen of a boy. Pasty-faced with skinny arms, this would be way too easy. The bell rang and any idea of pity or compassion was swiftly banished as I assumed my boxing stance and moved towards the victim. The eyes of a fighter say everything and his screamed terror at me. He didn't have a strategy for defeating me or any smart opening moves planned – puny boy's only game plan was to survive as long as possible.

In for the kill I went, landing a blow to his abdomen. 'Oooph,' he exhaled, his eyes squinting with pain. This was as cruel as beating up Bambi, but once I started the job I'd travelled to Plymouth to undertake, it had to be finished: jab, jab, cross, upper cut, upper cut, pivot to the side, upper cut, jab, jab, jab, jab, cross; hook to the body, hook to the head, jab, jab, jab … He hadn't landed a single punch on me. The bell rang to announce the end of the round.

Back in my corner, Eddie McGarry took to bellowing advice in my face but all I could think of was the smoke on his breath – the fumes he was belching at me were unbearable. Looking away, I tried to suck in some clean, refreshing air. The bell rang for round two and I darted away to see if I could bring the encounter to a rapid conclusion. This was to be a hallmark of my amateur and professional fights: an impatience to knock out the other guy and go home. Unless my opponent really merited it and put up a good account, I wasn't going to hang about long. In this case, it took three rounds to demolish my pasty adversary, who looked highly relieved as he staggered back to the changing room.

As we put our clothes on, an ABA official walked in and pressed a refreshment ticket into each of our hands. This would get us a tiny bacon sandwich and some pop, the latter being something called orange juice although it was packed with E numbers and colourings. For us kids, there was no alcohol.

It was a different story for the ABA officials, however, who treated themselves to what, in the 1970s, would have been a fine spread of nibbles washed down with wine and beer. The sight of it all irritated the hell out of me: those portly officials who scribbled on bits of paper and then stuffed their faces while the ones who had entertained the pundits, the evening's performers, skulked at the edges with a pathetic little sandwich and chemical fruit-juice concoction. Many of those officials had almost certainly come from modest backgrounds themselves, but they seemed determined to set great distance between their humble roots and newly found status on the boxing circuit.

All of us Christie brothers stuck on gloves and boxed for the Standard Triumph but the end results were very different. We had been street-fighters but boxing isn't about thumping the living daylights out of your opponent, though it often is. Somehow, I realised that skill and tactics were also involved and so I developed moves that I wouldn't be bothered about, if I was just rearranging a skinhead's features. In the ring, however, I wanted my fighting to have a certain style and finesse.

My oldest brother Des was a tough street warrior and after a handful of amateur fights he didn't really pursue a boxing career much further. Michael had more success: he and I were the first black kids to box in the England team, around 1980. For the first time, I found myself draped in the Union Jack, an icon also being paraded up and down Britain's high streets by National Front thugs. In truth, this left me with mixed emotions.

Michael performed well in the England team, but he lacked my ability to dance and, as Eddie McGarry conceded, the two of us were in a different class. Although Michael would go toe to toe with his opponent and whack the punches in, it was all very even-paced – just the same thing, over and over.

After me, Wesley was the most successful, fighting as 'Lloyd' Christie: his middle name. He was a professional welterweight and eventually won the British title in 1987. It's testimony to his skill that he got so far, given he spent crucial months of his form-ative teen years in Borstal following scraps in the street and hanging out with the wrong kind of blokes when he should have been training.

But the biggest handful for the Standard Triumph was my brother Andy. As Eddie said to me years later, he just wouldn't 'knuckle down'. And to be a great boxer, that's exactly what you've got to do. Andy was National Schools Champion by the time he was fifteen and we could have walked the same path to the top. Instead, he preferred to hang out with the bad boys on the street and I believe that's why he stumbled ultimately.

The NABC semi-finals were held at the Standard Triumph in 1979 with Andy Christie on the bill; the show had been publi-cised, posters and publicity sent out. All the local press and boxing writers were present and the audience was seated, waiting for the evening's entertainment. Instead, they gazed at a boxing ring that remained stubbornly empty: Andy was hanging out with his usual crowd on the street. Tom McGarry, meanwhile, was completely humiliated.

Tom's rage was loud and public. Turning to a reporter from the *Coventry Evening Telegraph*, he exploded and his rant duly appeared in print: 'What Andrew did was unforgivable – he let down himself, his club and his county. He has not been training for a couple of weeks but I fully expected him to turn up on Saturday. He did not even have the decency to let us know that he was not going to box – a simple telephone call would have been enough.'

The headline said it all: 'STAY-AWAY CHRISTIE BANNED FOR A SEASON'.

So, was blood thicker than water – or boxing? Not at all! I was completely on McGarry's side and as fed up with Andy as he was. On the same night, I demolished my opponent in a round, venting my anger towards my brother on David Tharme from Widnes. All he saw was a hurricane of punches, a thousand fists flying about his body and head. The local paper reported the match with some restraint:

Christie, cool, confident and deceptively casual, appeared to exercise the minimum amount of effort. Working behind a lethal left jab, Christie had Tharme down for a count of eight with a short right and when a left hook sent the Widnes boy flying backwards on to the ropes, referee Ron Winterburn rightly decided he had seen enough.

Simon was possibly the least suited to a career in boxing; he wasn't as athletic as the rest of us and was a whole lot more docile. The killer instinct that I myself took for granted just wasn't there in my youngest brother. Like Michael, he was more a man of peace than war. This might help to explain why he turned up late for a bout on the amateur circuit one day. Sheepishly, he told us that he'd overslept and couldn't make the fight in Whitley Bay, but I suspected his heart really wasn't in it. Faced with the dishonour of another Christie doing a 'no-show' at a boxing match, the rest of us decided to take action.

At the time I was working in a garage and so I knew how to hotwire the rusting old Volkswagen Beetle belonging to my boxing trainer. We then bundled Simon inside, took to the road and drove off like madmen to the North Sea coast. That car hadn't seen a road, let alone a motorway, for quite some time. With no regard to our safety, we hurtled across the country in icy conditions, passing several major road accidents along the way: one of which, I recall, involved a dead person sprawled out on the tarmac. But there was no time to gawp – we had to get Simon to the show on time.

When we got to Whitley Bay – in just about one piece – the Christie brothers burst out of the car and dragged Simon into the hall. He returned the favour by shaming us with a dreadful performance. In stony silence, we went back to Coventry. After that particular episode, Simon put the boxing gloves down and picked up the bottle instead – often bottles of wine that we brought back from boxing dinners, the ones the officials hadn't guzzled during the evening.

Those bottles of wine used to sit next to our trophies in the Cheveral Avenue living room as if they were awards in themselves, but what we didn't realise was that Simon was cracking them open behind our backs and swigging back the content, sometimes even before school. He was turning up tipsy for lessons.

I'm not sure at what point I realised that I was pulling ahead and away from my brothers, but I'd be lying if I didn't admit there was a growing awareness that my talent was unique. In 1977, HM Queen Elizabeth II celebrated her Silver Jubilee and I became Schoolboy Champion of England, a far more momentous event in my world. At thirteen years of age, I'd already chalked up the Warwickshire County Championship the year before. For the next four years, I wouldn't let anybody else near those trophies and brought them home time and time again, adding NABC (National Association of Boys' Clubs) National Champion to my collection for three years as well.

By 1981, I'd won every amateur title that a fighter could take, which earned me a place in the *Guinness Book of Records*, now known as the *Guinness World Records*. In the decade before, this book became familiar to every kid in Britain through a weekly BBC programme called *Record Breakers*. TV entertainer Roy Castle would invite young talent onto the teatime show to talk about the record they'd broken or even attempt to break a new record, there and then. This always seemed like a distant world to me, but all of a sudden I was now part of it.

Not long afterwards, Tom bumped into Roy Castle on a train. Never one to miss an opportunity, he sidled up and gingerly suggested a certain Errol Christie might make an interesting subject for a programme. Needless to say, we never heard back. In retrospect, it was sad: with the stormy summer riots still on the horizon at the start of that year, positive black role models on television might have made a difference.

Recognition in my home city of Coventry came through the sports pages of the local paper – although at school and at home, I was still the same worthless ragamuffin: 'wutless,' as my mother described me. At President Kennedy, I was an academic nobody, all but written off as just another black kid slowly heading for the dole queue or maybe a supermarket checkout job, if I was really lucky. Nightclub bouncers still turned the Christies away and thuggish white blokes continued to yell 'Nigger!' from car windows as they drove past. It was as if I was living in two parallel universes: one in which I was hailed a champ, the other where I was called a 'nig-nog'.

At this stage, I took to keeping scrapbooks of all my press cuttings so that after any really unpleasant street experience I could delve under the bunk bed, take them out and remind myself of this other world where I seemed to amount to something. I pored over those headlines:

'CHAMPION CHRISTIE TOPS TRIUMPH BILL'

'ERROL CHRISTIE – IMPRESSIVE RECORD PUTS OFF OPPONENTS'

'DYNAMIC CHRISTIE LANDS TITLE'

'MIGHTY ERROL CHRISTIE'

All too often, I could see only one black face in the newspaper photo: mine. An Afro-Caribbean oasis in a white sea, I had to ask myself what I really expected to achieve from these efforts. Acceptance by society at large seemed impossible in 1979 or 1981 – a black man was either somebody who was taking your job or just a figure of fun and so I ruled that out. Fame and fortune seemed phoney to me – and as we'd discovered with *Record Breakers*, nobody wanted to see black boys on TV.

So, I boiled my ambition down to money. I'd spent a whole childhood with my nose pressed up against shop windows while Dad flatly refused to give us 3p for a Curly Wurly. Everything I was doing now was geared to being able to walk into those shops, slap my money down on the counter and take whatever I wanted – legitimately, of course. There would be no more second-hand or borrowed clothes, for a start. When, after bringing another cup home to the city, I was invited to shake the Lord Mayor of Coventry's hand in his parlour at the Town Hall, I had to borrow a jacket from one of the trainers – I just didn't have one of my own. The arms were too short and the shoulders too tight. One day, I promised myself, I'd be able to afford my own suit.

Out of all the white kids at Standard Triumph, there was just one who visited our home. Raymond Satchell wasn't so much brave: he just didn't seem to be aware of the risk he was taking by walking across the threshold. With Mr Christie senior storming round the house, shouting crazy rubbish or silently boiling up a temper, I never brought mates or girls home – Raymond was the exception.

He and I shared a passion for boxing and, unlike other white kids, Raymond was happy to train with me down at the Standard Triumph. I liked the fact that he was free of any malice and had an open personality. As a fighter, he earned the nickname 'Kermit' and also 'Kiki' after two children's TV characters, both frogs. The reason for this was his comic appearance when he fought in the boxing ring: whenever he punched, his little eyes shut tight involuntarily and his throat made bizarre croaking noises that were slightly disturbing.

One press cutting has Raymond in his usual pose with closed eyes, but landing a killer punch on his opponent at an ABA semi-final. Everybody was sure that, despite fighting like a frog, Raymond would go on to great things. However, this was not to be. What happened to my friend came as a stark early warning for me.

One day, Raymond turned up at Cheveral Avenue with a cut near his eye. The ugly, fresh gash was hard to ignore.

'What happened to you?' I asked.

'Fell out of bed,' was his reply.

Of course, I didn't believe him. Raymond sat down on our sofa and I waited for him to spill the beans, but he wouldn't be drawn. Only later did I discover that he'd had an epileptic fit. It was a massive seizure: he hadn't led me on about falling out of bed, he'd just not told me the reason. Deep down, I'm sure he knew it meant curtains for his boxing career. The passion we shared could only be continued by me – from now on, he'd have to be a spectator from the sidelines.

Callous though it undoubtedly seems to me now, our friendship was also terminated, although not straightaway. Over time, I saw less and less of him, however. My focus became ever more narrow. What powered me forward was a determination to become the best of Britain's boxers and that meant I couldn't spend too much time worrying about those who fell away.

Raymond's fit may have had any number of causes, but boxing probably didn't help. That doesn't mean I would ever advocate closing the sport down – nor for that matter, would I want to see white-collar boxing banned, even though it's been heavily criticised by some doctors: forty-something males hitting each other is deemed dangerous, according to the British Medical Association. Whatever risks the sport carries, it's still more dangerous to sit at home in front of the TV, allowing yourself to get clinically obese. And for young guys like me, boxing was the key to the door out of the ghetto. Take that key away, and I'd have been left with nothing.

But I couldn't completely ignore what happened to Raymond, nor could I be deflected from my goal. No other path was open to me, no other way out of the drudgery and pointlessness of my daily existence in Coventry. The City boys that I've trained in recent years tell me: no risk, no reward. They picked up that motto trading derivatives in the markets and in my struggle to escape the Midlands, I took up a similar motto. The words of Winston Churchill became my own watchwords: 'No retreat. No surrender.'

With Raymond Satchell no longer by my side, I was back on the road. My fitness levels soared and, even at the age of sixteen, I looked to most people like a fully grown man. Eddie McGarry remembers one incident in Leicester, where a little kid was fighting me for the junior ABA title and he managed to land a couple of punches. Appalled by this indignity, I felt the need to take him apart bit by bit. At the end of the slaughter, the challenger's dad and the boxing club secretary marched up to Eddie and demanded to see my birth certificate; they didn't believe I was sixteen. Initially, he laughed it off but they persisted. Faced with the prospect of having the national ABA title stripped from me, the Christie family, plus Eddie was forced to take a trip to my birthplace in Leicester to obtain the relevant document. Triumphant, we returned with definitive proof that I was indeed a boy in a man's body.

In 1981, aged seventeen, I was with the England team when we took on Ireland. We were put up in a hotel and at some point during the night most of the other fighters started to yawn and began slinking off to bed. But I was having none of it. As usual, the excitement of being away from home was way too much. I was also showing the first signs of the insomnia that has plagued my adult life.

A skinny redheaded flyweight called Danny Porter yawned and announced that he was off for some shut-eye. He was a bit of a practical joker and that night I decided to turn the tables on him. We all carried on chatting for a while until I picked up the phone and rang Danny, who I suspected had now fallen asleep in his room.

'Hello – is that Danny Porter?' I asked, putting on my poshest voice.

'Yeah – hoozat?'

'Hello, Danny – sorry to intrude, but it's the *Daily Express* here ...'

Now I had his attention. All my mates were trying not to burst into hysterics.

'Oh right, is it? 'Ow can I help?'

'Well, Danny – we've heard so much about you: great puncher, great fighter – so please get dressed straightaway. We've got a photographer waiting for you. Come to room number 84, we want your picture in the paper tomorrow. Could you make it here snappy?'

Totally disorientated and incredulous, a few minutes later poor little Danny shipped up at number 84, his hair combed, shoes shined and wearing something that passed for a suit. At the sight of him ready for the non-existent photo opportunity, we collapsed in the corridor.

'You bastards!'

Eventually, I think he forgave me.

The partnership between Tom McGarry and me became like the father–son relationship I'd never enjoyed at home. Mentor, trainer and teacher, the big Scottish trade unionist took me under his wing. He was determined to make me into a first-class boxer and to tear me away from the endless street fighting that I constantly found myself drawn into. He and Eddie always seemed to know when I'd got involved in yet another scrap with the boot boys; it was as if they had antennae that sensed the moment when my fist planted itself into a skinhead's smirking face.

But now I began to take Tom for granted. After picking up so many trophies, I started to credit myself for all the glory and forgot how much I'd needed his help and guidance. Of course, I was young, maybe a bit arrogant. Behind all the goofing around, I think I believed that ultimately it was me alone who could ensure my escape from Coventry. Tom might help me on the way but if I really wanted to forge a new life then it would be down to me to achieve it.

One morning, he was giving one of his addresses to the boxers at the gym: how well we'd been doing, but how much more we could achieve. I drifted off and then started chatting away to somebody next to me. This show of indifference enraged the big man.

'Errol!'

'Yeah?'

I adopted the demeanour of a pissed-off, inner-city black kid – which is pretty much what I was. My head was held at an angle, lip curled in a sneer, a regular teenage rebel. But Tom had seen enough.

'Get out of here, lad!'

Momentarily stunned, I said nothing, convinced he was joking.

'*Out!* Did you hear what I said?'

A flicker of fear gave way to indignant anger on my part. Who was Tom to think that he could throw out the Standard Triumph's best fighter? He could try filling that trophy cabinet with the lesser boxing mortals around me but he wouldn't succeed. I'd show my surrogate father that he couldn't reject me so easily.

So, off I went to a rival gym: Coachmakers was linked to another motor factory. I would make Tom sorry for talking to me like that, especially in front of all the other young boxers. He'd be back on his hands and knees, begging for my return.

That vain fantasy never materialised. Coachmakers was awful – really, really terrible. A boxing gym needs an atmosphere of intense discipline and application with a man like Tom in charge to force the pace, to keep the fighters continuously training with the utmost dedication. Standard Triumph was a teeming hive of activity while Coachmakers was sleepy in comparison. Seconds after walking through the door to my new gym, I realised I'd made a terrible mistake.

There was no proper boxing ring; gloves and hand wraps had been discarded all over the place – a habit that infuriates me to this day. To my mind, a boxer has to look after his kit with the same care as a soldier in the Army; it's a matter of pride to keep your head guard, gloves, shorts and boots properly packed away. A disorganised mind can never make a top-class fighter.

I tried to make a fist of it, pardon the pun. Coachmakers was never going to work for me, though. Deep down, I knew where my spiritual home lay and it was only a matter of days before I returned to the Standard Triumph and stood in front of Tom, sheepishly shuffling my feet like a naughty toddler.

'Can I come back?'

Expressionless, Tom gazed at me. And then finally he said, 'Go and do your training.'

The only good thing to come out of the Coachmakers' episode was that I met a new trainer, who I now brought back with me to the Standard Triumph. Leon Thomas was to be the man who would take me to a professional standard. A quiet and mild black guy with a dry sense of humour, about my brother Michael's age, Leon upped my stamina by insisting I went running – something that was to become an obsession from then on. Like many boxers, I would be up in the small hours to pound the nearby pavements. Thanks to Leon, I was to reach the pinnacle of the amateur scene before turning professional.

Year after year, I was slowly but surely building a reputation as the boxer that no one could beat. By the end of the 1970s, the worlds of County, Schools and Junior ABA Championships had learned there was only one young fighter that you had to overcome to get your gloved hands on those coveted trophies. Kids would turn up and try their luck at taking the County or Schoolboy trophies from me only to be sent bouncing off the ropes and back to their corner.

By 1979, the national sports press had picked up on my existence. In that year, I fought Spencer Williams for the NABC cup. Ringside journalist Ken Jones captured what the Errol

Christie performance was all about:

> From the opening bell, it was one-way traffic. Christie, who is
> built like a Chieftain tank, attacked Williams' non-stop scoring
> to the face with piston-jabs and follow-up rights. Christie's domi-
> nance in the first round was almost frightening. He came out for
> the next in the same mood and Williams was left, literally,
> hanging on. In the final round, Christie even spat out his gum-
> shield as he threw himself forward again. He finished the bout as
> he started it, totally on top with barely a punch conceded and
> hardly a sweat on.

Hilariously, the judges awarded Williams 'honours for his bravery'
but this was understandable – by now, I'd lost just two of sixty
bouts and enjoyed a 100 per cent success rate in competition
outings. With more than bit of understatement, I was quoted in
one newspaper as saying 'My boxing has become more than a
hobby now.' Indeed, it was a passion that burned. With nothing
to go back to – on the streets, at school or at home – I had to keep
powering forward.

By the age of seventeen, the only trophy left to win was the
Senior ABA Championship but, despite my record, there were
plenty of naysayers around who thought I was about to bite off
far more than even I could chew. 'Just be happy where you are,
Errol,' they told me. 'You've done well, lad – now don't push your
luck.' Imagine the surprise then when I got to the semi-finals.
Now those cautious comments were modified.

'You're very lucky to have got this far.'

'Don't be sorry if you lose the next one – you've done really
well.'

Those sort of well-intentioned words annoy the hell out of me.
I wasn't prepared to acknowledge any glass ceiling on how far I
could rise; any barriers others thought insurmountable. With
Jamaican fire in my soul and a hatred of being kept down, I
regarded those otherwise friendly comments as patronising, a
nice way of keeping me in my rightful place. But I had no 'Massa'
and I tugged no forelock as my folks had done: Errol Christie was
going to the top, whether the people around him believed in him
or not.

I was seventeen years of age and this was 1980. To win the championship, I would have to take on mature men who were bigger than me and arguably more experienced. My opponent in the semi-finals was to be Joey Frost – a very strong man, physically, who had recently gone up to middleweight.

For most pundits, he was the man to bet on. After all, Joey Frost was boxing captain of England and had represented his country as a member of the 1980 Olympic squad in Moscow. No one in the right mind expected me to topple him. But suddenly, the people of Coventry sat up; now they took notice of a boy that many of them had once described as a 'nig-nog' and a 'coon'. Later, Tom McGarry informed me that the bars in town were eerily empty as men rushed home to switch on their televisions to watch the action unfold. This was an era when boxing was on the mainstream terrestrial channels at peak viewing times.

In my home town, TV viewers could switch to Central TV, where regional sports presenter Gary Newbon was giving his view of the fight. In the years ahead, he would become a keen follower of my career. He also appeared on ITV, broadcasting to the whole country alongside that moustachioed smoothy Dickie Davies, who presented *World of Sport* – a programme that filled the entire Saturday afternoon every week. Over at the BBC, Harry Carpenter was the undisputed voice of boxing as presenter of *Sportsnight*. As my career went stellar, I was to rub shoulders with all those personalities.

Coventry was glued to the box and I didn't intend to disappoint but Joey Frost had no intention of yielding, either; he was at the top of his game, better known and a hard man to boot. The moment the bell rang, the England captain stormed out of his corner to send me flying back to Coventry at the end of one of his powerful jabs. Blows rained down and I was left in no doubt as to his resolve. On two occasions, I had to pick myself up from the canvas. I was a boy fighting a man, but this was nothing new – the key thing now was to pull myself together and inject some self-belief into my fighting.

Remembering all the grown men I'd fought on the streets and left in a pool of their own blood, I turned on Frost. Using my whole body to drive jabs and crosses into his larger form, I worked over his torso from all directions in the way that the Standard Triumph had taught me. Keeping light on my toes, I buzzed round him like a killer bee. Down he went onto the canvas and then again. The second time, the England captain didn't rise.

Frost versus Christie was described by one scribbler as a 'humdinger' and I still look back on it as one of my greatest victories. I'd started off on the wrong foot, but then found the path to victory and followed it. According to Tom McGarry the roar from the frenzied audience was so loud that it was impossible for him to know when I'd actually knocked Frost out. The deafening noise from around the ring made the bell inaudible and he'd been worried that the decisive punch landed after it had rung, but as the referee raised my arms, it was clear that I'd won, fair and square.

At first, the sheer scale of what I'd achieved didn't sink in – I simply acknowledged the crowd and enjoyed the cheers. But then seeing the dejected figure of Frost in the other corner, I suddenly realised what I'd done. In sending him down, I'd left no option to the powers that be other than to make me boxing captain of England, the first black man to hold that position.

But there was to be no ceremony or grand dinner. Tom just came up to me later on and said that he'd been informed I was to be England captain. No official came up and patted me on the back or shook my hand to tell me the great news. All that happened was that some boxing bigwig told Tom, who relayed it to me. And that was that. But it still filled me with a burning pride: I had become top dog and shown England what a black man can achieve.

With Frost disposed of in the semi-finals, I now faced an even greater opponent in the finals for the Senior ABA. Cameron Lithgow ('Lucky Lithgow') was an experienced England international with twenty-one wins out of twenty-four international bouts. If I defeated him, 1981 would be the year when Errol Christie ruled supreme over the amateur boxing world. Lithgow was roughly the same weight as me but a fraction taller. Birmingham-born, he represented the Park Youth amateur boxing club. To lose to me would be nothing short of humiliation.

I was relishing this fight. Pumping with adrenalin, I climbed into the ring. Having sent Joey Frost down, I was no longer overawed by the big white boys that I'd only recently been told I was incapable of defeating. Lithgow's luck, as far as I was concerned, was about to run out. If I notched up this victory, I'd win the greatest prize the English amateur world could offer, crowning years of teenage achievements.

We began the fight and I discovered his style was all detached subtlety: spending more time on the back foot, never coming forward, retreating in the face of onslaught. It was an old tactic to wear out your opponent before turning the fight to your advantage. At one point, I felt as if I was chasing him round the ring. For an impatient individual like me, keen to knock out his opponent in round one and go home, Lithgow's chess-style approach was tedious.

It felt as if he hadn't come to fight me, just to out-point me. I preferred a thrilling tear-up instead of this dainty dance. To relieve my boredom, I did a little Ali shuffle: a rapid, walking movement in a stationary position that was one of the great man's trademarks. This didn't go down well with the audience. Afterwards, I was told there had been some catcalls, but in the heat of the fight I didn't notice anything else.

Already, I'd been warned by one journalist – Roger Draper – about my Ali shuffle after the fight with Frost. In the heat of the moment, I'd performed it over his prone body:

The only time his feet are likely to leave the ground is when he unveils an unscripted Muhammad Ali "shuffle" across a fallen opponent. I remind him that this suggested show of arrogance had not gone down too well with supporters of Liverpool's Joey Frost when he twice put down their Olympic hero on his way to the ABA semi-finals. A northern newspaper had blasted Christie for his unsporting attitude.

'I can't remember doing it but if I did, I didn't mean anything by it.'

Finally cornering my subtly performing prey, I let loose a combination of moves that sent Lithgow reeling. Off he went to find the ropes, struggling to prop himself up. After a little more punishment in round three, the fight was called in my favour. But it didn't feel like a proper victory: the sweat wasn't pouring off me, I wasn't gasping for air, there wasn't a single cut or bruise to show for my efforts. I wanted a clear-cut victory and always preferred an outright knockout, but Lithgow wouldn't give me that satisfaction. Throughout, he stayed on his back foot, which drove me nuts.

Afterwards, the mood in the dressing room was truly glum. It was as if I'd just lost the cup, not won it. Muhammad Ali once remarked that nobody knows what to say in the loser's dressing room but, on that night, they couldn't find the right words for the winner, either. When a journalist asked for my victor's comment, I was almost apologetic.

It must have been one of my worst performances. I just don't know what went wrong; I kept trying to put the pressure on Lithgow, but I just couldn't do it. Perhaps the occasion got to me, I just don't know.

Tom McGarry joined in the hand-wringing with this observation: 'A perfectionist will always find fault with his performance but having said that, it was not one of Errol's better displays.'

It was left to the BBC's Harry Carpenter – doyen of boxing commentators – to give a very different opinion. Summing up what the millions who had watched thought of me, Carpenter exclaimed: 'A star is born!'

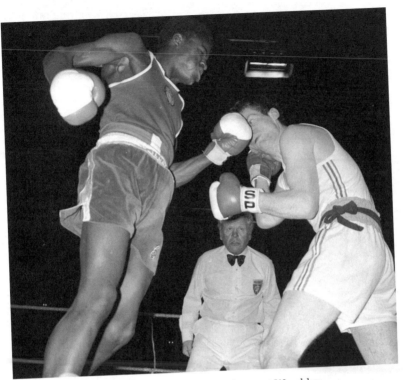

In action against Cameron Lithgow at Wembley,
1 May 1981.

PA Photos

4

RIOT!

'I've come to the conclusion that
We're gonna hunt yeh yeh yeh
The National Front – Yes we are,
We're gonna hunt yeh yeh yeh
The National Front
Cause they believe in apartheid
For that we gonna whup their hides
For all my people they cheated and lied
I won't rest till I'm satisfied'

'Steel Pulse' – Jah Pickney

I looked down at the leaflet in my hand: Asian Satnam Singh Gill had been set upon, killed in a racist attack. In the nasty language of the 1970s and 1980s, he was the victim of 'Paki-bashing'.

But something about this murder set it apart from all the other beatings that Asian kids had suffered, like a line had been crossed. Somehow we just knew a stand had to be taken against those thugs or they would walk all over us. A group calling itself the Coventry Committee Against Racism decided to organise a demonstration in the city on 20 June 1981 and I heard that The Specials would play a gig against the National Front at the Butts Stadium, where the city's rugby team normally played. It was to be the centrepiece of a day of long-overdue action against the new Nazis.

The Specials were a multi-racial ska band from our city, currently topping the charts with the hit single 'Ghost Town'. Their down-to-earth lyrics about clubbing at the local Locarno nightclub, or being chased through the 'Concrete Jungle' of the Hillfields district of Coventry, spoke volumes to kids like me.

I heard on the grapevine that the NF were mobilising for a big counter-demonstration; they intended to swarm into the Pool Meadow Bus Station from all over the region. By word of mouth, me and the other guys in Hillfields were told to gather at the old cathedral and be ready to greet the NF supporters as they arrived. Immediately, I realised there would be an almighty bust-up, right in the middle of Coventry.

It wasn't hard to convince guys like me to go down there and fight: months before, the tension in Coventry had been growing. There was an atmosphere of lockdown, with the police monitoring our every move. Stop and searches were on the increase, we had a harder time than ever getting into the clubs and any jobs that we'd once been able to get, even the lowest-paid ones, had dried up. Everybody was on the dole.

We were ready to riot.

Tom and Eddie McGarry had to be kept in the dark about it. The following weekend was the Senior ABA final, in which I'd fight Cameron Lithgow. If the sports media found out that I'd been in a riot, my boxing career would be over.

'Stay away from trouble on the streets,' Tom constantly cautioned me. 'Just don't get involved.'

Looking back on 1980 and 1981, many people can remember a feeling prevalent in all the inner cities that something big was about to kick off. But staying indoors when the streets exploded was not an option for me: this was the opportunity to get revenge on the boot boys – I could not walk away.

By then, the skinhead enemy, in their oxblood DMs, bleached jeans and green bomber jackets, had become better organised and more politicised. It wasn't like the old days when racist hooligans simply lashed out at us without much thought, from tribal instinct alone. Now they had leaders dripping poison into their ears about how we were to blame for them not having jobs and council houses. True, the factories were closing down and houses and flats becoming harder and harder to find, but then my black mates were also on the dole and living in dingy squats. In fact, they were worse off than many of the skins.

By the time I took on Cameron Lithgow in 1981, I knew a lot about those squats. In Cheveral Avenue, things came to a head, forcing me to move out permanently to Hillfields. It started with the realisation that my dad's untreated mental condition was getting a whole lot worse.

One night, I came back home late from a clubbing session with my mates and, as usual, broke into the house through the living-room window. Unlike Des, who was much bigger than me, I could slip in like a snake and drop to the floor fairly noiselessly; I'd done this a few times and never woken up the folks before.

In the small hours of the morning, I slithered through the gap like a big black serpent and rolled onto the carpet. The room was completely dark and silent. There was no sound from my parents' bedroom and so I flicked on the living-room light only to find myself face-to-face with Dad, who was sitting in his usual battered armchair, staring at me. Frozen with terror, I waited for the familiar words: 'Ay, bloody boy!'

But nothing happened.

Instead, his bloodshot eyes stared straight ahead, flickering oddly. They were wide open, but unseeing. Bolt upright, his hands gripped the arms of the chair. Years later, I found out that this is what the doctors describe as a 'catatonic fit'. In layman's terms, he was on another planet. Instinctively, I knew there was nothing for me to do except switch off the light and go up to bed. Afterwards, we never spoke about the incident.

As the trophies piled up in the living-room cabinet, Dad's reaction was not so supportive as you might imagine. Our tiny living room was now filled with cups, victory shields, framed photographs and all the other paraphernalia that came with boxing success. My prowess in the ring was there for him to see every day of the week. Then one day, another brickie turned round to him on a building site and jibbed him: 'I bet your son can beat you up now – see him in the papers!'

Mad as hell, he came home and found me in the bedroom, looking at my scrapbooks.

'Tink dat yooz a man now 'cos you can box!'

He was shaking with rage, but there was nothing that I could say or do to change things. From the beginning, he knew the cards were stacked against him in life. At least I had a slight chance to make it better for myself. Boxing had opened up an escape route from the daily drudge that I was determined to pursue and I wasn't going to let his feelings get in the way. After I refused to respond to him, he shuffled off.

Another day, Dad came home from the building site with a big gash in his head that required twelve stitches. His left arm was put in a sling, too. An Irish builder had made some racist remark and, unable to take it anymore, my father lashed back. The Irishman retaliated by grabbing an axe and then tried to split Dad's head open like a melon, but by all accounts he'd ended up the bigger mess. Mum said the cops had turned up and tried to arrest Dad, pinning the blame on him.

It looked like my dad would end up behind bars. Remarkably, he was able to walk free because a couple of his workmates felt sorry for the old man and spoke up for him. He certainly wasn't capable of doing it for himself. They said the Irish guy was a loose cannon and had been in the wrong, so the cops let the matter drop and Dad came home. But none of this improved his mood: in fact, all the frustrations in his life were leading to an explosive breaking point.

One night I was in bed but not sleeping very much when I heard a commotion downstairs in the living room. My mum let out a short scream and Dad sounded like a mad dog. Quickly, I bolted downstairs and pushed open the living-room door. Nothing could have prepared me for the sight in front of me. Dad stood there, his fists clenched like a prize-fighter. Mum was squirming on the sofa, sobbing and screaming, crying out the 'Lawd's' name, her clothes torn and her bra showing. As I walked in, she tried to cover herself up.

Then he started to hit her again. It was all some stupid argument about her not visiting a cousin of his when she'd been in Jamaica a while back, nothing that merited this treatment. I had to catch my breath and then I squared up to him as best I could.

'If *you* touch her – my mum – one more time, I'm gonna *kill* you!'

Enough of Honour Thy Father. Not if this was the way my father chose to behave. His snorting bullhead turned to me, eyes blazing. Unlike the night when I'd found him in a catatonic state, he knew where he was now and his own son had dared to tell him how he should treat his wife. Maybe the voices were saying something as well, but I suddenly realised the next swing of his fist was coming in my direction.

Terrifyingly, he made a weird, howling noise like a demented werewolf. His whole face contorted like I'd never seen it before. Then he grabbed the nearest object he could find: a tin of Vim – a scouring powder that Mum must have left on the table. He hurled it towards me with such force that it left a dent in our living-room wall for years. I ducked and the tin exploded, releasing a cloud of white powder that hung in the air around us, stinging our eyes.

I couldn't land a punch on my own father. Part of me wanted to, but for so long I'd been programmed to honour him that it was never going to happen. I'd had my fill of his madness, however. The sight of Mum quivering on the sofa, shouting, 'Lawd Jesus!'

and him like a vengeful God planning his next violent move was all too much. I shook my head: this was the end.

I exited the living room, then opened the front door and left the house. With one short backward glance at Cheveral Avenue, I fled the family home for good. My new life was to be among the drug dealers, prostitutes and small-time gangsters of Hillfields.

Hillfields made most middle-class people in Coventry shudder. If you were a respectable sort of person and found yourself driving through that part of town, you'd hit the accelerator hard and get the hell out of there. It was where the bad black people lived, and some bad white people, too. Drugs, knives and illegally acquired cash, all were in abundance at Hillfields. This was an unforgiving landscape of big concrete tower blocks surrounded by ugly, littered scrubland. The lifts in the blocks never worked, the graffiti was never removed and the rubbish stayed uncollected; it was a place where the rule of law didn't seem to apply.

So, I exchanged the family home for a rented room in a squat in the middle of a police no-go zone. And I'd never been happier. The rent went to a mate of mine, John Rawlins, who lived in the tower block with his girlfriend. He was white and she was black. I never really saw them that much as they appeared to live under a duvet cover most of the time.

I was up early every morning as my job at the Coventry Clutch Centre, a garage near Jubilee Crescent, had now gone full-time. Like my parents, I was determined never to draw the dole. No matter if millions were now unemployed and the British economy was going down the pan, I refused to become another statistic – I'd clean the streets first.

Having a room to myself was a magical experience. The bunk beds were gone, the psychotic father storming up the stairs to beat us even blacker and blue just a bad memory. I didn't have to make a mad dash for the fridge to get any food before my brothers and sisters got there. My mother's voice screaming 'Lawd Jesus!' all the time at some minor cause of irritation was no more. Instead, a lovely silence, just the purr of distant traffic and the sound of John humping away in the room next door.

Weekends were even better. In Cheveral Avenue, Saturdays had become a living hell: Dad found it impossible to work with other human beings and so he'd gone solo as a builder, a one-man contractor. When he couldn't cope on his own, he drafted in his sons as skivvies. Every Saturday, we found ourselves knee-deep in a sandpit that he kept in the garden, shovelling it into his van. Then it was off to Birmingham or wherever to help out on some job that he was making a mess of. But now, with my own job and flat, I didn't have to slave for old-man Christie anymore.

Sundays were also free of Elder Nicely, Deacon Kennedy and Sister Toff. No more interminable church services and 'hipopo-popopo'. Instead, the Sabbath became a genuine day of rest: religion-free and without that blond, blue-eyed Jesus staring down at me from the hallway in Cheveral Avenue; the Anglo-Saxon messiah who'd failed to watch over me at home.

Saturday nights became a little more interesting. The flats around us were permanent party venues. I'd walk into a stranger's home – there didn't seem to any concept of private property – and writhing bodies would be all over the floor, a sea of snogging everywhere. Free of the restrictions of living in Cheveral Avenue, I now began to pull in earnest.

I lost my virginity at sixteen. An older white woman, aged about thirty, had taken to walking past the Coventry Clutch Centre. One day, in the spirit of the times, I wolf-whistled at her. She glanced back coyly and before I knew it, I was in her flat and in her bed. The first time I found myself on top of this woman, I didn't shoot – but there was a good reason for this.

She'd just informed me there was a husband and he was in the Army, but fortunately he was away; that made me feel a little uneasy. Even though I was more than capable of handling myself in any fight, the thought of taking on a trained soldier still gave me pause for thought. So, I made by excuses, got dressed and left. However, I couldn't resist a return visit, a few days later.

We were back in bed and this time, we were definitely fucking all the way. All raging teenage hormones, there I was, banging away like a horny black rabbit. Suddenly, I had the oddest sensation as if I'd been smacked hard on the back of the head; there was a tingling followed by a shudder through my entire body. For a moment, I thought the husband had returned and hit me, but then I realised I'd shot my load into a woman for the first time. Finally, Errol Christie had lost his virginity.

The only thing that had delayed me in this was boxing. For years, us young fighters had our heads filled with rubbish about the dangers of sex from adults on the ABA circuit. One old bloke stands out in my mind – a trainer who would give us dire warnings about how our todgers would be the ruin of us. Sex can destroy your performance in the ring, he told us. Shooting your load too soon before a bout would make you too relaxed, more liable to be hit by an opponent: 'You got to stay sharp, boys! Sex weakens your legs, makes them go, saps all your energy. So, don't do it!'

Even though I had girlfriends, I was nervous about going the whole way as I was off boxing most weekends. However, after shagging this woman I went on to victory in the Senior ABAs so the nonsense didn't stand up to too much scrutiny. Once I'd punctured the myth, the fighting and fucking happily co-existed from thereon.

I started seeing a white girl called Alison Brooker, who was at President Kennedy School with me. This was still quite unusual. While white girls would go with black blokes for quickies, often they'd admit to our faces they'd never dare go out with or marry us; it just wasn't the done thing. Apart from anything else, their dads would have flayed us alive. To most white parents of the time, there was nothing worse than the thought of coffee-coloured grandchildren – it was as good as saying your daughter was a hooker or a heroin addict. Serious relationships and babies were reserved for white guys: we were stud-service only.

Alison was prepared to give our relationship a go, but more surprisingly, so too were her parents. They even came along to the Standard Triumph to watch me box. Possibly, the fact that I seemed to be achieving something in life and was obviously burning with ambition to get to the top made up for the colour of my skin. Or maybe they just didn't care. However, Alison and me were not to be, largely as a result of that ambition of mine. While she wanted to have weekends together on the sofa watching telly, I was off to yet another championship. Evenings would be spent in constant training at the gym or going off on long runs round the streets of Coventry. So, when her ultimatum came – settle down, or fight on alone – Alison was the inevitable loser.

Monday was the biggest clubbing night of the week for teen-agers in Coventry. That meant the youth of the city descending on Tiffany's or one of the other discos in the town centre. Sex would be on the menu, but so too would fighting. As we got ready to go out in Hillfields, I'd find myself with a group of black guys tooling up, ready for a big tear-up.

Flick knives would be placed inside jacket pockets. Some of the martial-arts types had homemade 'nunchucks' – two bits of broom handle with a chain link in the middle. They'd practise their moves with these improvised weapons, imagining heads being cracked open. I once had a go, but only managed to smash a light bulb overhead before I decided it wasn't my thing. Usually, I'd just watch these violent men going through the motions till one of them would turn to me.

'Errol, you tooled up?'

I'd raise my fists: 'I got my knuckles, ain't I?'

Those were my weapons of choice and, so far, they hadn't let me down. My brawny hands were already criss-crossed with small scars from other people's teeth. There was no need for me to carry knives or nunchucks: Mother Nature had designed me as a self-contained fighting machine.

Those men weren't friends, more like blokes you hung out with and mainly because there was safety in numbers. Some of them would end up dying well before their time – drugs overdoses, shootings or knifings. Others were to lose their minds or end up in prison. There was one guy, who we'll call 'Danny', who pimped girls, but then got mad when one of them (who he also thought of as his girlfriend) had an unpaid relationship with another bloke. Instead of taking it out on the other guy, he murdered her.

Before this, my brother Michael and Danny had been in a sort of disco-dance combo called the Funkateers. They'd take to Coventry's dance floors looking like Earth, Wind and Fire – all sweatbands, shiny shirts and way too much spandex. To see Danny moving to the rhythm, all cute smiles and knowing winks, you'd never guess what a demon was lurking inside.

I once found myself in the City Centre Club with Danny and Michael. A smaller venue than Tiffany's, it was located by a flyover, just off the dual carriageway that cut through the city.

Anybody who went clubbing in the Midlands or north of England in the 1980s will know what this place looked like: the mirrors, grotty carpet, everybody sharing a cramped dance floor, girls' handbags on the ground and blokes hovering to pull as the last song came on.

The three of us stood around with our drinks until Michael suggested we dance. Only we were big guys and the dance floor was full, so we strutted our stuff where we stood until a very unfriendly bulldog of a bouncer appeared and ordered us to stop.

'Can't dance on the carpet.'

Now this wasn't some Turkish hand-woven rug, it was a beer-sodden and very sad-looking piece of cloth that squelched underfoot.

Indignant, I responded: 'Nowhere else to dance, mate.'

Suddenly I found myself in a headlock. Taken by surprise, the bouncer managed to manoeuvre me, and very rapidly for a man of his build, to the reception, where he began ramming my head against the counter. I had just about managed to struggle free when two other bouncers popped up out of nowhere and joined in. Three against one struck me as very unsporting, definitely not Queensberry rules.

'Get off me, you bastards!'

Proud of my good looks, I didn't need Conan the Barbarian or his two mates ruining them for me. Michael wasn't going to stand by and let his brother be abused like that, either. He might be a Man of God now, but he was handy with fists and feet back then. A drop kick on the bulldog bouncer dealt with him: the other two surveyed their damaged colleague and just melted away.

Outside, I was cursing, burning with my old man's anger. I insisted we had to return to the club, tooled up, to really teach that threesome a lesson they wouldn't forget. Only the caress of a nunchuck would succinctly make the point. Within minutes, we were back at the Hillfield squats, where we grabbed every weapon we could lay our hands on. Off we went, full pelt, to mete out some revenge only in our absence, the club management wisely decided to shut up early. We returned to a venue that was prematurely silent, but there was something rather pleasing in the knowledge that at least we'd had an effect.

'Come back next week, then!' I snarled.

Making our way home, we strolled over the flyover. Below, cars and lorries and vans zoomed past. For a moment, I let their bright lights shine in my eyes. I wondered how many of those drivers were heading for London, hardly aware that they were shooting past this strange town, where rude boys and skinheads kicked ten shades of crap out of each other. Could I dare to dream that I'd be behind the wheel of a flash motor myself one day, making my own way to the Big Smoke?

'Come on,' said Michael, tapping me.

On the other side of the flyover, Samuel Vale House loomed: a 1960s concrete lump beside the Coventry canal. As we got closer, we could make out the sound of a party that was going on somewhere in the block. The three of us stared up and there, on the balcony, was a group of white kids looking back down. It took barely a second before one of them gave us the customary greeting.

'Fuck off, you black bastards!'

I sighed, a sort of resigned sigh. It was the sigh of a man who knows that he must go and punch somebody to the ground.

As a young black man, I often wondered if skin this colour was a curse; all it seemed to do was attract abuse. My response was always to fight – and win. But in spite of that, sometimes I craved the odd day off, a day when my hands could be something other than fists, but it never seemed to happen.

Michael was now counting the number of floors to the balcony.

'One, two, three …'

We all counted together now: 'Four, five…'

'Fifth floor,' I announced. 'Let's go teach 'em some fucking manners!'

Even my saintly brother Michael agreed. Needless to say, Danny was already making for the front door of Samuel Vale. In those days, there were no security locks on most of the blocks, or if there were, they weren't working. In no time at all, we were pounding up the stairs to get our blood pumping round our bodies before the fighting started. It's very important for boxers to get their heart rates up in advance of unleashing their fists.

On the fifth floor, we crept down the corridor listening at each door for the music. But all that greeted us was silence. Michael pointed to a door.

'I think it's this one. Reckon they've turned the music off.'

They'd obviously seen us coming. I flipped open the letterbox and to my amazement, saw a hallway full of people – frozen still, not saying a word; hoping we would go away. I could smell fear from inside the flat. Standing erect, I smiled at my accomplices.

'*Definitely* this one.'

Barely had I got the words out when the door swung open. On the threshold, a white bloke quivered with a beer bottle in his hand, held with violent intent. Behind him were other white partygoers, also wielding their drinks as weapons. Half of me found this funny, but the other half-realised things still had the potential to turn really ugly. Heavily outnumbered, at the same time we had managed to inspire real fear.

Michael showed his calm and controlled side, trying to reason with the man in front of him. He sounded like the future Man of God, come to bring peace and reconciliation.

'What's all this about then?' he asked, with a little smile.

'Wha'?' the white bloke replied.

'Shouting out things like that at us.'

'You're a fucking black bastard, aren't you?'

'Did we do anything to you?'

While the preacher of tomorrow tried to educate the man at the door, I was working out how to land an almighty silencer of a left hook on his jaw. All I had to do was get the right angle. Deftly, I moved to the side of the door. Leaning against the wall, I waited for the idiot's jaw to emerge far enough over the threshold to allow me to plant my fist on it and send his racist mouth to the other end of the corridor. Like a hunting dog, my eyes fixed on him. As he argued with Michael, the white bloke obligingly moved forward. Perfect.

Like a missile, my arm launched into his face but instead of catching his chin, I misjudged my aim and caught his throat. As he went down, he made a rather unpleasant gurgling noise. Danny and Michael stared at me just as a tsunami of beer bottles hurtled towards us from the partygoers. Definitely time to go.

As we belted down the stairs, I turned to Michael: 'I think I might have killed that guy.'

Calmly, he turned to me and observed in a matter-of-fact way: 'Well Errol, you did punch him in the throat.'

Days passed. I scanned the newspapers and watched the telly expecting to hear about the 'Samuel Vale Murder'. I was convinced I'd killed him. As I've already said, sleep has never come easily to me and that week, I'm not sure I got a single wink. The feel of his throat against my fist played on my mind – the crunch of cartilage, the gurgle and then his last breath. I could almost see him lying in a mortuary fridge, a hideous bruise on his neck.

After a week, I'd still heard nothing. Perhaps the bastard had survived, after all. It wasn't long after this that I heard about Danny's crime: the horrible killing of one of his girls. If a prostitute pissed off her pimp in Hillfields, it was a capital crime, a mistake paid for with a young life. That was the law of the Concrete Jungle. The brutal murder sickened me and was one of several incidents that would eventually propel me out of the ghetto. Needless to say, Danny disappeared from our lives and only recently emerged after many years spent at Her Majesty's Pleasure.

As teenagers, our whole week built up to Monday night when we'd have to get into Tiffany's at all costs. Squatting in a post-war pedestrian precinct called Smithford Way, Coventry's leading night club was a giant glass brick with three flights of stairs that led up to the entrance. At night, I used to think it looked like a lighthouse. Once up the stairs, you went across a glass walkway from the tower into the main part of the ballroom. The building was very modern and part of Coventry's attempt to shake off wartime memories of being bombed to bits.

If the bouncers at Tiffany's didn't let us enter, the disappointment would cast a long shadow over the week ahead. In your young, dumb way, you felt you'd missed out on any number of experiences: a quick fumble in the dark by the toilets or a dance with a rude girl to a song like The Beat's 'Mirror in the Bathroom'.

For me, drugs were out of the question and even the booze was kept to a minimum. This was a time before ecstasy, though some kids popped amphetamines. But not me – even dope bored me.

To me, it was like attacking your own body: I had enough adrenalin and rage inside to give me a permanent high without asking a dealer for help.

Early in the evening, before I left Hillfields, you might hear this kind of conversation:

'Wos 'appenin' tonight?'

'Check me later.'

Bored blokes would be sniffing out likely fights, rival gangs we knew were coming into town, scores had to be settled with racist bouncers. Somebody who'd slept with another person's girl was going to get killed for it. The word went round and somehow we always seemed to know where to find the action. This, you have to remember, was a time before mobile phones. Most of us didn't even have landlines: the only way you found out where a tear-up was occurring was when somebody whispered in your ear.

One Monday night, I was getting dressed up, pulling on my Sta-Prest Levis, legs looking like two pipe cleaners. For me, 1981 was all about ball-busting tight leg-wear. The Funkateers – Danny, Michael and their partners in dance crime – wore baggy pleated trousers, but Errol Christie liked vein-crushing denim. I also had a tank top and probably some kind of pork-pie hat as 2 Tone music was all the rage.

Like John Travolta in the opening moments of *Saturday Night Fever*, I strode towards Tiffany's with a good time on my mind. A few drinks, not too many, and some ladies. One on each arm would do.

The previous week, I'd been turned away because my trousers were too short. Bullshit, of course. What that bouncer really meant to say was 'You're black, aren't you?' But he just didn't have the balls to come out and say it. My pride had taken a bruising, but this week I decided bruising of a different kind was in order.

Before me loomed the big flight of stairs inside the glass lighthouse that lead up to the main door of Tiffany's. Running along the middle of the stairs was a rope chain, suspended from posts to separate two queues: one for Tiffany's, the other for a smaller club in the same building, called Bally Hai.

Both clubs once formed a much bigger venue called the Locarno, a legend in the history of Coventry's night time entertainment. By the time I reached my teens, the Locarno was defunct but the lads in The Specials, being a few years old than me, sang about the place in their song, 'Friday Night, Saturday Morning':

> *'I'm going to watch my money go.*
> *At the Locarno, no.'*

So, I joined the queue and with each step came a strange feeling of anticipation. One part of me looked forward to the club inside with all its delights. Already, I could hear the music thumping through the walls. At the same time, I had the uncanny and exciting feeling that I was going to have to reckon with those bouncers again. I wasn't alone in those sort of feelings: back then, most black guys in Coventry knew they stuck out a mile in any club queue and as far as the doormen were concerned, we were trouble.

I looked down at my trousers, nothing too short about them. I could hear Mum telling us Christies again how good we looked for Church. My shoes were shining, trousers pressed, shirt was ironed – however, it wasn't Elder Nicely I'd come to see, but the fine young ladies beyond that door.

Now I was face to face with the enemy, a type of 'German' I took great exception to. After all, down at the City Centre Club one of them had tried to demolish a reception desk with my head. In front of me was a squat little bloke, who was flanked by two overweight bubble-perm bouncers with spotted dickie bows. Shortie was apparently the club manager.

'You're not coming in,' he squeaked.

But that was his point of view, not mine – I was going through those doors even if I had to punch my way through. His face didn't betray any intention of giving way, so I stuck my fist in it. In a flash, his smug smile was all over my knuckles – his dentist would be quids-in. The two bouncers dragged their boss inside and bolted the door shut. I apologised to everybody around me for the inconvenience but then suddenly the door swung open again.

One of the bubble-perm monsters re-emerged. He picked up one of the posts with the rope chain through it and began swinging it at me like a mace. I dodged back as he continued towards me, red-faced and furious. At the top of the long flight of stairs we squared off to each other, him jabbing at me with the piece of timber. Finding my moment, I kicked it out of his hands. Now I considered us more evenly matched. Then, in the time-honoured Errol Christie tradition, I fired a right cross at him to send droplets of blood splattering across his perm. He dropped like a stone.

One of the Mighty Seven – Tony Burchill – was with me. At this point, he tapped on my shoulder and suggested we might want to leave. If I stayed, I'd end up fighting every bouncer from Tiffany's and Bally Hai. As that might prove suicidal, it was probably a good idea to call it a night. Tony was a guy whose opinion I always trusted. He was a nice, decent bloke, whose sister tragically died of cancer in her teens.

I think that loss made him mature more quickly than the rest of the old Mighty Seven. He saw a bigger picture in life and became a healthy restraining influence on my wilder self. Without him there, I'd probably have let my bravado get the better of me and taken on every German in the place. Instead, we found ourselves walking back to the squats of Hillfields and sharing a bag of chips.

However, Errol Christie was to have a third go at getting into Tiffany's. If every other kid in Coventry was there on a Monday night, then I had to be on that dance floor, too. A bit unwisely, I ventured back. Somehow I got through the door and pretty soon I was teaching an adoring girl how to shake her ass properly to the music. All around were other teenagers, gyrating to some now-forgotten disco hit.

I'd been spotted, though. At first, I didn't realise I was in a very dangerous situation. My eyes were all over the girl in front of me, my thoughts concentrating on how to get her back to Hill-fields. Already the bubble perms were moving in for the kill, working their way through the punters towards my good self. The first hint of danger was when I caught a glimpse of a spotty bow tie through the crowd: it was attached to a slab of meat in a crisp white shirt and black trousers with a mean expression.

Spinning round, I caught sight of another. Then, on my heels,

I wheeled round another one hundred and eighty degrees to be faced with yet one more bow tie and perm. At a rough count, there were four or five of these animals and they were closing in. One word screeched through my mind – *shit!*

Without uttering a word, not even 'Charge!', the bouncers made their move. As I punched for my life, they furiously fought to restrain me. The whole area became a scene of mayhem, girls screaming as I sent my legs and fists flying in all directions.

One of the bow-tied monsters made a comment that stuck in my head for years: 'This guy's crazy – like he wants to take on the whole world.' And he was right too. All the petty injustice, the racism on the streets and in school, I wanted to take it on and beat it up, smash it into small pieces. He couldn't have put it any better way. There was no room for discussion or polite talk anymore. Those who made my life, and the lives of all my brothers, a misery would only be addressed in one way now.

Tiffany's doors opened and I was sent flying down the stairs. As I picked myself up, I heard them slam behind me. My pride was a little bit dented, but there were no injuries to speak of, so I wandered off towards Hillfields. One moment I'd been having a nice time with a white girl and then this. Not far from me was a small gang of skinheads on a street corner with sullen, hateful expressions on their faces. Blowing a hole in their dole money with some shared cheap booze from the off-licence.

With my job at the Coventry Clutch Centre and the bits of cash that I picked up from the fights, I was probably in a better financial position than many of them. My thirty quid a week from the garage meant I wasn't scraping around or thieving to survive. I certainly wasn't sticking my head in a bag of glue to alleviate the boredom or shooting smack into my veins. My money was honest, my morals better than a lot of kids, and I didn't abuse my body. Every year, I was bringing back cups and trophies to my home city and my reward was to be thrown down the steps of Tiffany's.

The next day, I moped into town, still aggrieved at my treatment of the night before. Walking past the huge mock-Tudor barn of a boozer called the Tally Ho, I almost counted off the seconds in my head before the first drunk white knucklehead emerged to scream some anti-black abuse. The pub was often a flashpoint for racist taunting, usually followed by vicious fights. I didn't have to wait long: out came a middle-aged bloke, jabbing his forefinger at me.

'Come on then, you fucking nigger! Get back to your own country, eh?'

In a nearby chippie, several of my mates – all black – could see the tawdry drama unfolding outside, but I gestured with my eyes for them to remain where they were. I didn't need any help with this idiot.

'Not got any bottle, you fucking coon?'

Now I had plenty of bottle and he was about to find out. The creature lumbered towards me, the worst for four or five pints. I was expecting a well-telegraphed hook or cross, what non-boxers take to be a proper punch, but this moron thought he was a Kung Fu fighter.

Kung Fu was one of the big fads of the 1970s. There'd been a massively popular American TV series named after the martial art, which starred David Carradine. Kids all over the world had taken it up for a while until they'd inevitably become bored and moved onto the next thing. There was even a disco hit called 'Kung Fu Fighting' with a dance performed on *Top of the Pops* that involved lots of hand-chopping and comical kicking. Best forgotten, I think.

Anyway, our racist decided he could destroy me with some classic Kung Fu moves – or what *he* took to be Kung Fu. With one big bound, he launched himself and his impressive belly gut as far as he could into the air: which wasn't very far at all. The theory was to soar high above and kick me in the face. In practice, he went up about three inches before I promptly knocked him out with a brutal jab as he touched down. At my feet, lay another Christie victim.

Unfortunately, the evening brought me no respite. After some drinks, while walking home and talking with a white girl I knew, a group of skinheads came strutting towards us. As they neared, one of them snarled: 'Don't like that.'

Angrily, I turned to face him: 'What do you mean?'

But he looked past me to the white girl: 'Black man's mattress.'

The fists of doom clenched, ready for action again. Luckily for this mouthy skin, a little guy from my old church was walking down the other side of the road at the same time. And what Eric Brown lacked in height, he more than made up for with his deep and booming, gruff voice.

'Evening, Errol – everything alright?'

Coming from such a small man, this vocal earthquake confused the skins enough that they ran off. I glanced back at the little mob disappearing in their bomber jackets and hitched-up jeans, an army of identikit thugs. They had no right to tell me who I could hang out with but it was no use: they thought they did.

By pushing us down and abusing us, the skinheads hoped to get an edge on us, to stop us black boys rising up the social ladder as they fell down it, but they were doomed to failure. Now the jobs they'd always considered theirs by birthright were disappearing and the council houses they thought were being handed out to us were actually being sold off by Maggie Thatcher and her new government.

The Tories came to power in Britain in 1979 and they didn't seem to like us very much. This was a government of Germans, by Germans, *for* Germans. Like all my schoolmates and buddies in Hillfields, I felt as if white society was out to bury us, but I was ready to fight back with my fists.

To have met Errol Christie in 1981 would have been a potentially dangerous experience: the fury inside me meant that a wrong glance would have earned you a punch in the mouth. I expected nothing but hostility from the outside world and I gave it back in equal measure. My whole life had been defined by fighting – fists, my sole way of expressing myself. I didn't think too much about the deeper politics – I just knew who my friends and enemies were. And those enemies felt my wrath wherever I found them.

That summer started with one of the worst confrontations I ever got involved in – a fight in which I really should have lost my life. To this day, I gaze up at the multi-storey car park by the Leofric Hotel in Coventry's town centre and shudder at the events that unfolded there. In reality, they were only a dress rehearsal for the full-blown riots about to follow.

It was a blazing hot afternoon with a golden sun up above but the attention of my Hillfields' comrades and me was not on the weather but the white blokes standing aggressively in front of us. As had happened so often before, us black rude boys squared off to a bunch of snarling white skinheads. Unusually, we outnumbered them for once and it felt like a slaughter of boot boys was on the agenda.

Despite our larger force, they had been the ones to set things in motion by hurling abuse at us, the routine insults I needn't repeat again. Eventually, even their tiny brains worked out that there were more of us than them and so they high-tailed and ran for it. Smelling victory, we bolted after them.

Running behind the Leofric Hotel, they diverted into the multistorey. I don't know if they expected us to stop, but we certainly didn't. The concrete building echoed to DM boots thudding up, ramp after ramp. On the second floor, the white thugs made their stand and we got ready to give them a well-earned pasting: I was going to enjoy the beating I was about to deliver.

But then one of the boot boys grabbed an iron bar from the ground and before I knew it, he'd gashed my arm. I was shocked because I hadn't seen this attack coming, but his reflexes were fast. Besides, I was possibly too cocky and self-assured about the situation.

This was the worst injury I ever sustained in a street battle and the deep scar is still there to this day. I'd let my guard drop and paid the price. The pain seared through me. I looked down in horror at the blood gushing across my forearm, but didn't have long for self-pity as the sound of approaching sirens filled the air. With the Senior ABA Championships at Wembley Arena just weeks away, I couldn't risk being arrested. In any case, no black man wanted to end up in a police station with his head being introduced to the bottom of a flushing toilet.

The blood was now on my jeans. McGarry had been right: this was how to ruin my boxing career – taking on all the boot boys in the vain hope of defeating them. I had no idea what damage had been caused, but this was the first time it hit home that the street battles were taking their toll on me.

Below and getting closer, the Black Marias charged up the ramps, lights flashing and full of menace. I couldn't end up caged in one of those vans, so without looking to see where I'd fall, I jumped over the concrete wall to what should have been certain death.

For a few moments, I floated. Then with an almighty thud, I landed. Beneath me was a huge mound of builder's sand. I picked some of it up in my right hand and laughed: those fine granules cushioned my fall and saved my life. Maybe I had a guardian angel, after all. I couldn't imagine how else I'd managed to avoid breaking any bones or even ending up on a mortuary slab.

Dusting myself down, I fled the scene before the coppers caught up with me. Up above, the boys from Hillfields were being corralled into vans and carted off. I thanked my lucky stars I wasn't joining them. Then, turning a corner, I caught sight of Dennis McGarry, another of Tom's sons. That sent a bigger shudder of fear through me than the arrival of the cops, seconds earlier. If Tom had the slightest inkling of what had just happened, he'd be furious.

When I got to the gym the following day, wearing a long-armed sweatshirt to hide the gash in my arm, Tom strode up, red-faced.

'Hear you've been fighting in town.'

'Who said that – Tom?'

'Never you mind. I hope it's not true, that's all.'

As I shadowboxed into thin air, Tom continued to hover. I knew he had something else on his mind.

'I hear there's some kind of commotion gonna kick off in the town centre, anti-racist demo.'

'Yeah,' I said, trying to sound disinterested, 'something like that.'

'You're doing so well, laddie. Don't go ruining it, eh?' he said, standing in front of me.

I paused and we both looked at each other. Tom had known me since I was eight years old and life in the Christie family was to him an open book: the daily strife and woe we'd endured that I'd reacted to with my fists. He was constantly dismayed when my name cropped up over and over in accounts of various street battles, but I think he also knew the fighting was impossible for me to give up, that I'd never back down – not so long as I stayed in Coventry.

As I left the gym, I bumped into Calvin Lynch. He and his brother Colin were young black boxers, who trained at Coachmakers. I'd met them during my brief exile from the Standard Triumph. Calvin flashed a broad smile of recognition.

'Going on the riot then, bruv?'

I nodded. Already we'd heard that busloads of National Front members were heading towards Coventry for the big day. The fascists planned to descend on the city to break our heads open and disrupt the anti-racist gig by The Specials. It didn't matter if I was going to be on television the next week, fighting in the Senior ABA finals: if the NF thought they could take over our streets, I must be shoulder-to-shoulder with the anti-fascists: there could be no discussion on the matter. I was betraying Tom, but I was defending my community.

Calvin and I walked briskly into town and the sight that greeted us was like a scene from hell. A skinhead army spewed out of the coaches they'd chartered, giving their familiar Hitler salutes. Some were beefy specimens who looked like they could give a good account of themselves. Others were malnourished, skinny wretches that I could have flicked over. Together, they formed a mass of seething, ugly hatred.

'Sieg Heil! Sieg Heil! Sieg Heil!'

Hard to believe that in a city bombed by the Luftwaffe just over thirty years before, here were British kids chanting Hitler's slogans. Beneath the ruins of our ancient cathedral, deliberately left in the condition that the Nazis had reduced it to, this scum glorified the Third Reich.

I waded into the ranks of the anti-fascists. The two sides were sandwiched between the De Vere Hotel and the Pool Meadow Bus Station. This was normally the quieter end of the town centre, where buses calmly arrived and departed, but that day it was a battle zone. Approaching it was an unbelievably exciting experience. The cheering from the crowd at a boxing match was something with which I was well familiar, but this sound was like nothing I'd ever heard before or since.

The noise was deafening, roars of words you couldn't make out. On their side, occasional outbreaks of monkey

'Ooh-ooh-oohs!' and, of course, the 'Sieg Heils!' Then on our side, chants like 'The National Front is a Nazi Front – stop the National Front!' Fascist and anti-fascist leaders yelled at each other through megaphones and orchestrated chanting among rival supporters. And other than that, a barrage of constant shouting and jeering filled the air.

All around me were rude boys, 2 Tone ska fans, Lanchester Polytechnic students, left-wing groups and ordinary black guys. Facing us were boot boys organised by National Front types in cheap suits, trying to look respectable. One of them had a megaphone and was yelling about 'red scum' and 'too many immigrants'.

The cops held a thin blue line between us – boys in blue on horseback, who charged up and down through the middle of the opposing forces. Barging my way to the front with Calvin, I studied the twisted little faces opposite to see if I recognised any of them. I'd vowed to myself to hunt down the local boot boys like dogs afterwards, but it soon became clear that these piggy-eyed blobs were mainly from out of town.

Then some coaches started to pull up on our side of the road: reinforcements had arrived. The doors opened and out flooded a load of Asian lads, who had come to join us from all over the Midlands. No doubt they were fed up with having dog crap pushed through their letterboxes and the word 'Paki' spray-painted on their property. One Asian youth brushed past me, then turned and offered me his hand: 'Watcha, bruv.'

Instantly, I was in shock: I'd never heard an Asian call a black man a 'bruv' before; we just weren't that close as communities. I had Asian mates in the form of Suki and Pups, but by and large, we didn't mix to anything like the extent that we do today. There was often an undercurrent of hostility between us, if truth be told: black kids going into Asian-run stores usually felt they were under constant surveillance, singled out as potential shoplifters and general troublemakers. Often it seemed as if Asians saw us as being a rung or more below them in the pecking order and we resented that.

And so I shook the kid's hand: 'Go on then, our kid.'

Nearby, TV cameras were trained on both sides of the road. In the summer of 1981, reporters were having a field day. They didn't need to go to war zones in foreign places to find some excitement: Britain's cities were ablaze. Coventry was rioting, but at the same time and for the same reasons, so too were Brixton in London, the Toxteth district of Liverpool, St Paul's in Bristol, and so on. Even my birthplace – Leicester – joined in the fun. Night after night, the cops, the National Front, the Anti-Nazi League and Britain's angry unemployed youth were on the news as they left a trail of destruction in neighbourhoods throughout the country. At long last, years of frustration had erupted.

A TV camera turned in our direction but I didn't notice. Days later, it was pointed out to me that my shoulder made it onto national telly: part of me was on *News at Ten*. In full frame, Calvin Lynch was shouting at the Nazis. In retrospect, it was lucky only my shoulder got famous. If my face had been on the news, Tom McGarry would have gone ballistic and a question mark might have been drawn over my future fighting career.

Ahead, police horses reared up on hind legs, dumping turds all over the road, while a killer confetti of broken bottles and bits of concrete showered in both directions. Behind me, kids were chopping up the fancy paving outside the Leofric Hotel and lobbing it at the NF. The other side was returning the compliment. Nobody seemed concerned about the injuries they were causing: this was war, after all.

One of the Nazis yelled into his megaphone: 'Why don't they join their black brothers in Africa?'

Then a chant from the NF crowd:

'Ain't no black in the Union Jack!'

'Ain't no black in the Union Jack!'

'Ain't no black in the Union Jack!'

I bared my teeth: we had put our bit of black in there all right – our blood, sweat and tears too. From slaving on British-owned plantations to mopping the floors of their hospitals, the Union Jack was a flag that lots of us had mixed feelings about in those times, but soon I'd be lifting it high above my head many times as a professional fighter.

'Ain't no black in the Union Jack!'

'Ain't no black in the Union Jack!'

'Ain't no black in the Union Jack!'

If I could have shut them all up with one giant jab, I'd have done it.

As the bricks, bottles and masonry flew past us, I ducked and dived – more good practice for the ring. Then suddenly a copper was knocked off his horse by one of those airborne bricks. I didn't see who threw it, but the brick just sailed into his head and he fell clean off his nag. A trickle of blood oozed from under his helmet.

Unsurprisingly, this direct hit went down very badly with the West Midlands Constabulary. The cheering from our side didn't help, either. Pretty rapidly, they decided that we were the culprits and made for us, snarling from behind their shields. Bodies covered in Anti-Nazi League and Rock Against Racism stickers flew towards me as everybody on our side did a runner.

'Get the fuck out of here!'

'Cops are coming!'

So, we ran – ran hard, ran for our lives, our hearts beating out of our chests. Now there was only one refuge, a sanctuary even the police wouldn't dare enter, but to get back there, we'd have to keep up the speed and behind us came the menacing thunder of hooves and police sirens.

All those years of being chased by skinheads from the school gates to Cheveral Avenue had left me with powerful legs and powerful lungs, so as we poured into the badlands of Hillfields, I was at the head of the crowd. As if there was a force field around the area, suddenly the cops halted and turned away. Pre-programmed into their minds was the knowledge that this was no place for them. If they'd set foot on those streets and alleyways, missiles would have rained down from the tower blocks above, bloodying their heads. It just wasn't worth the hassle.

For the country, the boil had been lanced. Finally, the anger contained in the inner cities burst out. Even I felt a bit of calm in the days that followed. However, I'd been left with a badly damaged arm after the car park fight and this set me thinking about how I was going to lead my life from now on. I wanted boxing to be my sole focus but somehow I kept getting drawn into what was happening on the streets, the riots being the biggest bust-up so far.

Reaching the end of my teens and with a major trophy like the Senior ABA to fight for, it was time for the boy to become a man: if I was going to leave Coventry and realise my promise in the ring, I had to change. It seemed as if one more defining event was needed to turn my life around and a few days after the riot it presented itself.

Outside a club – it may have been Tiffany's or the City Centre Club – a white man pushed in front of me. I'd been queuing for a while and I certainly wasn't going to tolerate this rudeness.

'Oi!'

He turned round and curled his lip contemptuously. Could he really be so stupid as to insult the soon-to-be Senior ABA Champion of England? It seemed he could.

'Fuck off, you black bastard!'

With my index finger, I turned his shoulder so he was facing me. Before he could raise any objections, I slammed a jab into his mouth. Without a second's thought, he slid to the ground, out for the count. A little bored, I checked my knuckles but there was hardly a graze. As far as I was concerned, the matter was closed and he would wake up, knowing there were certain things he shouldn't risk saying in public.

But another black guy – from Birmingham, as I recall – decided I hadn't finished the job. Before I realised what he was doing, he stamped down hard on the lifeless guy's head. There was a disturbing crunching sound as his boot made contact.

'What d'you do that for?'

I looked at the stupid grin on the Brummie's face, but no response was forthcoming. He couldn't even put into words why he'd done what he'd done. It was the sort of dumb, cowardly thing that happened on the streets: you saw your enemy lying on the ground and so you kicked his head.

But I felt sickened: this wasn't the way I wanted to fight. Never was it my intention to kill or permanently injure anybody; I just wanted to shut them up, to get them out of my face. The only reason for letting my fists fly was to get a bit of respect or, failing that, some peace and quiet. I expected my victims to survive, maybe learn something about their bigoted behaviour. To stomp on a man's skull when he was already concussed just went against everything I'd learned, both in the ring and on the streets.

Tom McGarry was right: it was time for me to grow up, to become something different. A better man, I hoped. The years of senseless violence were behind me now; they had to be. If things didn't change, Mum's worst fears would be realised: I'd leave Coventry all right – but in a wooden casket.

5

GANGSTERS AND MANAGERS

'We're all given some sort of skill in life.
Mine just happens to be beating up on people.'

Sugar Ray Leonard

Outside Burt McCarthy's mansion in Danbury: Burt *(far left)*, me, sporting a cap, in the back row and Andy Straughn *(far right)*.

Errol Christie, personal collection

Burt McCarthy and Frank Warren *(to my left)* and Burt's brother, Leslie *(far right)*.

Errol Christie, personal collection

Me *(left)* with Andy Straughn in our basic digs after coming to London.

Errol Christie, personal collection

Sparring with my hero Sugar Ray Leonard at the Thomas A' Becket, 29 September 1982.

Mirrorpix

UNIT SALES D.I.Y. LTD.
are proud to welcome

THREE TIMES
WORLD HEAVYWEIGHT
BOXING CHAMPION

MUHAMMED ALI
"A Living Legend"
to our
D.I.Y. SUPERSTORE on
THURSDAY 11th AUGUST 1983

Sparring with the greatest. Muhammad Ali came to Coventry – to open a DIY Centre.
Mum and my sister Annette are visible in the background.

Mirrorpix

My Mum meets
Muhammad Ali.

*Errol Christie, personal
collection*

Through the streets of Coventry prowled a shiny blue Rover TC. A chauffeur was behind the wheel and a man called Mickey in the back seat. Balding, with strands of black hair across his pate, gleaming teeth and a robust chin, Mickey Duff had once been a boxer. For decades ever since, he had dominated the game as its leading UK promoter. Nothing moved in the world of boxing unless he said so.

I was working in the Coventry Clutch Centre in Jubilee Crescent, fixing some un-roadworthy motors and checking out any women who sloped past. In the background, I could hear the phone ringing, but I just ignored it – one of the other blokes would pick it up.

The ringing stopped.

'Somebody called Mickey Duff on the phone for you.'

I sniggered – the lads had obviously found out who Mickey Duff was and were playing a prank on me. I wasn't going to fall for it.

'Yeah, *right!*'

'Nah, really, Errol: phone call for you, it sounds important.'

I wiped my hands of oil and grease, then picked up the receiver, half-expecting a mate of mine to be laughing himself stupid at the other end. Instead, I found Mickey Duff: he launched straight into a stream of sales patter about what a great talent I was and how well we'd work together, then it was all about signing on the dotted line and the fantastic future that lay ahead of me as a world-class professional boxer.

'Got to speak to my manager, Tom McGarry,' I mumbled meekly. Like my parents before me, suddenly I found myself disorientated by this figure of authority but my gut feeling was that I shouldn't agree to anything until the manager of the Standard Triumph had given it his blessing.

'We'll talk some more,' Duff answered and then the phone

clicked dead. Not knowing what to think, I wandered back to the car I'd been attacking with my tool kit, sliding underneath to get a better look at the mechanics. I carried on until one of my workmates nudged me with his foot.

'There's a bloke in a blue Rover TC says he wants to see you.'

This definitely didn't feel right. Sure enough, in front of the Coventry Clutch Centre and looking completely out of place was a big, smart car. Inside was the fifty-year-old boxing titan. He didn't get out, but rolled down the window and surveyed the grease-covered teenager in front of him. All of a sudden, I felt like a slave being looked over: for a moment, I thought he'd want to examine my teeth and eyes then get me branded and shipped off.

'Hello.'

'Errol Christie?'

'Yeah.'

'This where you work, then?'

'Yeah.'

'Nice. You wanna reconsider my offer, then?'

Not there and then I didn't: to him, I was just another signing but I'd built up enough pride to think the least he could do was get out of his car and ask me those questions face to face. Uppity nigger? Yes, guilty. If this man wanted Errol Christie on his books, then he could show me a bit of respect. Instead, Duff drove off.

Left standing on the kerb, I wondered if I'd blown it. Ten years of fighting to get to the top of the amateur game and I'd pissed off Mickey Duff – badly. I saw my chances of going professional quickly disappear down a plughole. He'd really caught me off-guard. The last place I'd have expected him to show up, offering me a contract, was the Coventry Clutch Centre.

What I feared, more than anything else, was being 'mentally mugged'. Duff had signed up stacks of boxers in his life and was the smoothest of talkers. While I had my own way with words, I just couldn't risk being tied in knots by one of the boxing world's great silver tongues.

I thought he'd vanished for good, never to be seen again, but I hadn't reckoned on the man's power of persistence. A few minutes later, the phone rang once more. This time it was Tom

McGarry. By now Mickey Duff had made his way round to his place. Clearly, the country's top promoter was refusing to leave Coventry empty-handed.

Packing up early for the day, I went over to Tom's place and there was the blue Rover TC parked outside: waxed, polished and gleaming in the sunlight. Inside, Tom and Mickey were exchanging forced pleasantries and chatting about recent fights. I walked in awkwardly and then it was all back slaps and knowing grins from Mr Duff, who clearly thought I was in his clutches already.

However, the negotiations that followed were far from friendly and throughout I couldn't shake off the feeling that I was like a bit of meat in a butcher's shop window – one with a price tag the customer didn't like. Tom, the veteran shop steward, wanted the best for the amazing young talent he had nurtured for so many years. But Duff had incredible power: it was in his hands to decide whether I would ever be seen on the BBC. He was my gateway to a world of pro-boxing fame and fortune – and he knew it.

So, sitting with my gob shut and a dumb expression on my face, I watched in horror as the two men steadily fell out.

Eventually, Tom cracked.

I remember my amateur manager hauling up his bulky Scottish frame and bawling: 'Ach, away with ya, Duffy!'

From the sofa, we both watched the country's leading promoter walk away. Outside, the engine of his Rover purred as he prepared to slink off, back down the motorway to London. I should have been terrified that we'd blown it or, more to the point, that McGarry had torpedoed my chances of turning pro and finally escaping Coventry, but instead I felt strangely exhilarated. So did Tom. He had stood up for what he thought I was worth: in the end good would surely triumph and Duff could stick his contract – we'd find somebody better to go with.

But the news somehow leaked and a shocked sports press couldn't believe we'd sent Duff packing. It was said McGarry and me were switching the traditional roles, with us interviewing prospective managers instead of the other way round.

'CHRISTIE REJECTS £20,000 PRO OFFER' screamed one headline in the *Boxing News*. And in reference to a Midlands' boxing legend of the past: 'The kid they're calling the new Randy

Turpin is in no hurry to conquer the world.' Now that simply wasn't true: I was in a mighty hurry, but as McGarry explained to one journalist at the *Coventry Evening Telegraph*:

> 'Every week, somebody asks about Errol and it's true we have turned down a £20,000 offer. When and if Errol wants professional boxing as a career, then the man who can guarantee him a secure future is likely to get him. Money isn't everything when we talk about a kid's future.'

With Duff firmly out of the picture, Tom decided to pay a visit to a man called Frank Warren. The year before, he'd emerged as a new face on the boxing scene when he promoted his first licensed show between two American heavyweights at the Bloomsbury Crest Hotel in December 1980. We thought, like a lot of people in the sport, that Warren was a breath of fresh air, an alternative to the dominance of Duff. So, off we went to see him.

At first, I was impressed. Warren was polite, welcoming and there were lots of handshakes. He seemed more like the sort of person I'd want to be associated with; there were none of the bad vibes I'd felt with Duff. McGarry went through various terms and conditions and we left, satisfied we'd arrived at a good deal. But when the whole thing was set down in writing and arrived in the post, Tom experienced a sudden change of heart. The stout Lanarkshire trade unionist growled his head off: '*No.* Not having *that*! No, not at all!'

What McGarry was upset about, I can't remember now but the door was also slammed shut on Warren as a manager. I did begin to wonder if Tom was having difficulty letting me go. After all, I'd grown up with this man as my surrogate father and he'd been a guiding influence who moulded me into what I'd become. Without him, I'd have slid into crime and ended up in borstal. Instead, he had given me direction and hope: through boxing, I'd found a purpose in life. However, the time had come for me to cut loose from the Standard Triumph. This would mean a new manager, moving to London and spending a lot less time in Coventry. The old factory gym that had been my second home since I was eight years of age would become a fading memory, a place I'd look back on fondly but rarely, if ever, visit. None of this gave me any heartache in 1981: I was straining to get away and build a new life but I think Tom found the transition much more painful than me.

While I thought he was right to turn Duff away, something I never questioned him on, his approach troubled me a bit. I wondered whether he secretly hoped we might carry on as usual, that the transition to a professional career could be postponed. There were others who also thought I should hold off on the big leap – pundits who believed I ought to stay amateur and join the British team at the Olympics – but that didn't interest me in the slightest. My ambition was to become a pro like my boxing heroes and that meant splitting with Tom.

It seemed like fortune was tipping me the wink when we got a call from Burt McCarthy. A tycoon with a mansion in Essex and a business importing silicon chips, he offered to come up to Cheveral Avenue to meet me. It didn't seem right to have him over to Hillfields, where he'd probably lose the hubcaps on his car. Instead, he turned up at the family house, where I now had to trudge back. I was in time to find Mum nervously pouring out tea to her special guest.

The living-room table was adorned with an old-fashioned teapot, china cups sitting on top of doilies and fancy little cakes to eat – old-time Jamaican hospitality. While most English people had forgotten how to do a high tea, their former subjects kept the Imperial traditions alive. Mum was chattering away about this and that while our visitor slurped. Tom McGarry was also in the room, sizing up the prospective manager.

McCarthy seemed to handle the situation in his stride and held forth: 'Must come to my place in Essex, I've got a few boxers on the books ... I'm a self-made man, that's right – worked for everything I've got ... Errol's a brilliant boxer.' And so on.

Over tea and cakes we got to know each other and he seemed quite convincing. There was none of the high and mightiness of Duff. Gradually put at our ease, I could sense things were rolling to a successful conclusion, even Mum must have realised this son of hers was no 'bad breed kroff' as she topped up her best teacups yet again. Finally feeling we'd met somebody on our wavelength, McGarry and I agreed to stay at the aforementioned mansion in a place called Danbury.

'Southfork' might have been a better name for the Essex home. My new manager's pile in the country resembled the famous ranch in the American TV soap *Dallas*. There were pillars and marble, a swirling gravel drive led up to the house. He had his own private woodland, greyhounds in the outbuildings for dog racing; there were garages full of posh cars I'd never seen the like of at the Coventry Clutch Centre. McCarthy even employed staff to look after his house and grounds. My first visit to Danbury was an eye-opener as to how the other half lived: if I'd ever doubted the Christie family was dirt-poor, those delusions were now dispelled for ever. We really were on the bottom rung of society.

Quite a posse turned up in Danbury that day: Tom McGarry and my brother Michael, still staking his claim to be recognised as a boxing talent in his own right. There was Leon Thomas, the trainer I'd found at Coachmakers, and another boxer who was to become a great friend and my flatmate in London – a cruiser-weight with a calm and even temperament called Andy Straughn. Plus Tony Adams, an up-and-coming welterweight also going pro at the same time with McCarthy.

At long last, we felt, things were getting better. Like most boxers, we'd all come up from the gutter and now had a glimpse of the high life. The surroundings gave me a vision of what I wanted in my future. The only person who might have had misgivings on that day would have been Leon, with whom I would part company. From now on, I'd be working with a trainer recommended by McCarthy.

Burt McCarthy emerged from his mansion, all broad smiles and slaps on the back. He was a man in his early fifties with a comb-over hairdo that would often make me chuckle in the years ahead. Often he used to disappear into the loo with a little toiletries bag to re-do his hair and then re-emerge with it all neatly plastered down.

McCarthy was always well dressed, immaculate even. The conversation frequently chimed with remarks about his self-made status: 'When I got my first Rolls-Royce we had nothing', 'We came from nothing, same as you, Errol' and even 'You've got to work hard, you see. That way, you'll end up with what I've got.'

Old money might have found this talk vulgar but I understood what he meant. In fact, I wanted to be what he'd transformed himself into: Burt had achieved his status through silicon chips but I'd get there with my fists. One day, I'd have Roman columns of my own and garages stuffed with flash motors. There was no doubt in my mind that I deserved all of it. And so, we signed up to McCarthy. Which meant Tom now had to bow out of my life. Truthfully, I'd been champing at the bit for a while. In the months before I went professional, a newspaper article hinted at the tensions that had begun to arise between Tom and me. Clearly, my growing unwillingness to take orders from my old mentor could be read between the lines.

The tabloid piece went under the headline 'ERROL PERIL!' There I was, photographed in nothing but swimming trunks, sitting on the ropes of the boxing ring. The journalist wrote the article because I'd just been voted Best Boxing Newcomer by the Writers Club – the organisation of journalists who wrote about boxing for the newspapers and sports press. This was a huge vote of confidence in my ability from the scribblers on Fleet Street. I attended the award ceremony in a bow tie and dinner jacket, still feeling as if I should be serving the drinks instead of being the guest of honour. The trophy was the biggest I'd ever won: a heavy piece of silver in contrast to the plastic or tinny tack I'd taken home in the past.

Typically for a black man in the early 1980s, it was assumed in the article that I was 'jobless, but full of dreams'. Possibly this was intended as a compliment but I was very much in work – unless being a car mechanic at the Coventry Clutch Centre wasn't regarded as a proper job. Like my parents, I'd never lived off the dole.

> *Clutching his tea in a Coventry café last week, Errol Christie displayed none of that blank despair you associate with the unemployed. Black and out of work, Christie is one of the idle thousands in a once-affluent city.*

It was like being flattered and insulted at the same time. The article then went on to describe Tom as a 'squat Lanarkshire man with an echo of Jock Stein in his voice' and 'burly beneath a blue anorak zipped to his chin'. When Tom was asked if we talked a lot, he replied: 'No, I talk. He listens.' And that was the line that really grated: Tom could have said that a year before and I'd have nodded humbly in agreement but not now. As I stood on the threshold of becoming a pro boxer, my ego couldn't withstand being addressed like that, as if I was a naughty child who had to be put in his place by his surrogate dad.

Tom and I were due for a split, then. I'd got my pro manager lined up and very soon I'd be moving to London, a city I'd always dreamt of living in. It was far from Coventry, far from Radford, far from Cheveral Avenue. Meanwhile, there was one last act to be played out in our story: the 1982 European championship and a boxing battle that took me to East Germany, as it was then, deep in the heart of communist Europe.

Having called my racist enemies 'Germans' all my life, I now flew to the town of Schwerin to be surrounded by the real thing. But a pleasant surprise was in store for me when I was treated with respect by everybody I met – the real Germans weren't at all like the ones in Coventry.

The European Junior Amateur Championship semi-finals saw me up against a giant from the Soviet Union with the forbidding name of Ossubek Kilimov. This was three years before the movie *Rocky IV* pitched America's Rocky Balboa against the Soviet Ivan Drago in a fictional fight to the finish.

Well, my bout in Schwerin was very real, my opponent bigger than Dolph Lundgren. He'd been described in the press as 'unbeatable' but I immediately detected a weakness: it was in his sheer size. He was built like a tank but I figured Kilimov would find my dancer-fighter approach hard to keep up with. If I buzzed around him, landing an endless flow of combination punches, eventually I'd bring him crashing down. However, most of the pundits were convinced Kilimov would flatten me. All his fights leading up to this bout had been single-punch knockouts. He was a regular one-hit wonder. In a typical Kilimov encounter, the other man would come out of the corner only to be carried back in seconds.

His record was remarkably similar to the twenty-first-century Russian, 7ft-tall fighter Nikolai Valuev, who demolished all in his path until he ran into south London boy David Haye in a 2009 encounter that dominated sports headlines. Like Valuev, he was a gigantic slab of a man.

Before our bout, I saw the Soviet pound up and down the corridor like an angry bear. He was huffing and puffing, a big scowl on his ugly face. I returned to the changing room and went through my usual pre-fight routine of idle chat and joking around. Through the walls, I could hear him in his changing room, practising jabs on his trainer's pads and making 'woof' noises as he exhaled. This was a well-worn tactic by fighters: make loads of aggressive noises in your changing room to intimidate your opponent next door, make out you're a caged animal about to be unleashed.

Once we got into the ring, I was forced to appreciate the physical scale of what I was up against. He had to be a heavyweight. Surely there had been a terrible mistake here? For a middleweight, I was regarded as big but this monster made me feel a whole lot smaller. As the bell rang, I threw caution to the wind and went at him with some upper cuts, which had to be delivered at maximum thrust to make an impact. There could be no let-up in the punch rate if I had any hope of tenderising his tree trunk of a torso.

Bouncing around on my feet, I darted in every direction to avoid his jabs. One punch from those gigantic Russian fists and I'd have woken up in Moscow. Unused to a boxer who moved like I did, the Soviet's face had gross irritation written all over it as if to say, stand still, I'm trying to hit you, comrade. Occasionally Kilimov would lash out wildly, but his fists only swung through thin air.

In effect, he ended up shadow boxing, while I bruised him up good and proper from every direction. This was the way I'd always worked over the punchbags at the Standard Triumph. Never content to stay in one position, I'd leap to another side of the bag to deliver my next punch. To me, jabbing and crossing from the same place was lazy as well as boring for the crowd. Keep 'em guessing, I thought. Will it be his left side that gets punched or maybe his right? Will I go for his head or the body?

In the second round, this Russian Goliath began to succumb to

Coventry's David. He caught me once and it definitely hurt, but events were moving in my direction. In just a few seconds, I landed ten clear shots and not one came back. At the break, I could see a small group of extremely annoyed Soviet advisers screaming in his ears – he must have come back out with them ringing.

In the third round, things went from bad to worse for Kilimov. Like so many boxers I'd come up against, he went through the same motions, over and over again, showing no flair or initiative. But I refused to stand still. From all angles and to his head and body, I pounded away. Sometimes, when fights went like this, I could hear a James Brown song thumping away in my head and my feet moved to the imaginary sound:

I feel good, I knew that I would, now…
Whoa! I feel nice, like sugar and spice…

Just as my feet shuffled to the beat of any number of disco hits in Tiffany's: I was up dancing and now I was up fighting.

Neither of us ended up dead on the canvas and it fell to the judges to make a decision. Kilimov hadn't impressed them and only a glum-looking Hungarian judge voted in his favour, probably afraid the Soviets would invade again if he didn't. The rest of the judges threw their votes behind me and it was my gloved hands that were raised upwards in triumph. I was ecstatic, leaping in the air and whooping. Meanwhile, my opponent looked like a man facing an execution squad.

To win the European championship, I had to crush Italian middleweight Moe Gruciano. When I entered the ring, it was to cries from the audience: 'Ali … Ali … Ali …' My technique in the semi-final had reminded them of my hero, the greatest boxer of all time. To say I was chuffed would be putting it mildly.

Gruciano proved a bit of a disappointment: the guy was in reverse gear, almost running away from me on occasion. All five judges awarded me the championship and threw in an extra award for Best Boxer of the tournament. Covered in glory, I returned to England.

Back home, I brought my record-breaking amateur career to an end. I'd won more cups than any amateur boxer before me or since those days. In fact, due to a change in the rules, my record may stand for ever. For example, I fought three championships in one season, which can't be done now. My record was also made possible by an early start to boxing, which would be illegal under today's regulations.

Despite some voices urging me to do the Commonwealth Games or the Olympics, I knew a pro career was what I wanted – not least for the financial security I hoped it would finally bring me. Pro boxing equalled money, which equalled escape from Coventry. It meant having what had always been denied me. I never wanted to be the kid with his nose pressed against the shop window, staring at what he couldn't afford: it should be me in that shop, getting my big fat wallet out and buying whatever I wanted.

It seemed Burt McCarthy shared the same vision: he wanted me to finally escape from the ghetto, to make something of myself. I duly repaid his confidence by unleashing a torrent of knockouts in my first professional fights. In some ways, it was just business as usual – a continuation of my amateur form. Almost like clockwork, I'd turn up at the ring, advance from my corner, then leave my opponent kissing the canvas and go back home. In my first six pro bouts, I didn't fight for more than eleven rounds in total.

My first professional fight was against Swansea's Terry Matthews on 18 November 1982. This encounter brought me into contact for the very first time with a TV reporter who would champion my fights from the very beginning. Gary Newbon was a familiar face on ATV, the local independent TV channel covering the Midlands. Later it became Central TV, then part of ITV. Gary was not only a reporter, but also assistant head of sport at ATV – he'd seen my amateur record and decided my professional fight must be televised.

No money changed hands on this occasion – he just agreed to send the crews for free. This would kick off not just a media relationship but genuine friendship; it was also the first time I appeared on TV (the Senior ABA final has been broadcast by the BBC, but I'd managed to exclude myself by not signing with Mickey Duff).

Matthews took a speedy and savage pounding, going to a technical knockout in three rounds. It was even written that my fists were drawn to his face like magnets. The boxing fraternity soon had me marked down for greatness. It didn't take long before I heard my name bandied about as a future world champion. After all, the experts said, I'd demolished everything in my path as an amateur and my pro career seemed to be going the same way too.

Then in flew an American boxer from Chicago by the name of Harlein Holden. I was nineteen at the time, February 1983. Holden was a known figure with a decent enough track record. McCarthy told the press that he hoped Holden would help with my 'boxing education'. It seemed the American had arrived in the UK intent on winding me up from the outset, repeatedly asking, 'Who is Errol Christie?'

One journalist quoted him saying, 'Who is Errol Christie? We have never heard of him in America – what can you tell me about him? He is just a name to me but I have come here to do a job. I have a good punch and I can assure everyone that I am not just here for the ride. I am no pushover.'

Of course, this was all part of a calculated wind-up by the older fighter. But like my dad, on occasion my sense of humour failed me, especially if I was being roundly mocked. One morning in the lead-up to the fight, I picked up a newspaper only to gaze wearily at the headline:

'"WHO'S CHRISTIE?" ASKS OPPONENT.'

Really, I'd had my fill of this joker – he needn't book a return flight to Chicago because my fists were about to send him home first-class, at the speed of sound. It would be like flying Concorde all the way. I'd post him his chin later on.

On the night, the grinning irritant strode into the ring at the Sports Centre, Coventry – a huge new venue at that time in the improbable shape of an elephant. ITV cameras were positioned nearby to capture all the action.

Gary Newbon was there, clutching his microphone and giving a running commentary on the night's events. The ATV reporter was in no doubt that his decision to televise my first fight for free had paid off – I really was the Coventry wonderkid he'd hoped and believed in. I had discovered that Gary had a similar goofy sense of humour to me and also thought he was irresistible to women. We both might have been mistaken on that score.

That night then, Harlein Holden strode in with 'The Hammer' emblazoned on his blue gown. He was punching the air and jumping up and down like an idiot. Seeing my disgust at this display, he took to skipping around me and staring right into my face. This was going to be a short fight, I resolved. No mercy would be shown now.

The bell rang. I began by removing his grin with a strong left jab, followed by a killer right cross. For a few seconds, he gripped the ropes and shook his head, blinking slightly to try and remember exactly where he was. Waiting for him to find his composure again, I followed through with two fast punches from my left hand. Then no longer thinking consciously and in a pure animal state, I pummelled his body and sent his gum shield whizzing off. In the sixty-fourth second of our fight, he went down to defeat.

One report said my tormentor sat in his corner rather confused and whimpered to his trainer: 'It was a left hook, wasn't it?' The next day, the headlines were more to my taste:

'IT'S A KNOCKOUT – NOW HE KNOWS WHO CHRISTIE IS!'

Throughout 1983, the victories kept coming. Oklahoma security guard Sam Leonard was sent back to Tulsa with a sore head. Then Nicaraguan middleweight Lino Cajinas suffered a similar fate at the Crest Hotel in London. And back in my hometown, I saw off Vince Gajny in nintety-two seconds.

Those fights ended so quickly that it's difficult to talk about them in huge detail. It really was a case of I came, I saw, I conquered. Or more accurately, I climbed into the ring, I touched gloves, I laid him out. A mate of mine told me he once popped out of his seat to get a drink and by the time he came back, my fight had started and finished. The punters were picking up their coats and leaving to go home.

Gajny was very much a case in point: I caught him with a right cross and soon enough he was looking for his shoes. Sportswriter Jack Steggles said I was using him 'as no more than a punchbag when referee Paul Thomas leapt in'.

It was during this fight when I realised that Coventry was rallying, full square, behind the boy from Cheveral Avenue. The cheers from the local crowd were resounding, solidly behind me. I left the ring, finally feeling that I was getting the recognition I'd always longed for.

Each morning, I found myself soaking up the glowing copy in the newspapers:

'CRUSHER CHRISTIE.'
'CHRISTIE SO IMPRESSIVE.'
'CLASSY ERROL IS SO QUICK.'
'ERROL'S AT EASE AGAIN.'
'CHRISTIE SHOWS HIS CLASS.'

Any boxer today racking up that kind of victory would demand the rewards to match, but our living conditions were spartan compared to the lifestyle enjoyed by successful fighters nowadays. On moving to London, Burt McCarthy placed me in a house in Greenwich. This was no swanky pad by the river. Instead, a crumbling old pile that showed only the barest signs of once having been grand. Sharing this humble abode was Andy Straughn. I'm convinced to this day that Burt had a master plan at work here: Andy's calm and even temperament would tame my animal instincts and give me more self-control. Meanwhile, I in turn would give my new friend a bit more fire in his belly and turn him into a tougher fighter.

I must have mentioned to Andy our family belief in duppies (mischievous ghosts, a bit like poltergeists) as one night he scared the brown stuff out of me by pretending to be a ghost in the dark hallway. Eventually, the freezing cold of this creepy Amityville Horror proved too much and we both went off and found digs in Brockley.

To see photos of us now, we look like a right pair of country bumpkins. The young London guys we saw around us were sharply dressed: neat, short haircuts, power or tonic suits, depending on their preferred style; yuppie or mod – all accessorised with top-of-the-range watches and fashionable shoes.

Coming from Coventry, we seemed to have emerged from a time machine – one that had just materialised from the 1970s. We were living proof of the yawning divide that was opening up between the huge wealth in the capital and the industrial decay spreading across the Midlands and the North.

To start with, the money was hopeless. Back then we had no concept of television fees or sponsorship deals. A flat fee was pressed into my hand for every knockout. To make ends meet between fights, Burt McCarthy came up with the ingenious idea of getting Straughn and me to work at his jewellery business, Goldcraft. We were paid a weekly wage of £150 and earned our keep by soldering precious metals together.

Goldcraft was one of several companies owned and operated by McCarthy and it specialised in necklaces. Picture this: two muscular boxers with big hands trying to link a lady's delicate gold chain together. Today's boxers might baulk at this as a method of paying your way, but us two country boys simply accepted this was the way of the world. As far as I was concerned, Muhammad Ali himself might have had to thread necklaces at the start of his career.

The promised riches of professional boxing seemed a long way off. I was on TV and winning all my fights, but scrimping to pay the monthly rent, bills and other outgoings. Every morning, before going to the gym, Andy and me were at Goldcraft and McCarthy even escorted Andy down to a bank in Clerkenwell to arrange an overdraft facility for him. Like my folks, however, I wasn't prepared to live on loans – I wanted to pay my way as I went along and so I rejected the idea of a bank loan to keep me going.

The state-of-the-art gym facilities I had expected turned out to be a rather basic affair in an outhouse on McCarthy's estate in Danbury. An affable bloke called Don Davis was the trainer assigned to me. A laid-back Caribbean, what I loved about him was his ability to keep up with my dancer-fighter techniques. He was like a perfect shadow to my every move. But what I also wanted from Don was his inside track on what I could expect to earn in the future, as he himself had been a professional fighter. He, in turn, could see my impatience to get the riches that I felt I rightly deserved, but he counselled patience – not a virtue I suffered from:

'You're too aggressive, Errol – calm down.'

'Don't worry – it'll come.'

'You'll get what you want, eventually.'

He reminded me of those Bob Marley lyrics:

> 'Don't worry about a thing,
> 'Cause every little thing gonna be all right!'

I'm afraid I didn't believe those sentiments: I felt I had to turbo-charge my professional career forward, this was a race against time. In small ways, I tried to take back control of parts of my life. Training was a start and I coughed up out of my own pocket to use the no-nonsense facilities above the Thomas A' Beckett pub in south London. The place was compact and hot. In the corner was a ring, four punchbags nearby and also a little room for skipping in. Nearly all the boxers there were white so I stood out like a sore thumb from day one.

The man in charge was Danny Holland, Henry Cooper's trainer, and I'd throw him out of the little room when I was there so that I could use the scales in private. Like a lot of fighters, I didn't want my weight publicised between fights. If I was too heavy, then I'd spend hours hitting the bags followed by long runs round London with sweat pouring like a stream from my body.

Finding that everybody trained in silence, I decided to introduce a groundbreaking departure from tradition. In came my portable tape deck to liven things up a bit. This was an era before gyms throbbed to pumping house music, as most do these days. The result was instantaneous – all the boxers hated it.

'Turn it down – can't hear myself think!'

'That bloody jungle music you lot play!'

The pub had a long association with Eddie and Charlie Richardson, the gangland bosses from south London who became embroiled in a notorious turf war with Ronnie and Reggie Kray, the more famous east London gangsters back in the 1960s. All four earned themselves impressive jail sentences for their activities.

Eddie's love of boxing was well known, as was his generous

and kind-hearted support for up-and-coming talent. One of those talents was my good self. As a Coventry boy, ignorant of London's criminal history, I had no idea that the man who turned up to so many of my pro fights in a big brown Mercedes was Eddie Richardson, brother of Charlie and a man whose enforcer was the infamous Mad Frankie Fraser.

Eddie was a highly personable and charming gentleman, who cheered my performances from the ringside and often celebrated over a few drinks with Burt and me afterwards. He and McCarthy had known each other for more than two decades and were the firmest of friends. Years later, I found out that Eddie was such a huge fan of my fighting that he'd gone round selling tickets to his mates to get as many of them as possible along to my bouts.

He'd completed a long stretch behind bars after being convicted in the so-called 'Torture Trial' of 1966. So-called because it was alleged that people were lifted from the streets and put in front of a kangaroo court by the Richardsons before 'justice' was meted out in brutal gangland style. But I knew nothing of this at the time. To me, Eddie seemed just another well-off boxing fan, one who was refreshingly free of any negative attitudes towards me on the grounds of my race. An unassuming man, he addressed me as an equal. In the years since I've heard a lot of things about Eddie, Charlie and Frankie Fraser but I must confess nothing has altered my view of them, not one bit.

When I went professional, Mad Frankie Fraser was still finishing off a twenty-year sentence. Originally it had been fifteen but he'd led a riot in HM Prison Parkhurst and once again found himself in front of a judge, who added five years to his sentence. Eventually, he was to end up spending an astonishing forty years of his life behind bars.

When I was training down at the Thomas A' Beckett, Frankie's name would be mentioned in respectful and hushed terms. The short man with a wiry frame inspired a mixture of awe and fear in the boxers, but the support that the gangsters gave to the sport and the natural distrust we all felt for officialdom back then meant that there was an odd sort of affection, loyalty perhaps, towards the likes of Eddie and Charlie.

After my fights I'd often go to one of the Richardson's clubs in

Catford, a place called J Arthur's, to chill out and relax. It was there that Mad Frankie had his big party when he finally emerged from the nick in 1985. As McCarthy's star boxer, I was invited and introduced to Frankie for the first time. We got on like a house on fire. Like Eddie and Charlie, he'd had a go at being a boxer in his youth and had later been in prison with Henry Cooper's uncle, who he once remembered receiving the cat-o'nine-tails – a multi-tailed whip commonly used in the British Navy and prisons during the old days.

Frankie also served time with Frank Warren's uncle Bob for their part in the attack on a man called Jack Spot in the mid-1950s, a well-reported trial at the time. He maintains Bob was totally innocent of the crime for which he was convicted: 'Terrific guy, never complained.' Warren was a huge boxing enthusiast and, according to Frankie, it was he who'd introduced Burt and Leslie McCarthy to the sport and the idea of getting into management, hence me ending up in their stable.

Frankie's party was one of the best nights of my life. Catford may not be the most salubrious part of London in some people's eyes but these were people that I enjoyed mixing with. Later, I would hear details of what Frankie had allegedly done involving pliers and toes, but as we raised our glasses to toast his release after two decades in prison, he was just a jovial cockney geezer with an evil twinkle in his eye.

Patting me on the back, he said that boxing was the best way for a working-class boy like me to avoid getting banged up. Having spent forty-two years behind bars, I suppose he was something of an expert. And he told me about his own failed attempt to make it in the ring: 'When I was a kid, I loved going to the Blackfriars ring, but I always cheated. Had a lump of lead in my glove ...'

With my star in the ascendant, I began to mix with boxing royalty. Names I had only read about and people I aspired to be now crossed my path. The first magical encounter was with a man for whom I've always had unqualified respect. One day, McCarthy announced that he'd fixed up a sparring session – in the presence of the media, of course – with Sugar Ray Leonard. I was speechless. My manager wasn't lying when he told the press: 'Sugar Ray wants to meet British boxers of potential. Errol will love it.'

We met at the Thomas A' Beckett and the photos show me in an almost trance-like state: my fist posed affectionately under his chin, his hand on my shoulder. Inside, I burned with an ambition to match his achievements, to come within reach of his greatness. I couldn't imagine meeting a boxer as magnificent as Sugar Ray but then things just got a whole lot better.

In August 1983, Muhammad Ali announced that he would visit Coventry. Among several engagements were trips to the Coventry FC ground and a local chippie owned by veteran heavyweight Jack Bodell. Must have been the first and last time that Bodell had thousands queuing outside his shop. All I could hear were cries of 'Ali, Ali!'

The former World Heavyweight Champion was also pencilled in to open a DIY store: the Unit Sales DIY Store in Rotherham Road, to be precise. I still have that flier. Even now, it makes me laugh. The classiest fighter that ever lived, the man who gave us 'The Rumble in the Jungle' and 'The Thrilla in Manila' was in my hometown to cut the ribbon at a shop selling floor tiles and Cuprinol!

For me, the highlight of the day (and hopefully, for him too) was to spar with a certain Errol Christie in the town centre. Surrounded by my family, I traded a few mock, even slightly comical, blows. We both seemed to enjoy deflating the whole pomposity that can sometimes surround boxing. He pulled aggressive faces and I just burst out laughing.

'You're pretty,' Ali said to me, 'but you're not as pretty as me.'

Staring into his eyes, I didn't see aggression but friendliness, a real warmth that I hadn't expected. He was much bigger than me in every direction: a tall and broad, powerful figure. This was way before the illness that beset him later in life.

Ali was still very much in his prime. Extremely fit, he would have been in his early forties and, for me, it was incredible to think that in a career spanning two decades he had achieved so much: first, as Cassius Clay and then Muhammad Ali. He put an arm on my shoulder and I guided him to meet my mum and Annette, who were just as much in awe of this legend as me. For once, I was unable to find the right words – everything coming out of my mouth was semi-garbled. But he wasn't chattering away, either. I'd expected a loud-mouthed preacher such as we'd seen so often on TV, boastful with lots of clever putdowns, but he was very down-to-earth with none of the flamboyancy assumed to be part of his character.

Aside from the official press photos on the day, there's a Polaroid snap of Ali with my mother. She could hardly have imagined her 'bad breed kroff' would one day introduce her to the man who literally rubbed shoulders with Malcolm X. However briefly, the delight that showed on her face must have helped make up a little for the years of torment and frustration in our family home.

As we sparred and goofed around, I couldn't help glancing at the faces in the crowd. It was hard to forget it was people like this who stared over the garden fence at me when I'd first arrived in Coventry as a small child in Cheveral Avenue. Skinheads and boot boys were there, too – the same animals who had chased me home from school every day but were now roaring their approval. I found it difficult to accept their applause with good grace. By now, the damage ran way too deep.

Muhammad Ali and other American boxers blazed such a magnificent trail through the 1960s and 1970s that they were able to command huge sponsorship deals and TV rights. To me, it felt like black boxers in Britain had some catching-up to do and so I took it upon myself to convince the marketing and advertising types that black faces, especially mine, were bankable.

I never stopped talking to people, banging my head against all sorts of walls in the hope that I'd get a slice of the money that the white boxers were earning. I'd have countless polite chats with those who could have made something happen but their expression said it all: black faces didn't sell products. Throughout the early 1980s we were invisible on the front of fashion maga-zines or TV ads. In the end, Frank Bruno would break through: meanwhile, Errol Christie and others were not wanted.

So, the doors to the mega-wealth I craved stayed shut. Instead, there was the constant suspicion that I was earning way too little. I didn't know how to take this up with McCarthy or even what I'd say to him; the whole financial thing seemed like a maze to me and nobody could give me solid and reliable advice. All I got was chat from other fighters who'd say that after all those knockouts I should be earning a lot more, but I just couldn't figure out how to go about it.

Of course, I wasn't the only boxer who felt like this, particularly black boxers. Michael Watson, a boxer I'd later fight, said he once received a cheque from a bout and was almost in tears at how little it was. But I didn't do tears: I did anger, although I understand how he must have felt. At that time, there was a constant sense of frustration shared by all boxers of my skin colour. Above was a glass ceiling and none of us knew how to break through.

I got to a stage of frustration where I just thought: sod it, I'll go ahead and waste what money I've got, anyway. A Porsche 911 was an early purchase. It was the most curious sensation to drive around Coventry in this luxury car, remembering how we'd all crammed into Dad's beaten-up old Wolseley as kids. Now I was surrounded by the scent of new leather with an engine that purred instead of coughing and spluttering.

It amused me to see white folk staring at the black man in his Porsche. I knew they were asking themselves whether I was a drug dealer or if I'd stolen it. At best, maybe I still worked for a garage and was taking a rich white man's car for a spin. On the motorway home from Coventry to London, often I'd spot a nightclub owner called George Henry in another lane. He owned a club in Coventry called George's, as well as the Limelight in London's West End. We'd become good mates and I'd toot him as I drove past. He'd step on the gas in his white Rolls-Royce convertible and race me down to the capital.

Keen to get the sort of financial security that my parents had never enjoyed, I started eyeing up the property market. Like most British people, I figured out the best place to put your cash was in bricks and mortar and so I ploughed my earnings into an impressive house in Dulwich, south London, and another smaller place in Lewisham, which I intended to rent out. In the true spirit of the eighties, I even dabbled on the stock market, buying a few shares. It seems odd to say it now but my newfound status as a homeowner put me on cloud nine.

Around this time, I formed a new posse for night-clubbing that I now refer to as the black boxing equivalent of the Rat Pack: me, welterweight fighter Lloyd 'Ragamuffin Man' Honeyghan and heavyweight Trevor 'Hughroy Currie' Curry. We got on like the proverbial house on fire and saw ourselves as a trio, helping to change the face of sport while also having a good time.

Lloyd was a party animal. Jamaican-born with a heavy patois accent, we would be returning home with some girls from a club and he'd declare: 'No spend no money upon them!' and then proceed to buy a very expensive meal and more champagne than you could possibly drink as I watched on in awe.

'I thought you weren't going to spend any cash on them?'

But that was Lloyd spending no money. When he pushed the boat out, it was an evening with royalty. In contrast, when I didn't spend anything the girl was lucky to get a bag of chips. Needless to say, with his spendthrift ways Lloyd had the most success of us three on the pulling stakes. Women stumbled at my feet but they fell at Lloyd's, I sometimes said.

I suppose I could have had a string of girlfriends, but I didn't. Other fighters accused me of being 'too fussy', but my pickiness probably saved me a lot of money and hassle. I was completely focused on my career – on reaching the 'big time' – and as Alison had found out back in Coventry, I couldn't afford to let women get in the way. I sometimes felt there was a reckless streak to some of my fellow boxers' partying that I just couldn't share. Dare I say it, Errol Christie had a bit of a moral streak. Early on, I decided that when I had a kid, I'd be around for him or her 24/7.

While I was doing well, Lloyd did a lot better in terms of TV coverage. I used to say Trevor and me were too black for the telly: TV preferred the paler skin of Lloyd Honeyghan, though his superb boxing played a part as well, but ultimately even he couldn't charm the BBC like Frank Bruno did. When he opened his mouth and dropped into Jamaican patois, his choice of words and way of expressing himself were too full on for 1980s' TV audiences.

The Raggamuffin Man was prone to using words such as 'pussy' and 'bumba blot' to describe any number of people and that directness was not always acceptable. To me, his honesty and frankness were great qualities but for the media and PR folk, this presented a potential problem. When he gave an opinion, he didn't coat it in sugar. A commentator on ITV's *World of Sport* once said I'd been 'tested' on another fighter. Immediately, Lloyd rose from his studio seat and barked that I shouldn't be treated like an experiment. Naturally, this brought the discussion to a premature close.

Lloyd had strong political opinions: he was very anti-National Front, not to mention the apartheid system in South Africa. His principles would be tested after he won the WBA Welterweight World Championship in September 1986 and was to defend his title in South Africa against Harold Volbrecht shortly afterwards. Rather than do that, he threw his welterweight belt in the bin, saying: 'Me no go there!'

You couldn't help but admire his courage even if he was also throwing away a good part of his career prospects. The amount of money on the table to go to South Africa could have made him comfortable for a long time afterwards, but Lloyd just walked away. I think I'd have turned it down as well but, for me, it would have been greater agony to push away all those riches.

In the years that followed I'd see him after fights, hardly able to speak. Not because he was punch-drunk, but out of sheer physical pain. He put everything into his fights and beat his opponents up so badly but, in the course of all this, he exhausted himself. Sometimes it tired me out to watch Lloyd expend every ounce of energy in his body in the ring. He really was a 'Ragamuffin Warrior'.

During my childhood, birthdays had never been a big deal. My parents couldn't afford to shell out on flashy presents and later on, I was too busy boxing to notice the date. Even if I did, I ignored it. But in my new life, things would clearly have to change.

My first birthday as a professional boxer in 1982 involved Burt McCarthy throwing a big bash at his mansion in Danbury. There, I found myself surrounded by his business associates and friends, none of whom I knew. The only person in the room that I could really talk to was the TV presenter Gary Newbon, to whom I attached myself for the rest of the evening, along with

Andy Straughn, who also had no idea what to say to any of Burt's wealthy buddies.

A year later, I organised a party more on my own terms. My chosen venue was J Arthur's in Catford and this time I got all my new boxing mates down: Trevor Curry, Lloyd Honeyghan and Frank Bruno came, the latter with his wife, Laura. Frank spent quite a bit of time trying to fix me up with one of her friends. 'She'll do rice and peas for you,' he said. To a black man this was certainly a selling point, but not quite good enough on that occasion.

I liked Frank, but he managed to wind up a lot of black boxers on account of his goofy routine with TV sports presenter Harry Carpenter; the centrepiece of which was his corny catchphrase: 'Know what I mean, Harry?' These words became nationally famous, even featuring on the comic puppet show *Spitting Image*. But it drove boxers like me nuts. Here was an intelligent black guy cast in the image of the safe pliant negro; a figure of fun white society could embrace. Maybe I was more militant in my attitude, more uncompromising, but it annoyed me to see a fighter as great as Frank projected like this. In truth he was a bright guy, I just wished white folks knew that as well.

While Lloyd and Frank increasingly dominated the BBC's boxing programmes, I was fast becoming part of ITV's regular entertainment output. That, however, had not been a given after turning professional. When Tom McGarry turned down Mickey Duff, it really was an enormous risk which might have sunk my professional career at the outset: Duff had the BBC's boxing output sewn up and if you weren't signed to him, you didn't get on the Beeb. That's how it went.

Signing to Burt McCarthy raised the immediate question of where my fights would appear. Fortunately, the answer to that particular conundrum was to hand: it turned out McCarthy was working closely with the new rebel promoter Frank Warren. He found the doors of the BBC locked on him, but resolved that dilemma by talking to ITV.

Fortunately, Warren and ITV were able to strike a deal and ushered in what now looks like a golden age, for both the channel and the sport. In turn, I became one of the main faces on *Fight*

Night and we traded blows across the airwaves with the BBC. It's hard to believe, unless you're of a certain age and can remember, just how popular boxing was in the 1970s and 1980s. Overnight, TV made household names out of boxers.

On the BBC, Frank Bruno was the leading black boxing face: he was managed by Terry Lawless and promoted by Duff, after Bruno rejected McCarthy. Herrol 'Bomber' Graham and Lloyd were also regular fixtures. Back at ITV, I was the main black boxing face – the first, in fact – alongside other fight talents like Terry Marsh, Joe Bugner, Keith Wallace and Jimmy Price. Often I'd find myself being interviewed by presenters that I'd watched on telly throughout the 1970s, like Dickie Davies, the front man of *World of Sport*.

With his well-groomed hair, big moustache and fashionable suits, Dickie was regarded as smooth and sophisticated, back then. Every Saturday afternoon he went head to head with Des Lynam on the BBC's *Grandstand* programme. More than anything else in the world, I wanted to fight live on Dickie's show.

The audiences for *World of Sport* were up to 20 million in those days – often for the knockabout British wrestling matches that featured the likes of Giant Haystacks and Big Daddy. On the first occasion when I was interviewed in the studio by Dickie, it felt completely bizarre. There I was, inside the TV screen as it were: on that famous programme set with the gigantic *World of Sport* logo behind me, part of a programme I'd watched as a kid.

Later Dickie flew with me, Trevor Curry, Lloyd Honeyghan, Frank Warren and Terry Marsh – who would be falsely accused of shooting Frank in 1989 – to the Isle of Man. This was a couple of years on in 1986, when Trevor lost the British Heavyweight title to Horace Notice at a fight in Douglas. On the same trip, Terry Marsh triumphed over Francesco Prazioso to gain the European Light Welterweight belt. Meanwhile, I chatted up Dickie and hung out with Norman Wisdom who lived in retirement on the island as well as getting in a bit of training with Lloyd.

Two other presenters on *World of Sport* were the hugely popular Ian St John and Jimmy Greaves (more commonly known as 'Saint and Greavsie'). Greavsie interviewed me on the new ITV breakfast show, *TV-am*. The only memory I have of that early-morning encounter was my impression of the main presenter, Anne Diamond. Maybe I'm mistaken but I got the most horrible vibes off her. We were very definitely from different sides of the track.

A while after my interview, I ran into Greavsie's son, who asked me point-blank: 'Do you have a problem with white people?' Despite the friendly persona I was trying to project, clearly I was coming across to the TV crowd as a bit chippie. I didn't know how to respond to that comment and so I just grunted, before walking away.

Despite that exchange, the channel was coming to regard me as an audience draw with the advertising revenue talked above all else. When ITV organised a group photograph of its leading stars in the mid-1980s, I was asked to pose along with the likes of David Jason, Eamonn Andrews, Ernie Wise and Anneka Rice. The only black man in the picture, I hasten to add.

I found myself becoming one of a new wave of black faces on TV. No longer content with bit parts, increasingly I was taking centre stage. One of those other black faces was the footballer John Fashanu. I soon struck up a friendship with him, especially when I discovered that he lived in Blackheath.

In 1984, John Fashanu played centre-forward for Millwall Football Club. Two years later, he joined Wimbledon at the time when they were known by the media as the 'Crazy Gang' because of the players' well-known love of practical jokes. But John never struck me as much of a joker, unlike his fellow players. In fact, he was deadly serious and enormously driven: his main focus in life was money, not hilarity. And he was always ready with a doom-laden warning about my finances: 'You better sort yourself out now, Errol. Be too late one day, got to do it all now, like I have. You just never know when it's all going to end.'

As kids, he and his brother Justin, also a footballer, had been sent to a Barnardo's home when their Nigerian parents split up. Unlike my dad, who was just an illiterate brickie, their father was a barrister but when he and his wife went their separate ways, the small brothers were put in care. They were then fostered by a white couple in Norfolk: Alf and Betty Jackson.

Justin eventually came out as gay and subsequently committed suicide. By that point we were no longer friends, but I can imagine this wouldn't have been an easy time for John. Attitudes to homosexuality weren't too liberal back then and in the black community; they were downright hostile. Sadly, I can't claim to be any different and one incident still sticks in the mind.

I'd just read about HIV and AIDS in one of the tabloids. This was when it was being described as a new 'plague', with gays often seen as the main carriers. Before Lady Di did her hand-holding bit, sympathy was still in short supply from most quarters. I was slightly naïve on the whole subject and, sitting in a pub one day, asked another boxer what all this AIDS stuff was about. He just slapped me on the back:

'You don't have to worry, Errol – what with being heterosexual.'

My blood surged: 'You fucking *what*?'

Next thing he knew, the boxer in question was bouncing off the nearby fruit machine and I was putting my fist away. I had to be calmed down and gently informed that a 'heterosexual' was actually a straight person. I'd never heard the word before! In my simple upbringing, there'd only been 'bent' and 'straight'. Young, black, aggressive and often incapable of taking a joke (a trait I'd inherited from my dad), I'm afraid my response was entirely predictable.

During the time that I knew Fash, a decade before the tragedy with Justin, the two brothers were coining it. John had a place in a smart part of south London that wasn't far from my newly acquired homes in Dulwich and Lewisham, so it wasn't too long before I was popping round for a drink.

'Fash', as I called him, asked me to come and see him play at Wimbledon. This was a new experience for me – I'd never been to a football match in my life. Even though I played the game at school, the terraces had been so infested by skinheads in the 1970s, I'd no wish to go and stand among them. If I'd gone to a Coventry FC game in my teens, I'd have spent more of the match fighting the crowd than watching the action.

For the players, things hadn't been a whole lot better up to that time. There were the monkey noises every time they walked on the pitch or took possession of the ball, plus the racial abuse from other players in the changing room. Then the lower expectations that black players had to contend with, but things were starting to change. Footballers like Fash were winning the grudging respect of fans through their playing, but I wouldn't want to overplay that. There was still a long, hard battle ahead before multi-racial teams ceased to be an issue.

So I went to Wimbledon with some trepidation. As the man I was, my aggression was at the same, if not a greater, level than the beered-up, chanting fans around me. We got to the ground and there were thousands of blokes who I'd always regarded as the enemy. All I expected was to hear the insults with which I was already way too familiar. To my surprise, I didn't hear a single monkey noise or see a banana skin land on the pitch. I had to concede that, at long last, things might be starting to change.

Outside Fash's house was a smart-looking car with his name emblazoned down the side. That I didn't like, it was way too showy. I was pleased to have reached the big time as a boxer, to have got on television, but I didn't need to rub my fame in other people's faces – that sort of naff self-promotion was almost a disease of the decade. If you had it, you flaunted it, back in the eighties. And if you didn't, you just looked on at those who did, feeling like nobody. I didn't like this kind of yuppie (or 'buppie', if you were black) behaviour – all I wanted was a bit of respect and a lot more money.

But Fashanu adored the limelight. He'd enter a club and make sure everybody knew that he'd just arrived. I'd be walking behind with a little nod to anybody who recognised me, but otherwise I'd be way more discreet. But there was another, more sinister reason for my discretion: with the fame that attached to me, I still got some very unwanted attention. Once my address was known through press coverage, local racists took to scrawling some very unpleasant graffiti on the front of my house.

I came home from one fight to find 'nigger' written on my front gate. So, Britain had not buried its bigots yet. I opted for a certain amount of privacy to protect myself and those around me when I met people who asked if I was Errol Christie. I'd tell them no, I wasn't. Then they'd start telling me stories about Errol Christie, making out they knew me well and how strange it was that I looked so much like him. They'd even say they were best friends with Errol Christie and I'd never clapped eyes on them before. Back in the eighties, celebrity culture was driving people mad, much as it does today.

Fash continued to be horrified by how little we were getting as boxers. Often he said that if I needed him to speak up for me with the powers that be, like a shop steward or negotiator, then he'd put his verbal skills at my disposal. Shrugging my shoulders in resignation, I would point out that footballers had plenty of support from each other and their professional associations, but boxers were on their own. We were ghetto boys, who were swallowed up by the system, chewed and then spat out when our bodies were too broken to carry on; that was a fighter's lot.

Despite his money and fame, Fash was always a bit suspicious of people. He was a restless man, whose trust had to be earned. He'd bought these surveillance gadgets for monitoring phone calls and other conversations. Once he insisted on lending me one to see if it would come in useful, but there was nobody I wanted to spy on – apart from Burt McCarthy, perhaps. I was always keen to know what the management were up to.

While hanging out with Fash, I met a girl called Mary from Wales at some club on the Old Kent Road. She was mixed race and fiery, with an ambition to be the new Shirley Bassey. Aside from singing on stage, she also designed clothes. That gave me an idea. With Fash's constant warnings about coining it while I could ringing in my ears and still no sponsorship or TV deals in sight, I dreamt up a money-making ruse whereby me and Mary would stage fashion shows.

She designed and made the clothes, while I sorted out the music and lighting. I wasn't massively qualified to do this, but threw myself into it and somehow we pulled everything together. On the night of our first show at a south London venue, we got a mixed crowd along from West End clubs, where we had publicised the event. The champagne flowed but I'm not sure how much clobber actually got sold – not that much, I suspect, certainly not enough for me to retire on. The ticket sales gave me a nice financial boost, but I soon realised this would be another dead end.

It was 1983 and I was leaving my teens. Not since I was a schoolboy had I been beaten in the ring. From the first time I'd stuck on the gloves, the overwhelming majority of my fights, including six pro bouts, had been victories. On 15 October 1983, my dream of fighting live on ITV's *World of Sport* programme came true. They did a live link to my bout against Doug James in Coventry.

The opportunity to box live on ITV had come about through some behind-the-scenes lobbying by Gary Newbon. Aside from being a TV presenter, he was something of a mover and shaker inside ITV and eventually became deputy head of sport on the channel. Newbon wanted to 'freshen up' *World of Sport* and he believed some action in the ring would do the trick. He convinced the programme producer that as Frank Warren's hottest promotional property I could be the new face of boxing on ITV. Gary was given the green light, but now he was landed with a little problem: having flattened a good number of boxers, Burt McCarthy couldn't find anybody to go up against me. According to Gary, Burt managed to tear out what little was left of his hair in phoning around to find me an opponent.

Up to 24 hours before we were going live, McCarthy sat on the floor at home, phone pressed to an ear, going through every contact he had in the industry to find a fighter with the balls to take me on. In the end, between him and Frank Warren they got Doug James to agree to stick on his gloves and give the TV audience some Saturday afternoon entertainment.

Burt quickly managed to book a venue, too: the Willenhall Social Club in Coventry. When I turned up, the place was packed to the rafters, not so much standing room only as barely any room to breathe. By the ring, the TV cameras prepared to whir into action. This being the era before pay-per-view telly, James and me had to wait twenty minutes in a corridor to fight while a horse race at Newmarket ran its course. Then from the studio, *World of Sport* presenter Dickie Davies introduced the big event in Coventry.

Fresh from some training in the United States, I ploughed into my opponent with little mercy to give the audience of 3 million strong what they wanted. Inside the first minute, a Christie demolition jab sent James down to the canvas, proving all those managers who kept their talent away from me had good reason.

Unwisely, he got up a bit too quickly and I nearly laughed

when I heard him ask: 'What happened?' He was also facing the wrong way for a moment, which convinced me this was going to be another Christie victory. The start of the third round saw my jab plant itself in the middle of his face while in the fourth round, three whacking great left hooks ended his torment. Afterwards, James had the good grace to say: 'Make no mistake, I didn't fight just anybody out there, he is someone special.'

In the same month, the *Boxing News* front page served notice on the British Middleweight Champion Mark Kaylor that either Jimmy Price or myself, 'the young lions of the middleweight division', would be matched against him in the next eighteen months. A prophetic article, if ever there was one.

So, I had everything to look forward to, including the World Championship that all the sports scribblers thought was within my grasp. Recognition also came from the most unlikely sources, including those I had once regarded as my sworn and implacable enemies.

One night, Mum was at home in Cheveral Avenue when the doorbell rang. She opened the front door to find an older, apparently slightly wiser figure of Broosky. The Yogi Bear lookalike racist was now very ill and, as it turned out, closer to death than maybe even he realised. Looking a bit sorry for himself, he held up a newspaper with a big photo on the front of it to my mum.

'See your son's in the papers,' he remarked, with a broken voice. This was followed by an attempted smile before he shuffled off. Mum watched him go, not knowing what to say – the words just didn't form in her mouth. Shortly afterwards, having shown there was some spark of humanity in him after all, Brooksy was off to meet his maker.

So, my success was winning over the most unlikely converts but if I needed to be brought down to earth, luckily there was always one organisation I could rely on: Her Majesty's boys in blue. Although I'd left Coventry and Cheveral Avenue behind me, I still suffered from insomnia. As I've said before, it's a battle I've been fighting all my life. I've never really got over having to share one small room with all my brothers: the constant interruptions, the noises in the dark and my mad, violent father wandering in every so often without warning. None of this was conducive to sound sleeping patterns. Even as I achieved my youthful ambitions, I couldn't just roll over and fall asleep. Instead, I'd stare at the ceiling and fret, brood or just think things over – opportunities I felt I was missing as a pro boxer, nagging doubts that my management could be doing a lot more for me, the amateur nature of the training and physio care I was getting.

One night, unable to shut my brain down, I got out of bed and decided to go for a run. For me, nocturnal jogging had become a regular alternative to sleep. Sticking my tracksuit on and grabbing the house keys, I slipped out into the quiet London streets and began pounding along the pavement.

I'd been going for a while when I became aware of two coppers, one female and one male, walking towards me. To this day when I think of them, I always refer to that duo as Dempsey and Makepeace after the British police drama that was on ITV in the mid-1980s. But the two coppers in front of me were far less likeable.

The male policeman smirked: 'Which house have you burgled, then?'

Stunned, I halted in my tracks. 'You can see I'm in my training gear, can't ya? I'm jogging,' I told him.

They exchanged knowing looks: black man running at night, the only thing he could be doing is running from, or to, the scene of a crime. The worst thing was I'd been so long an object of suspicion to the police that I'd almost convinced myself I might be a criminal. Before moving on, I blurted out another retort: 'Free country – innit?'

Furious, I went back home and stood outside, gazing at my Porsche 911. No doubt they'd think I'd stolen it. While I contemplated it and ground my teeth in fury, the gruesome twosome passed by in their patrol car. I jabbed my forefinger at the Porsche.

'It's mine, you know. *Mine!*'

The next morning, I considered a visit to the cop shop to give them all a piece of my mind: I was Errol Christie. Yes, the boxer from the telly, *Fight Night* – earning my way and paying my taxes, a decent law-abiding man. But now, as I opened the front door to my house, I felt like a kid again – like a no-good ragamuffin from the streets of Hillfields.

ITV commentator Gary Newbon gets a K.O. from me.
Errol Christie, personal collection

Lloyd Honeyghan *(left)*, me, ITV *World of Sport* presenter Dickie Davies, Trevor Curry and Frank Warren – off to the Isle of Man.
Errol Christie, personal collection

The black boxing 'Rat Pack': me *(left)*, Trevor Curry *(middle)* and Lloyd Honeyghan *(right)*.

Errol Christie, personal collection

Me *(left)* with Lloyd Honeyghan – boxing rings by day and clubs by night.

Errol Christie, personal collection

Meeting veteran comedian Norman Wisdom on the Isle of Man.

Errol Christie, personal collection

Frank Bruno *(right)* – a great boxer, but his catchphrase made other black fighters cringe.

Errol Christie, personal collection

Me training with footballer
John Fashanu.
*Lawrence Lustig/Daily Star/Express
Newspapers*

Desperate to make money, I venture into the
fashion business . . .

Mirrorpix

The stars of ITV: right at the back – behind the likes of Anneka Rice, David Jason and Ernie Wise – who's that?

Thames Television

6

SUCCEED OR DIE IN DETROIT

'We get into the ring and we say
— "Welcome to big time boxing!"'

Emanuel Steward — owner of Detroit's legendary Kronk Gym

EMANUEL STEWARD

The head of the legendary Kronk Gym, Detroit.
Kronk Gym

THOMAS HEARNS
WORLD CHAMPION

'Hitman' Hearns – bunches of punches.
Kronk Gym

DUANE THOMAS

Shot and killed aged 39 in 2000.
Kronk Gym

DAVID BRAXTON

'Machine Gun' Braxton – defeated by Mike McCallum in 1985.
Kronk Gym

MIKE McCALLUM

Often called 'The Bodysnatcher', and for
good reason.

Kronk Gym

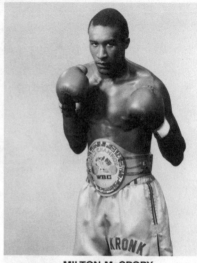

MILTON McCRORY
WORLD CHAMPION

'Ice Man' McCrory - a brilliant
welterweight.

Kronk Gym

Me with Kronk fighter Mike McCallum.

Errol Christie, personal collection

It certainly wasn't anything to look at. In the basement of an old tenement, in a run-down area of the murder capital of the USA, here was Detroit's world-famous Kronk Boxing Gym. But as Andy Straughn and I approached it, we were thrilled to bits. In Detroit, there were plenty of car-making production lines, but this particular production line turned out world-class boxers.

Names like Tommy 'Hitman' Hearns and Milton 'Ice Man' McCrory originated from Kronk. They were in a whole different league to anyone I'd come up against back home. From Muhammad Ali to Sugar Ray Leonard, I'd always been in awe of American boxers – thrilling fighters who knew how to move with grace and ease while delivering killer jabs and crosses. They were in huge contrast to the boring 'head hunters' as I called them that I'd got used to knocking out in Britain – boxers who were rooted to the spot, with no idea how to work over an entire body, just programmed to punch at the other man's head. The Kronk fighters, however, brought a skill and beauty to the sport that has never been equalled. Not for nothing have many commentators claimed this was the period when the sport reached its height.

Hours before, Andy and I had arrived in Detroit and we were driven from the airport to the home of the Kronk's manager, the legendary Emanuel Steward. It was late 1983 and Burt McCarthy had decided my talents needed an injection of what the Kronk had to offer. He'd listened to my frustrations about the training I was getting as a pro fighter and accepted if I was really going to take my place among the world champions, then I would have to start mixing with some of them.

Driving through Detroit, Andy and I stared wide-eyed out of the windows. I can only describe our reactions as a mixture of horror and wonderment: the city was a vast metropolis with skyscrapers and flyovers choked with traffic. In between, the clusters of buildings were huge vacant lots of land that were grassed over. Later we discovered they were mockingly called 'urban prairies', sites where buildings had been demolished. Not just because the previous standing structures had become derelict, but also on account of the drug dealers hiding out in them. The city's leaders figured the only way to flush out the dealers was to level big chunks of the place.

It was impossible to ignore the street crazies, pill-heads and alcoholics stumbling along, their stolen shopping trolleys piled high with all manner of rubbish. Detroit had gone through three decades of terrible decline and only years after we left would the city show any visible signs of recovery. As we drove along, it became painfully clear that, in this particular society, you either succeeded or lost very badly.

We hit a particularly grim ghetto, which made Hillfields look like a holiday camp. Despairing faces – most of them black, of course – stared back at me. This was the world from which many American boxers were trying to escape, covering themselves in the trappings of the good life in the hope they'd never end up back where they came from.

Suddenly, like the Emerald City in *The Wizard of Oz*, a gated estate appeared, right in the middle of the ghetto but a world away. It was an oasis of extreme wealth, oblivious to the poverty outside. We were ushered through the gates by security and drove on towards Emanuel Steward's palatial residence.

The pillars, marble and gold fittings that greeted us shamed even McCarthy's pad in Danbury. We drove up to a huge garage housing his limousines: it had bullet-proof glass screen in front to keep out the local armed criminals. Getting out of our chauffeured car, we were escorted to the house where Steward put up all his fighters. As we unpacked our things, Andy and I could barely talk to each other – we were still thinking about the city we'd seen outside.

Even though we'd just arrived, we were in no mood to hang around the gated estate. Both of us were itching to get down to the gym and look around – which was how we ended up outside such an unpromising building in a raw and edgy part of town. We went through the doors and down some dingy steps. The gym, we discovered, was a windowless sweatbox of a place. Hot, hot, hot!

As I entered, the beads of perspiration on my brow were as much to do with the boiling temperature as my mounting excitement.

If I thought the air conditioning was on the blink, I soon discovered there was another reason for the stifling heat: that was how Emanuel liked it. He believed when his fighters were training, they had to go through something of an endurance test with their physical stamina pushed to the limit. If you wobbled on your feet in that basement furnace, you simply weren't good enough for the Kronk.

There was an incredible din of thumping and thwacking as muscle-bound boxers assaulted the bags or sparred in the ring. In contrast to the first day at the Standard Triumph, I found myself in predominantly black company. All around me were brothers: maybe a couple of Hispanic guys, but mainly black men.

I was genuinely startled to hear some of the guys addressing each other as 'Nigger'. Remember, this was life before hip hop and Public Enemy. The only time I'd hear the n-word used was from the mouths of Radford Boot Boys and they certainly didn't regard me as a 'bruv' or 'homie'.

Standing at the entrance to this hive of activity, I wasn't sure what we were supposed to do next, though my gut feeling was to quickly change and set to work. From the other side of the gym, I was aware of a presence moving towards us: a big smile was getting ever nearer, then an outstretched hand.

'Welcome, Errol.'

There before me was Emanuel Steward – a stocky man, but with gentle facial features that belied his tough approach to creating champions. Behind him was a larger figure that I hadn't taken in at first, but now my jaw began to drop involuntarily. I gaped at the majesty that was Tommy 'Hitman' Hearns, the fighter who had been taken under Emanuel's wing in 1977 and turned into a legend, carrying off championship belts in six different weight divisions. While Muhammad Ali was a god, Hearns was his representative on earth – a man I could more easily identify with, but one for whom I have huge respect at the same time.

'You two gonna spar, then?' Steward asked, gesturing back to the boxing legend. I could hardly refuse. In no time, I was binding the wraps round my hands and sticking on my usual 16oz gloves. I'd always been a bit self-conscious about the size of my hands – they're huge. As the rest of me got bigger, they hadn't looked so odd, however. Back when I was a kid though, they looked scarily enormous.

But nothing matched the size of what I could now see at the end of Hearns' arms: fists the size of footballs donned 18oz gloves. They might have looked comical if it wasn't for the fact that I knew what damage they could do. You really wouldn't laugh after being on the receiving end of a Hearns' punch.

Through the sweltering gym and into the ring, the two of us strode. The other fighters stopped what they were doing and gathered round to watch the master in action. In the middle of them was the all-powerful figure of Emanuel Steward, waiting to see what I was made of.

Afterwards, Andy Straughn told me that he was convinced the Americans thought we were two plucky Brits who deserved nothing more than to be flattened for daring even to walk into the Kronk, but Emanuel must have had some regard for my abilities to immediately invite me to spar with the Hitman. Hearns and I tapped each other's gloves and sprang into our stances. The only thing I can remember him saying before the first punch was: 'How *are* you?'

We then went into battle: fast and sharp for four intense rounds, with a constant exchange of blows. Eager to impress the lads in Detroit, I employed all my dancer moves, staying on my toes and coming at Hearns from all directions. Unlike other adversaries I'd faced, he knew exactly what I was up to, though. They were his moves, after all. Like a true fighter, his eyes fixed on mine and with utmost skill, he predicted nearly all my tactics. But I kept on going and fought with a determination far beyond a mere sparring session.

The four rounds over, I turned to Steward to see what he'd made of my performance. My heart leapt for joy at the expression on his face: he was beaming from ear to ear. He pointed at me and turned to the other fighters standing around.

'If I'd been a judge of that fight, it would have been a draw!'

Hearns was expressionless. Meanwhile, I had to restrain myself from doing a triple somersault across the ring. From that moment on, the man in charge announced that I would be allowed to wear the coveted golden shorts of the Kronk Gym. That meant I was now a member of the so-called 'Kronk Wrecking Crew'.

Returning to the gated estate, Andy and I were once more escorted to the house. This was another distinctive approach that Emanuel Steward took to Kronk boxers. When we trained, it was hell on earth but outside the gym he lavished a standard of care on the boxers that almost had us living in the lap of luxury. Our fitness and diet was carefully monitored, with junk food strictly off the menu. Emanuel even went so far as to cook our meals himself on occasion. Many boxers spoke in glowing terms of the dishes served up by the Kronk boss, but his attention to detail went far beyond that. Emanuel was a man to whom you could take your grievances, have a moan about things in general and even get your spirits raised, if you were feeling blue.

He made all his fighters feel good about themselves: maybe because he'd struggled to build his own business, Emanuel understood the journeys we had taken. He knew that deep down many of us were insecure in our own ways and every so often needed a bit of a psychological boost.

Like me, Emanuel had started boxing very early: he was eight years of age, too. So besotted was he with his new-found sport that he used to sleep with his boxing gloves on in bed. He told me that he beat up so many of his friends that they didn't want to box with him anymore – a similar problem faced by the Christie brothers in Radford. Also like me, Emanuel ratcheted up an impressive amateur record. By 1963, the year I was born, he had become National Golden Gloves Champion of the United States and was talked about as a possible member of the US Olympics team for 1964. Twenty years later, I would face the dilemma of whether to go for the 1984 Olympics or turn professional. As things turned out, Emanuel wouldn't opt for either of those routes.

Another thing we had in common was that we both came to big cities determined to make something of our lives. Emanuel was originally from West Virginia and his voice has a southern twang that he still had when I was with the crew – that must have made him stick out when he first got to Detroit. So, we were both small-town boys who knew we had nothing to lose and a world to win in the big metropolis.

For whatever reason, Emanuel left the sport at the end of his teens to become an electrician at Detroit Edison, where he rose to become a supervisor. This would have been in the mid-1960s. Thankfully he couldn't stay away from the sport and worked part-time as a trainer and manager much as Tom McGarry had done and built up a reputation for being a good fight mentor. By 1972, he was able to quit the day job and the rest was a glorious history.

My involvement with the Kronk was at the tail end of what might be called its early history. Over the previous five or six years, Emanuel had made his name with Tommy Hearns. Together with Tommy, the crew was made up of names like David Braxton, Mike McCallum and Milton McCrory. They were the ring heroes of the mid-1980s, the bridge between Muhammad Ali (who hung up his gloves in 1981) and the generation that would come after us. Needless to say, 1990s' names like Oscar De La Hoya and Evander Holyfield were protégés of the Kronk.

Andy and me found ourselves living with middleweight southpaw Michael Nunn, welterweight Tyrone 'The Butterfly' Tryce and rising amateur talent Ricky Womack: it's worth noting that Womack, whose name doesn't trip off the tongue much these days, beat Evander Holyfield twice early on in that man's career: 1983 and 1984. I'm only sorry I didn't get to see either fight.

From the word go, this trio of housemates was obsessed with our English accents. What they discovered was that they could use the mere sound of our voices to pull local girls in Detroit, so Andy and me would be wheeled out in restaurants and bars and asked to speak, while Michael, Tyrone and Ricky would point at us, exclaiming: 'Will you listen to these guys talking – this for real, ladies – wad'ya think?'

I was happy to fit into the role, if it made them happy, but taking girls back to the gated estate and our house was a whole different affair. Also resident in the house was a minder called Alex, a short moody guy whose job it was to keep an eye on the young and restless talent. That seemed to involve making sure we used the washroom in the basement to keep our kit clean and were not bringing back girls for all-night sex sessions. It seemed the view that sex and boxing didn't mix wasn't simply confined to the United Kingdom.

Emanuel would often take us off for meals and evenings would frequently end with everyone watching fight videos. We were never allowed to forget that this wasn't some kind of holiday camp: we were on his estate to learn our craft and perfect our techniques. That said, once a week we would go to a party, nothing too wild, and all the other boxers would be there. I think Emanuel thought this was an essential bonding exercise between all of us and so I got the chance on many occasions just to wander up to Hearns and chat about the boxing scene. Tommy may have been the Kronk's top-draw for audiences but with his guard down, so to speak, he was a remarkably down-to-earth, unpretentious man. Big and tall, to stay within the welterweight class he had to sweat his guts out in the Kronk to shed the pounds – which he did to alarming effect. Sometimes before a major bout, he looked like a matchstick with gloves on.

Another member of the Kronk Wrecking Crew was David 'Machine Gun' Braxton – a brilliant fighter who used combination punches to devastating effect but he lacked the sheer power of Hearns. That's not to say that he didn't put on a great display for the punters, but when it came to knocking out his opponents, he lacked the slammer of a punch that the Hitman could deliver.

Mike 'The Body Snatcher' McCallum was another member of the crew. There's a saying I always subscribed to – 'Kill the body, the head will fall' – and that's how McCallum destroyed other fighters. He worked their bodies over till they crumpled with one lethal punch to the trunk after another, assaulting the kidneys and liver first then leaving the brain as the final course. Unlike other body pulverisers, he didn't leave his head exposed to any shot and was a brilliant defensive tactician.

McCallum was about six years older than me and originally from Jamaica. When I was swapping the short trousers of Hill Farm Junior School for the long trousers of President Kennedy, he'd been attending the 1974 World Championships in Havana.

Two years later, as I took home the first of many schoolboy trophies, he represented Jamaica at the Montreal Olympic Games. By the time we met, he had quite a record – so much so that promoters demanded big purse money to stick any of their fighters up against his lethal fists. As a result, he was literally priced out of the ring and spent more time watching than he should have done. That said, I saw him make mincemeat out of a few opponents, including Sean Mannion at Madison Square Gardens – an incredible fight where he took the WBA World Light Middleweight belt. Two years later in London, I would introduce myself to Mannion and also defeat him.

McCallum was one of the fighters that I could chat to very easily. Maybe it was the Jamaican connection and the fact that he was less hung up on my Britishness. He didn't haul me up in front of women and make me jabber a bit for their entertainment. In fact, he seemed pretty unfazed by my foreign tones and we got on famously.

Milton 'Ice Man' McCrory got his nickname from a reputation for knocking his opponents cold, but I wasn't so sure. McCrory was the same height as Hearns but not the same animal. He was a teddy bear, while Hearns was a real bear with big claws to match. Milton couldn't punch anywhere near as hard as the main man: Hearns threw atom bombs while it was flour bombs for McCrory. As Tom McGarry might have put it, and indeed did on one occasion about another kid: 'Ach, he couldn't crack an egg with those fists!'

Lack of a tough build and his gentle personality would prove his undoing. In December 1985, he went up against Donald Curry in Las Vegas for one of the great fights of the 1980s: the World Welterweight Championship. I'm told there was an electric atmosphere among the crowd. Milton was just twenty-three years old and his chances of winning were seen as good, particularly as Curry had recently broken his hand. But Curry was an old lion – the Mike Tyson of his day, I often thought afterwards. In the first round, he roared out of his corner and backed McCrory onto the ropes before sending him reeling. Then, in the second, Curry's left hook smashed into Ice Man's head and down McCrory went. There he stayed, while commentators with huge microphones strapped to their heads wondered if he would ever get up again. Two long minutes passed before he did so.

Duane Thomas was another young boxer I sparred with. On the surface, he was the most placid member of the Wrecking Crew, a good-looking black guy with a calm temperament, but I could sense a volcanic rage just waiting to burst out as it frequently did in the ring. I wasn't surprised when he went on to become WBC Middleweight Champion. Duane knew how to control his mood until the moment he had to unleash it.

Of all the crew mentioned above, Duane and I were probably closest in terms of character. I wouldn't say much until I had to, I was reserved in a way that could unnerve some people, and Duane was the same: economical with words until he needed to use them. Both friendly on the outside until you set an opponent in front of us when the story dramatically changed.

Having trained at the gym and sampled enough of Emanuel's good cooking, it was time for me to earn my spurs for the crew. I was pencilled in for two fights in front of capacity American crowds. My first opponent would be Robert Thomas and I'd face him in New Jersey. The second fight, just four days later, would be against Fred Reed in Michigan. Faced with my first trials as a Wrecking Crew member, I decided to go and get my hair cut. After all, I had to look my best.

It was sitting in a barber's chair in downtown Detroit when I saw my first full-on display of violent crime, US-style. Staring out of the window, daydreaming, while the clippers buzzed around my head, I witnessed a carjacking right in front of the shop. Andy was in the chair next to me and we both exchanged numb glances. A woman had just been dragged from her car by screaming thugs and dumped in the road. They then climbed into the motor and sped off.

We went outside to help but there was nothing we could do. As boys from the Midlands, we'd seen our fair share of crime, but nothing so brazen as this. Carjacking at gunpoint was not common-place in eighties Britain. The lady was shaken, but not too stirred: it seemed this was almost expected in the Detroit of those years.

The venue in New Jersey was Ice World, in a place called Totowa, and was adopted by Lou Duva, a man who managed nineteen boxing champions. He was also believed to be the last person to speak to boxing great Rocky Marciano before he was killed in a plane crash. Duva's company, Main Events, put on impressive line-ups at Ice World, which were televised by the US cable sports network ESPN.

This was my first taste of boxing stateside and I walked through six easy rounds with Robert Thomas before winning on points. Thomas was a southpaw, a left-handed boxer, but that didn't throw me. I could pivot and move around in a way that would confound any southpaw. Less experienced boxers are often unnerved by a left-handed opponent, but only because they don't dance around enough.

Coming back through security at the airport on the return journey to Detroit, I heard a voice to my side:

'What you niggers doing here?'

For a split second, I thought it might be a black man being friendly, although the word still made my adrenalin flow and my fists clench. Andy Straughn and I turned to find we were in front of a squat, heavily overweight and white security guard with an unpleasant sneer on his face. He was using the n-word in the very old-fashioned way that I'd grown accustomed to in Coventry. Clearly, New Jersey wasn't so enlightened as Detroit.

I made towards the racist goblin to teach him some manners in the same way that I'd educated so many skinheads back home. But Andy grabbed my arm and silently gestured with his eyes towards the gun in the goblin's holster as if to say, don't become another dead black statistic. I took the hint: everything was going so well and I had to learn to rise above under-achieving racist mediocrities like him. I could leave him and board a plane in the company of sporting giants whereas he and his bigotry would be left behind to sneer at other law-abiding folk.

For me, the incident brought into sharp relief how mixed up the situation was for black people in America when I was there. As boxers in Detroit, we were treated like minor royalty: the local people, black and white, worshipped the ground we walked on. The city itself was depressed and the Kronk brought much-needed glamour to the place. But you only had to take a short plane hop, mainly southwards, to find that people weren't quite so welcoming in other parts of the country. I'd summarise it by saying that for black blokes then, it was a case of when things were good in the United States they were very good, but when things were bad they were extremely bad – no happy medium. Back home in Britain, attitudes still weren't good but no one was seriously going to shoot us.

Three days later, I faced Fred Reed in Southfield, Michigan. Southfield had started out as a suburb of Detroit, but so many middle-class people had fled there from downtown Detroit that it had successfully incorporated itself as a new city. Only in the 1990s would black people begin to move in significant numbers to the place.

The bout was as unspectacular as the city. My opponent was eight years older than me, his record hadn't been too hot and I flattened him in about three rounds. The only memorable aspect of the fight was that Fred Reed managed to cut me above the eye. This injury would now start to recur and eventually contributed to my undoing.

Having earned the respect of the Kronk, Burt McCarthy now called me back home to face the Welsh champion Doug James on my home turf. On returning to the UK, Andy and I faced the painful realisation that we were hopelessly in debt. During our months in the States, we'd had to keep coughing up the rent and paying the bills on the flat in Brockley. With my bouts in the US, I'd managed to keep my head above water but Andy struggled badly. Whatever else the Kronk might have been, it certainly hadn't been a money-spinner. We came back as world-class boxers, with little or nothing in our pockets.

Still, I had a fight in the offing, which provided a financial lifeline. The Doug James bust-up was to be screened live on *World of Sport*. Finally, TV audiences in the UK would be able to judge whether Emanuel Steward had truly worked his magic. The answer, I think, was a resounding 'yes' for I demolished James but the one bit of damage he did manage to inflict was to re-open the wound I'd suffered in New Jersey.

McCarthy decided I needed to keep out of the ring for a few months to let it heal. This proved an unbearable gap for me. At a time when I felt that I needed to show the world what I'd learnt in

Detroit, I was stuck in the Thomas A' Beckett or round at the Danbury mansion, taking my irritation out on the bags.

It was during this time when I began to realise that it wasn't just the eye injury causing me problems. Twinges and aches all over my body, none of them boxing-related, now appeared to torment me further. Finally, I was paying the price for ignoring Tom McGarry's advice and the years of street fighting were beginning to take their toll. The injury from the car park in particular had never really healed and was now causing some real agony around my elbow. Often I'd have to stop hitting the bags and would instead stare angrily at the huge scar from the iron bar still running down my arm, a great gash that concealed shattered fragments of bone beneath. The boot boys really were having the last laugh now.

But no one beyond McCarthy and Andy knew that my body was playing up. To the outside world, I was still a great British hopeful. After four months of twiddling my thumbs, I re-emerged to take on Joel Bonnetaz at the Crest Hotel in London. It was a Frank Warren line-up of three 'cracking fights'. Warren had now formalised his relationship with McCarthy and in the introduction to the programme, he began with a special announcement to the fans:

> Tonight I am happy to inaugurate what I believe will be an exciting development in British boxing: Burt McCarthy, manager of the present Heavyweight Champion, David Pearce, and the next Middleweight Champion, Errol Christie, will from now on be my partner in all promoting.

He also revealed that Andy Straughn would become a regular fixture in his shows. The event was called the 'Show of Strength' and Warren breathlessly went on to say that it would bring together the best of his and McCarthy's talents: '… from Burt's side there's Errol Christie, the most exciting young fighter in the country, bar none'. Warren was no doubt impressed by the fact that readers of Boxing News, the industry's bible in the UK, had just voted me the Best Young Prospect for 1983. I'd received ten times more votes than my nearest rival.

So far, only two boxers had managed to take me beyond three

rounds: Robert Thomas in the US and Doug James, who left me with the eye injury. With Thomas, I'd almost tried to keep the fight going just to get some more experience and also because even I was getting bored of the rapid string of knockouts that I kept on delivering. Already McCarthy was waving wads of cash at certain fighters to persuade them to come and meet me. Most notably, he'd put £20,000 on the table if West Ham's favourite son, Mark Kaylor, would climb into the ring for a dose of the Christie treatment but Kaylor's people seemed in no hurry to pick up his offer.

I turned up at the Crest Hotel to take on French light-middle-weight champ Joel Bonnetaz. The week before the fight, *Boxing News* predicted a 'quick march' for the Frenchman: 'Christie should find him easy to hit and anyone Errol can hit is in a great deal of trouble.' After seven weeks under Emmanuel Steward's wing, people at home felt that I'd come back, looking like the real deal: 'Errol can hurt with either hand and the blows are fast and unpredictable.'

Boxing News predicted a win inside four rounds, but I had Bonnetaz saying 'au revoir' in three. Draping myself yet again in the Union Jack, I drank in the applause. Later, I discovered some fool from the National Front had put it about that I carried the Union Jack the wrong way round. As if a black man would have any idea which way up it should be! All I can say in my defence is that when you've just defended England's honour against France, does it matter which way up you're holding the flag?

The victories in the ring were turning into another day at the office for me: I'd show up, hang up my coat, lay my opponent flat on the canvas, then leave for home. My memory of the next two fights against Dexter Bowman and Stacy McSwain is totally hazy. Not because they landed any punches on my head but because it was getting all too easy. Time and again, I broke open the bubbly and celebrated yet another pro boxing notch on the bedpost.

It was beginning to look as if no one could touch me and the only question was: how far could I rise? Which was when the call came from the United States. A fight of epic proportions had been lined up between Tommy 'Hitman' Hearns and Roberto 'Hands of Stone' Duran on 15 June 1984. In the parking lot of Caesar's

Palace in Las Vegas, an enormous 26,000-seater boxing stadium would bring together two of the greatest boxers of their age to slug it out in front of a global television audience of millions. This was to be one of the great encounters of the decade.

There would be another fight before the main act and it had to be a classy affair. Half a million dollars' worth of tickets had already been sold for this massively hyped event and the crowd expected value for money. Hollywood celebrities, politicians and every kind of mover and shaker had snapped up seats. One of my all-time heroes, the comedian Richard Pryor, announced he would be there in person to witness this titanic event.

When I got back to Detroit, it was to discover that Hearns only wanted to spar with one man as he prepared to take on Duran and his reputed hands of stone. Later, Steward confided in me that Hearns had told the Kronk boss: 'If I can box with Errol, Duran will be easy.'

Unbelievably, he chose me above all the other heroes in the wrecking crew to hone his moves. With my constant dancing around, I was the fighter that he found hardest to control or predict. Like him, I liked nothing better than to create a flow of punches that differed every time. This was the workout he wanted before facing both Roberto Duran and a huge global TV audience for one of the greatest fights of the twentieth century.

He also insisted to Emanuel that I was to be added to the bill: 'Emanuel, put Errol on the card.' And so with Hearns rooting for me, I was placed on the undercard. For any British boxer, this was a huge honour and beyond the reach of most. But Emanuel didn't need convincing: he was only sorry that I'd returned to Britain and remarked on another occasion that I should have stayed with him in the United States, full stop. 'You've got a rhythm that nobody else here has,' he told me, 'you remind me of when I was a young boxer. I've never seen that rhythm anywhere except in you and me.'

On 14 June 1984, I checked into Caesar's Palace with Burt McCarthy. We were joined by none other than Eddie Richardson: the veteran gangland boss wasn't about to miss out on a moment of boxing history and I genuinely appreciated him taking the time out to come and watch me fight, thousands of miles from home.

The rest of the Kronk Wrecking Crew descended on the place and soon they were giving me advice on the best places to get some easy sex in Las Vegas: 'They got some class hooker here, buddy.' They were certainly a cut above the prostitutes I'd seen in Hillfields but Errol Christie doesn't pay for sex. As the lads kept referring to hookers, I'd smile weakly and say: 'Not interested in rugby players, mate!' But that didn't put them off. One boxer, who shall remain nameless, tapped me on the shoulder: 'See my friend, if you want some pussy, don't get a cheap one – there's always something wrong with it. You gotta pay top dollar.' I shook my head. The night before any fight was about turning in early and building up energy, not entertaining a lady of easy virtue. Yeah, those women might be stunningly attractive but I wasn't about to enter the ring in front of 26,000 people for the fight of my life with a roaring hangover and the memory of a night's hanky-panky on my mind.

Instead of satisfying my lust, I had dinner with Eddie Richardson and Burt McCarthy. There was another good reason for my sensible behaviour too: the fight was to be televised live for British audiences on *World of Sport*. I could hardly disappoint Dickie Davies by turning up groggy and hungover for the event. Unfortunately, given the time difference between the UK and US, I was required to don my gloves in the small hours of the morning to satisfy the ITV audience. As a result, I said goodbye to the dinner guests and sneaked off to bed way earlier than everybody else.

At the crack of dawn, I was up and heading over to the Caesar's Palace parking lot. It was with a mixture of anticipation and disappointment that I walked up to the ring. About 10 million people were sitting back at home in Britain waiting to watch me, but the Americans were either still in their hotel rooms or enjoying an early breakfast. With the Hearns–Duran bout still hours away, I got down to business in front of a half-empty house. In the front row, Emanuel Steward and Burt McCarthy looked on as I went about the job of dispensing with White.

Initially, the normally blistering Nevada sun was low in the sky, but out of the corner of my eye I could gradually see it rise like a menacing beast. As this was a city built in a desert, it didn't take long for the temperature levels to rise too and I began to feel this was a match that I had to end as quickly as possible, no matter how much heat training I'd received in the Kronk.

For an undercard fight supporting one of the greatest battles of the decade, I imagined I might have to struggle with the man pitted against me but during our five rounds, my punches seemed to cause White severe pain, whereas anything he landed on me hardly registered. With depressing ease, I strolled to another victory.

From the ringside, Steward was convinced I was now destined for greatness, having lasted the rounds and won. In his view, I had what he dubbed a 'star status mindset' and he assumed that I would want to grow my talents with him Stateside. Probably the biggest mistake of my life is that I didn't stick with Emanuel, but instead flew back to the mother country.

The Kronk's supremo not only valued my style but also approved of that fact that I was very much a team player, a respectful member of the Wrecking Crew. 'You always got a nice smile and don't hide away in the locker room,' he'd drawl in his Virginia accent. Emanuel thought that I fitted in so perfectly with the other fighters and his view was that I'd be insane to step on a plane and speed off. But that's exactly what I did, without a second thought.

Another Kronk boxer on the undercard that day was Duane Thomas, with whom I'd sparred in Detroit. Like me, he saw off his opponent with ease. It felt as if I was watching my American brother cruise to victory that day: a fighter who oozed the same temperament as myself, a self-contained boxing talent who just got on with the job in hand. But Duane was to fall victim to what I sometimes call the 'Curse of the Kronk' – the sad roll call of boxers who passed through the Kronk's doors and then, after achieving success in the ring, went on to die in unfortunate circumstances or fall foul of the law. At the turn of the new century, he was gunned down outside a store in Detroit.

According to the *Detroit News* he'd been shot in the head, chest, forearm, hip, thigh and flank by a 9mm gun in what they claimed was a drug-related dispute. To be honest, I'm not a man very often moved to tears, if at all, but Duane's death hit me hard.

It left me feeling very empty inside: that such a fine human being could be snuffed out so easily, it brutally summed up what a terrible world we live in.

As if that wasn't sad enough, two years later in 2002, Ricky Womack killed himself after his last fight. I'd shared the house on Emanuel's gated estate with him. The reason wasn't too hard to understand: a year after I left Detroit in 1985, he was sent to prison for armed robbery. He was only released in 2000 and then had to pick up the pieces of a broken boxing career. Incredibly, he won all four of the bouts he fought but nothing could be done to reclaim lost time. The sense of all the opportunities that had slipped through his fingertips must have crushed him.

Clearly, the backgrounds of many of these boxers came back to haunt them, no matter how well they seemed to be doing in the sport. J.L. Ivey, a super featherweight who was around when I was at the Kronk, was murdered in 1990. Wilson Bell was murdered in 1989 and Darrell Chambers was sentenced to life imprisonment for drug conspiracy in 1994. William 'Caveman' Lee was sent down three times for armed robbery. He was given the name 'Caveman' on account of his sideburns and was last reported to be working at a car parts yard. Alvin 'Too Sweet' Hayes did time, also for armed robbery; he died in 2004, aged just forty-four. John Johnson got two years for retail fraud.

Milton McCrory – 'The Iceman' – buried his younger brother Steve in 2000. The thirty-six-year-old had been a Kronk boxer, too and also an Olympic champion. He'd contracted some kind of wasting disease and at one point, even pawned his Olympic medal to raise some much-needed cash.

As I'd seen in my own family, poverty and deprivation leave deep scars. And even when the riches of boxing success appear to be on offer, it's all too easy to slip back into the old, familiar ways. Only someone from the most comfortable of backgrounds can fail to understand how this might happen.

After the Vegas bout against Stan White, I boarded a plane back to Britain: on my way to my first major upset. The bout that blotted my so-far unblemished record was against a Belgian light heavyweight, Jose Seys, at the Britannia Leisure Centre in Shoreditch. It was never intended to be a clash of any great importance just a filler between other, more significant fights.

Compared to Caesar's Palace, the venue was pretty modest. Maybe it was arrogant but at first, I didn't overly concern myself with the man I was up against. My main task ahead of the fight was to get my weight down. Once more, I was pounding the pavements of London with a vengeance. Other boxers would sometimes join me on my mini-marathons and be dismayed when, after we'd finished the long circuit, I dashed off while announcing that I was doing it for a second time. Those long runs of mine became a talking point among my fellow boxers, who thought I was overdoing it a bit.

In those days, we were weighed just before a fight and often I'd deliberately dehydrate to lose a few pounds more. This reduced me to a dried-out husk before my fights and medics nowadays wouldn't permit that kind of self-abuse. When a boxer enters a ring, it's to start an endurance trial that involves losing pints of water and, on occasions, I have to admit that I went a bit giddy because of what I was doing to myself.

The Seys' fight saw me use every possible weapon to lose weight: rigorous exercise, plenty of sparring and a refusal to drink so on the night, I got down to 11st 6lb. Seys, in marked contrast, weighed in at over 12st. In terms of body mass, this was a complete mismatch – I was definitely in the middleweight category while he was very much heavyweight. When we faced each other, it was obvious to me that the disparity in pounds wouldn't swing in my favour; I'd never been this light. Clearly, I'd overdone the weight-loss programme.

The ITV *Midweek Sport Special* covered the bout with presenter Brian Moore correctly pointing out that I'd not been beaten in thirteen fights with all but one finished inside the distance. I'd said that I was looking for tougher opposition and, in answer to that, they put me up against Seys: he'd lost only two of his fifteen professional fights so, in that regard, he was a worthy opponent. During the fight on ITV, Jim Watt and Reg Gutteridge commentated. As it got under way, their manner was casual and relaxed, clearly expecting another effortless Christie victory but I was to cruelly let them down.

The Belgian with the blond 1980s' perm, not unlike one of the bouncers I'd once fought at Tiffany's, emerged from his corner and it was all very workmanlike for just under a minute. Then, at fifty-one seconds, he caught me with a southpaw cross and I simply hit the deck. Seys ran back to his corner and stood there to see what would happen next, possibly unable to believe victory was coming to him so easily.

Stunned and showing no emotion, I got up again but barely ten seconds later, it happened once more. I was getting an object lesson in why this man was referred to as the 'Belgian Banger'. Having floored me again, Seys ran back to his corner while I struggled to get up.

'Whoah – southpaw!' shouted Reg as the left-handed Belgian got me with a cross from his left hand. 'The man we considered the best prospect in the country is down. What a sensational fight!' Not from where I was staggering, it wasn't. At that point, the referee decided it was all over and the Belgian had won inside a round. To his credit, Seys was reported as saying before the bout: 'Why is this little fellow fighting me? I thought he was a light heavyweight.'

Jim Watt observed that McCarthy would now need to give me every word of encouragement in his armoury: 'He'll need some persuasive words to say this is where you get stuck in again. They were talking about fighting for the championship, but I'm afraid this has turned it all around.'

Afterwards, this analysis from Watt was echoed, but much more viciously, in the press. I hadn't been beaten since I was fourteen years old but now it was open season on Christie. The sportswriters duly dipped their pens in poison and began writing my premature obituary. It seemed the only person who still believed in Errol Christie was me: it was my first taste of what might happen if ever I allowed myself to be floored in such a manner again.

Years after the Seys fight, it was amusing to see the tabloids compare Amir Khan's knockout at the fists of Breidis Prescott to my own performance against Seys. But there were key differences between my fight in September 1984 and Khan's defeat of September 2008. After my fight, there was nothing like the public-relations offensive that put Khan back on his feet. The shame of the knockout soon became history as both management and family rallied round him and hit back. In contrast, I had to carry the Seys' defeat like a bell round my neck for months afterwards. And whereas many pundits already suspected Prescott was too dangerous an opponent for Khan, I should have defeated Seys, regardless of the weight difference. He was subsequently described as a 'Belgian banger' but I could have bruised him all the way back to Brussels. But the reason I failed was a fatal mixture of pride and dehydration.

Re-establishing myself as a credible figure in British boxing was a painful process. My confidence had taken a knock and while Amir Khan was given emotional support from those closest to him and a decent physio, those two things were not open to me. I begged McCarthy to get me a qualified medic. My calves were overdeveloped, almost fit to burst out of my skin, and I subsequently discovered that I was suffering from a condition called 'compartment syndrome', an ailment that many athletes succumb to. Without going into too much gruesome detail, the nerves, blood vessels and muscles all become compressed in a confined space in the body (in the case, my calves). It's almost like everything is bursting to get out, but there's nowhere to go. In extreme cases, the treatment is a fasciotomy, a surgical procedure where the pressure on the affected area is relieved by a huge incision and skin graft.

The reason I'd developed this condition was constantly training for years. And my obsessive mini-marathons probably hadn't helped matters, either. With legs now horse-like in size, I was finding it hard to sustain my dancer-fighter approach. Instead of bouncing around, I was starting to lumber as I had done with Seys. In desperation, I asked Fash if I could use his physio. When I walked through the door, the man was amazed at the condition of my legs. He'd never seen such huge calves and right away, he understood the agony I was going through.

Then in November 1984, I finally got an opportunity to put the Seys' defeat behind me. In a glittering return to form, I despatched Bobby Hoye from Detroit in a single round and wandered over to the ITV camera to give commentator Gary Newbon a piece of my mind.

'I'm pleased to be back,' I told the ITV audience, 'solid punches, smacked him in the head, this is the real Errol Christie – a man full of aggression. Mark Kaylor, Herrol Graham, you bring them down here, I'm ready! I've been through hell.'

Then McCarthy sidled up to Newbon and dropped his little bombshell: he was putting £40,000 on the table if Mark Kaylor would come and fight me. Now we'd see if the West Ham middleweight had time in his hectic schedule to face me.

Back at the Thomas A' Beckett, certain voices were still telling Andy Straughn and me that the two of us were earning far less than we should. Well-known boxers, including British champions, thought I was losing out badly and that hit the rawest of nerves, so when word went round that former middleweight champ Maurice Hope had set up as a manager, I waited for the call. But I didn't have to wait long: the Antigua-born boxer was keen to bring me into his stable.

Hope was an elder statesman in the boxing world. Back in 1972, he had represented Britain in the Olympics, blazing a trail for black British boxers in the seventies. He'd retired from boxing in 1981 after losing the WBC Light Middleweight title to Wilfred Benitez at Caesar's Palace. So, I waited for his offer to materialise. Hope by name and by nature, perhaps. However, salvation was not at hand: the amount he held out to me was disappointing. I thanked him for his interest and then shut the door, thinking this was the end of the matter – but I was wrong on that score as well.

Having got wind of what had been going on, Burt McCarthy hurriedly organised a press conference. He told the sportswriters present that an attempt had been made to lure me away from him, offering a hundred grand. That figure was certainly news to me. McCarthy went on to say that he wouldn't be making a formal complaint to the Board of Control as he regarded the whole affair as 'an act of desperation'.

Hope's offer was in no way attractive enough to make me want to quit McCarthy. Not that I was having such a great time with Burt, but something about frying pans and fires came to mind. Lurking in the background behind Hope was the shadow of Mickey Duff, who had never really given up on trying to sign me: I was the boxer that got away and he wanted to put that right.

Frank Warren waded in behind McCarthy: 'I don't blame anyone for trying to lure Christie away. He is the most exciting fighter in the country and this shows just how highly regarded he is.' To prove he meant it, Warren went on to announce that he was also putting big money on the table for established middle-weights Mark Kaylor or Herrol Graham to come and fight me – they only had to say the word.

The only good thing to come out of the Maurice Hope episode was that it woke up my management to how desperately I yearned to move up a level. I was fed up with being described as a man with a brilliant amateur record who yet had to prove himself on the professional plane.

Although I never ceased to worry that Coventry would drag me back into its clutches and a return to poverty was never very far away, I almost dared to think my future could actually be a bright one. Was it too much to dream that one day there might be a world championship belt around my waist? As I pondered on this highly agreeable scenario, Mark Kaylor finally agreed to meet me.

Flanked by Frank Warren *(left)* and Burt McCarthy *(right)* – when I was still hot property.

Jerry Munson

The night before my fight at Caesar's Palace, Las Vegas. On the left side: Eddie Richardson *(second from front)* and Burt McCarthy *(at the back)*. On the right side: Andy Straughn *(at the back)* and me *(front)*.

Errol Christie, personal collection

Demolishing Joel Bonnetaz then draping myself in the Union Jack,
1 February, 1984.

Mirrorpix

7

RACISM LIVE AT WEMBLEY ARENA

'Back in those days you thought nothing of hearing people shouting, "Kill the black bastard" from the crowd. I heard it loads of times.'

Trevor Curry — Heavyweight Champion and friend

January 27, 1984   50p

BOXING
NEWS

Vol. 40   75th year   No. 4

PEARCE TAKES
THE SHOW ON
THE ROAD
– page 24

Christie comes to town!

And he's gunning for champ Kaylor

MIDDLEWEIGHT sensation Errol Christie (left) shares top billing in London for the first time when he meets Joel Bonnetaz at the Bloomsbury Crest on Wednesday. Christie is out with a £20,000 challenge to British and Commonwealth champion Mark Kaylor (right), who takes on American Ralph Moncrief at the Albert Hall on Tuesday. Previews of both the big shows on pages 2 and 3.

West Ham lad Mark Kaylor *(left)* and me show exactly what we think of each other at a press conference.

PA Photos

Summoned to meet
the Board of
Control to get my
ticking off.

Saying sorry, with fingers crossed. The grim line up: Terry Lawless *(far left)* next to Mark Kaylor, Burt McCarthy *(far right)* next to me, 18 October 1985.

Mirrorpix

A handshake to keep the Board of Control happy.

Mirrorpix

Errol Christie and Mark Kaylor – best of
friends. I don't think.

PA Photos

The programme for the fight they
tried to ban.

On 18 October 1985, both of us arrived for the photoshoot at London's Stakis Regency Casino, pumped up and ready to win the real first round of any boxing match – the stare-out. Two fighters face each other, eyeball to eyeball, with fists planted theatrically under the other man's chin. But the added tension between Mark Kaylor and me meant the event was bound to end badly.

To begin with, Kaylor and I were managed by two rival camps. Terry Lawless was Kaylor's manager. Lawless worked closely with Mickey Duff, who promoted his fights and managed many of the big names in the sport, including Frank Bruno, Maurice Hope and Charlie Magri. Duff worked alongside other promoters, including a bloke called Mike Barrett, who would co-promote my bout with Kaylor. Essentially, Lawless and Duff were the old guard of British boxing whereas McCarthy and Warren were still regarded as the upstarts who had burst into that cosy world.

It wasn't just our different backers but Mark Kaylor's temper that would make this fight stand out. Mine was bad, but his was possibly worse. Kaylor told a reporter that he was annoyed at me constantly goading him to fight. The comment, 'I'm ready for Kaylor' drove him crazy, he said. Also, McCarthy and Warren had been teasing his side for months on end with wads of cash, daring him to come and take on their boy.

Kaylor's rage aside, something more fundamental was at stake. The Londoner was the cocky, assured and swaggering white kid typical of West Ham, still a strongly working-class swathe of the East End. Back then, West Ham Football Club was notorious for its fans' violence and goading of black players, and many of Kaylor's supporters numbered among them.

Like a bad omen, the last issue of *Boxing News* before the fight warned the bout would put the entire sport on trial. An editorial thundered that an outpouring of racism from the football terraces into the boxing arenas would not be tolerated. The paper pointed its finger at Kaylor's supporters and the 'extreme right-wing fascist element in Britain, an element which is represented in Kaylor's home territory of West Ham'. This came as no revelation: it was an open secret that organised thuggery existed in that part of London, much of it targeted at black people. Not for nothing did the National Front try and recruit from the terraces at West Ham – they knew they were on fertile ground.

In truth, racism had already arrived in boxing. Back in 1980, white English boxer Alan Minter had declared about black American opponent Marvin Hagler: 'No black man is going to take my title.' Their fight at Wembley Arena saw the venue packed with Union Jack-clad skinheads. Amazingly, they'd been allowed to bring whole cases of beer cans inside, which quickly became projectiles when the fight went against Minter. The BBC's Harry Carpenter rightly described the event as 'a shame and disgrace to British boxing'.

Among many, the fear was that my fight against Kaylor would be a re-run of Minter versus Hagler. Only three days before our photo shoot, huge riots had taken place in north London. Tottenham's Broadwater Farm Estate exploded into violence, mainly between local black youths and the police. During the bust-up, PC Keith Blakelock tripped over and was hacked to death. Reports at the time said the rioters attempted to behead him.

It seemed as if the riots of 1981 would be replayed in 1985. This time, I wouldn't be on the frontline but the old hatreds seemed determined to suck me back in. There was an ugly mood in the country and that day it seeped into our photo shoot.

Fists held out, cameras flashing, I stared at my adversary but Kaylor kept glancing away. The photos over, I joked to the snappers: 'Think I came out on top there.' At first, Kaylor ignored me and chatted to someone across the room. But then he turned back and I could see he was furious. His reputation for having a short fuse was well known, but my own temper wasn't too far behind. Bending down close to my ear, he muttered three words that instantly made me see red. In a recent interview, he claimed that he called me 'an ugly bastard', but let's just say that what I heard at the time was enough to make me leap from my seat and take a well-deserved swing at him.

Suddenly, we were grappling on the floor, tearing at each other's jackets. No words were exchanged. Like mad men, the two of us wrestled in front of a press pack that couldn't believe their luck. The lens caps back off, lights started flashing again: Kaylor and Christie were giving them all a fight free of charge with ringside seats.

It was reported that Herrol Graham split us up, but if he did then I certainly didn't notice. This was unfinished business and if anybody thought this was a PR stunt, they were soon disabused. Outside the casino, Kaylor tried to barge me into a water fountain in the courtyard. Then we were off again, desperate to beat the other man to a pulp.

You could say this was a clash of cultures that was being played out time and time again on working-class streets throughout Britain. White boot boys who wanted to put uppity niggers back in their box and black rude boys who weren't going to take their shit anymore. They were two distinct parts of British youth, and in 1985 they were about to come to blows in front of a huge television audience.

While the promoters secretly rubbed their hands in glee, the British Board of Boxing Control was beside itself. McCarthy soon received a letter summoning me to appear before the Board to explain myself: I had 'brought boxing into disrepute'.

But it wasn't just the Board that was having kittens. Al Hamilton, a respected sports figure in the black community, called on the British Government to halt the fight. He rightly predicted Kaylor fans would dominate the Wembley audience just as when he faced Roy Gumbs (another black boxer) in 1983. Hamilton claimed Gumbs had admitted to him 'that he was scared of what would happen, if he won'.

Hamilton, who set up the Commonwealth Sports Awards to celebrate the sporting achievements of men and women from the Commonwealth, made a comment clearly designed to make me re-think the fight: 'But what about Mr and Mrs Christie coming down from Coventry to watch their son in the most important fight of his life? What happens if one of these thugs flings a bottle or anything else and hits them on the head or in the eye?

The innocent people, these are the ones I worry about.'

As Hamilton wrote at the time, the pubs and clubs of the East End of London buzzed with talk of the fight. It seemed the boot boy could at least extend a grudging respect to me as a black man who wasn't going to run away from the local boy – this nigger wasn't going anywhere. Hamilton told a journalist about one conversation he had eavesdropped: 'I was in a pub in Hackney last night and Christie–Kaylor was the main topic of the talk. They were saying, "At least now we have a man who is not going to run away from the situation."'

Kaylor's fans had recognised form. When their man lost to Tony Sibson a year before, two hundred of them had to be thrown out of the venue for 'unsavoury scenes and scuffles'. In boxing, we have become so used to peaceful audiences that to recall the mayhem that sometimes broke out in the past, particularly if a black man defeated a white man, might sound fanciful but there's plenty of TV footage from the time to convince any doubters that these hooligans were very much part of the sport's history.

Former Heavyweight Champion Trevor Curry sums it up: 'Back in those days, you thought nothing of hearing people shouting "Kill the black bastard!" from the crowd. I heard it loads of times, just learnt to ignore it. Even outside Wembley, I'd see a couple of black guys leaving a fight and they'd be bottled by white guys, who'd been there, too – that's just the way things were. You couldn't change it then.'

There were calls on the Minister of Sport, Richard Tracey MP, to ban my fight against Kaylor. It was too racially charged, they said, the national mood was too raw. Now the rioting in Tottenham had spread to other parts of the country and it seemed sheer lunacy to further stoke the fires of racial hatred. The brawl at the photo shoot provided a small snapshot of the hatred boiling over on the streets and did little to calm the nerves of the great and good. Even the Wembley police controlling the event called on the promoters to reconsider. But this was the eliminator for the British Middleweight Championship – the industry knew we were now a guaranteed audience draw, both Wembley and on TV. The promoters stood to lose around £30,000 if the fight did not go ahead and so they were in no mood to cancel. Neither were Kaylor or myself.

We had unresolved business to settle: this wasn't a boxing event, it was a grudge match. I'd never disliked an opponent or his fan base as much as I hated Kaylor and his West Ham army. Days after the bust-up, we went through the motions of a staged handshake, but there was no reconciliation in the air. As we made our public display of good manners, we could barely look at each other. This was just a publicity stunt to get the Board of Control off our backs, nothing more.

The fight was also a crossroads in our respective careers. For me, it was a chance to show the world that my stellar amateur record and near unbroken run of pro wins was no fluke. There had been constant attempts to denigrate my achievements, including digs at the quality of my opponents, but I'd knocked down whoever was put in front of me, including my last opponent: American Barry Audia, a fighter with a record almost as good as my own. After just two rounds, Audia came a cropper. I'd also earned my creds on both sides of the Atlantic and the right to wear the coveted Kronk shorts. Somehow that wasn't good enough for the sneering cynics back home; they were still waiting to see the arrogant black kid from Coventry finally trip up.

For Kaylor, a defeat really would be terminal. Already, he had seen his European Championship hopes take a battering at the fists of Buster Drayton and Tony Sibson. A defeat at my hands would leave him in the dustbin of boxing history. The stakes couldn't have been higher, for both of us.

Meanwhile, the industry showed its determination to press ahead by putting up a record pot of cash for a British title final eliminator: £82,000 would be split with 60 per cent going to the winner, while the loser would receive 40 per cent. To give an idea of just how much money that was in 1985, the total would have been enough to buy three family homes in a nice part of any British city. Or maybe two in London as the prices were always higher. Even the chosen date upped the ante: 5 November, Guy Fawkes Night.

During the build-up, the press swarmed round McCarthy, pressing for his views on the likely violence, on and off the canvas. Broadwater Farm was still smouldering, the East End full of testosterone-charged white geezers in vengeful mode and the bulk of the tickets snapped up by Kaylor fans. Meanwhile, the talk was of fascists and organised West Ham thugs, groups like the notorious Intercity Firm, turning up in full force on the night. Al Hamilton's prediction would come true, or so it seemed.

'I hope this is rumour, not fact,' McCarthy blurted out to the press, before asking my fans to 'come down in peace'. But the ticket sales revealed my supporters were staying away. Better to sit in the safety of their living rooms and catch the action on television than be bottled in a repetition of the Minter versus Hagler débâcle. This would leave me dangerously exposed on the night.

The programme for the event couldn't have been more succinct: 'Few fights have captured the imagination in recent years as much as the Mark Kaylor–Errol Christie clash'. The winner would go on to fight Herrol Graham, the man who pulled Kaylor and me apart at the photo shoot. 'It promises to be an excellent scrap, too, between two punchers with a great deal of pride.'

Scrap? We'd certainly succeeded in setting the tone for what followed.

While I should have been relishing the coming combat, behind the outward bravado I felt as if my body was falling to pieces: my calves were bursting out, my arms constantly ached. My weight was like a yo-yo, refusing to stay where I needed it, and my feet were in open rebellion. Since childhood, I'd spent years running mile after mile in cheap plimsolls and, finally, my beleaguered arches were collapsing. As if that wasn't enough, even my nose decided to give in. I began to suffer severe nosebleeds. The outpourings of thick blood left me staggering round the gym, clutching my face to stem the flow. I wasn't helped by a particularly crude piece of medical advice: in this instance, I was told to flush salt water through my nostrils.

After the Kaylor fight, it got so bad at a later date that I had to pay a proper doctor to hack cartilage out of my nose. This wasn't a unique condition for a boxer, certainly not one who'd compounded it by scrapping on the streets, but it came at the worst of times. From my head to my toes, it seemed my body had been driven to the point of crisis. From an early age, I'd given it no respite and now it was time to pay a heavy price.

The significance of the fight that I was about to face was not lost on me in the days before the big encounter. Looking back, some people – including Burt McCarthy – have pointed to later fights as turning points in my career. My manager thought the Charlie Boston fight that lay ahead was when my fate was truly put in the balance. But to me, Mark Kaylor was the devil I had to vanquish and it would be no understatement to say this wasn't just professional, it was very personal.

Finally, 5 November came round. My mission was to damage and hurt Kaylor in ways he'd never imagine: within the Queensberry rules of course. Entering the arena reminded me of a story that Elder Nicely recounted in one of his never-ending services – Daniel in the den of lions, sent to a certain death by the King of Babylon. The only difference was that Daniel tamed the lions whereas the beasts howling around me that night were in no mood to do my bidding; they wanted blood liberally splashed across the canvas, nothing else would do.

I strode confidently towards the ring, knowing that display of self-confidence would get right under their white skins. Tuning out the Kaylor fans' odious jeers and cat calls, I tensed every muscle as I approached the centre of the arena. Around the illuminated square of canvas were two lines of blue uniforms. That level of police presence sent a shudder down my spine. It was partly an old aversion to the cops from my street-fighting days, but also the chilling realisation that they really were expecting trouble.

Stepping through the ropes, I padded up and down on the balls of my feet and became all too aware of the malevolent buzz from the crowd. My eyes darted around, looking for an oasis of support, but there was none. In the whole of my boxing career, I'd never felt so isolated.

I watched McCarthy walk over to his erstwhile enemy, Terry Lawless. The two seemed to be getting on famously. Then he strode over to Kaylor's second, Jimmy Tibbs, and threw his arms around him. That scene has stuck in my head for years: it was the moment when I realised that we fighters really are just ring-fodder. Whatever happens to us, the managers and promoters live on. They had more in common with each other than they ever would with us.

Kaylor entered the ring like a conquering hero, acknowledging the wall of cheers from the West Ham ranks around him. I noted his size. At our weigh-in, I'd come in at 11st 4½lb compared to his 11st 6lb. Arguably, I'd lost so much weight that I was too light to be matched against my opponent, but that was pretty academic now.

Harry Gibbs was the referee. At his signal, we both moved to the centre of the ring, bobbing up and down and fixing a mutual stare of loathing. We knocked gloves in the traditional manner. The whole place erupted. To the best of my ability, I ignored the noise and simply locked onto Kaylor with my predatory glare, as if to say 'I'm coming for you'.

The key to winning that night was to approach the fight in the same way as I'd gone about all my victories: turn up, put the gloves on and knock out my opponent as quickly as possible. My eyes continued to burn two holes into Kaylor and I let him sense the wall of hatred that he was up against. It was at this point that Gibbs did something completely unexpected. Barely perceptible to anybody else, he tapped my face. I'd call it a slap, actually. In the quarter century since, not a day has gone by when I haven't looked back on that as an act of sabotage.

Gibbs knew this was a crucial moment: the moment in the fight when a boxer is psyching himself up, taking his concentration to a level that's hard to explain in words. Like a chess player works out his opening gambit or a poker player constructs a face that either betrays nothing or misleads. More than anything else at this time, a fighter is figuring out how to remain conscious and upright.

In any bout, the first round is key. Whether Gibbs' action was innocent or not – and I know my own view – that tap to my face completely disorientated me before I'd even thrown a punch. I returned to my corner, brooding on why this man had put his hand anywhere near me. Always easily provoked, now my temper was building to a fury. I found myself thinking about Gibbs instead of Kaylor, a fatal mistake as the bell rang to announce round one.

I sleepwalked towards Kaylor, still thinking, why did Gibbs slap me? As Kaylor's fist hurtled towards me, the punishment for not thinking straight was swift and savage. He caught me sharply and I reeled, my legs giving way momentarily. For a split second, I had the shocking realisation of just how cumbersome and hulking my calves really had become. Instead of dancing as I had done for most of my career to date, I now heaved around awkwardly for a few moments.

So, I tried to shake off the daze as fast as I could: I had to put the impact of Kaylor's killer right fist behind me, to come back at him, but it was difficult to regain the initiative so quickly. When a boxer spots an opening, he pursues it relentlessly and I'll concede that to his credit as a fighter, Kaylor didn't let the window of opportunity close on him.

As I steadied myself on the ropes, he delivered another right cross and this re-opened the wound I'd sustained from Fred Reed in Michigan. The blood started to flow but at first I didn't notice. Instead, I was distracted by a firework exploding behind me. Clearly, the West Ham contingent thought their man was about to do to me what I'd done to so many – slaughter me in the first round. I wouldn't give them that satisfaction.

Now it was Kaylor's turn to drop his guard. Sensing a premature victory, he acknowledged the crowd just long enough for me to deliver a sledgehammer blow that sent the London lad to his knees. Almost genuflecting before me, now it was his turn to feel the acid taste of humiliation. Looking down at him, he seemed almost appalled that I should have the temerity to claw my way back from such a disastrous opening.

Furious at myself as much at him, I rained jabs, crosses and hooks down onto his head and torso, hoping to terminate our encounter as quickly as possible. I desperately needed to offset my early indignity and I could almost hear my supporters in living rooms around Britain whooping with joy as Kaylor took a beating. But he absorbed everything. Other opponents might have run up the white flag but, with his future as a boxer at stake, this was a do-or-die situation for the Londoner. Like Lazarus, he rose and came back at me. After a brutal series of exchanges, leaving no doubt as to our mutual loathing, the bell rang to end the first round.

Back in my corner, one of McCarthy's lackeys screamed incoherent advice in my ear. The mood was one of pure panic: no words on tactics, just a stream of meaningless rants about 'going out and getting him'. I stopped listening: The only thing that would deliver victory was to become an emotionless killing machine, the fighter who hacked down countless boxers and removed the teeth of an army of skinheads. If West Ham's favourite son was to be destroyed, that grimly determined ghetto boy from Coventry had to come back to the fore.

The second round began. As *Boxing News* later described it: 'Christie and Kaylor provided such epic battle that it left even the spectators feeling drained: there was more than enough violence in the ring to satisfy the most psyched-up fan.' Throughout the second round, we landed king-size punches on each other but it was in the third that I got the desired result. Watching him move with an agility you didn't normally see in white boxers, I suddenly spotted my chance. With a right-handed express train of a punch, I sent Kaylor back down to the canvas for a second time. He remained on his knees for a couple of seconds, but then rose once more. It was impossible to deny his tenacity, but I was sure one more demolition job would see him counted out.

But far from succumbing to defeat, Kaylor seemed to react to this setback by redoubling his determination. Before long, we were slogging away like maniacs, loading on both physical pain and mental torment. The anguish in our faces revealed neither of us would consider yielding to the other: this was to be a fight to the bitterest of ends.

From the fourth round, I felt my legs getting heavier. Desperately, I tried to dance but those once-fluid motions now evaded me. The cut above my eye that I'd been largely unaware of now began to bleed in force, sending a scarlet trickle into my eye. Worst still, my nose started to let me down as well. Now I could see and taste blood – not an auspicious sign for any boxer.

In the fourth round, Kaylor hit me after the bell and I now saw a different kind of red. Furious, I moved to trade a return blow but McCarthy intervened and held me back, an incident later noted by *Boxing News*. My opponent seemed pleased with this dirty little manoeuvre and I, as the black boy, had to give ground.

At least that's how it felt as I glowered towards my corner.

By the fifth round, it felt as if the Queensberry rules had been torn up. At one point, I ended up dodging what I took to be an oncoming head-butt. Gibbs heaved us apart as we ripped into each other, over and over and over again. In an attempt to psyche myself up as the round went on, I tried to reprise my much-loved Ali shuffle, but here it seemed strangely inappropriate. This wasn't a fight of skill and dexterity: it had become the equivalent of trench warfare for boxing – all sound and fury, the kind of fight where tactics and talent weren't required so much as sheer stamina.

In the sixth, I tried to reintroduce some showmanship, to teach the crowd what I'd learnt at the Kronk – that boxing wasn't just a mean slog down to the finish. With a Hearns-like elegance, I delivered an unexpected right to Kaylor and followed this up with an almost balletic uppercut, my knee jerking upwards in perfect rhythm with my fist. Once more, Kaylor was left bewildered and clearly used to a cruder approach, which his fans undoubtedly adored. Frankly, they'd have preferred a bare-knuckle fight in a backstreet tavern.

Once more, Kaylor delivered the final punch of the round, though this time he managed to get it in before the bell. In the next round, I let loose a stream of jabs to which the other man responded with a few blows that many commentators felt hovered suspiciously around the belt. 'Kaylor hit back with three lefts to the body, at least two of which looked low, and then rocked Christie badly with a right,' as *Boxing News* reported. My manhood could painfully testify to those foul blows.

The eighth round transformed into my personal armageddon. Somehow I realised the initiative had been lost. I'd never liked going anywhere near the distance in any fight – a short, sharp shock was what I preferred to deliver, but this bout had dragged on interminably and I was running short of ideas. Maybe because of the huge animosity between us the whole thing descended by degrees into a slugging match.

The longer the bout went on, the more I became aware of the noise from the crowd, the referee, the lines of police, the blinding lights above and all the other things that normally I completely ignored. Instead of facing a single opponent, Kaylor and his fans seemed to meld into one big mass: I wasn't just fighting him, I was taking on the whole of West Ham.

But time was working against me. I'd gone into that ring to be victorious, to knock Kaylor out as I'd done so many others. Deep down, I knew that I couldn't last the full ten rounds because of the body pains that were racking up. As I left the corner for the last time, I was only too aware that if I didn't land a knockout blow on him pretty quickly now, I'd be utterly doomed. He'd gone down twice: somewhere inside me I had to find the old Christie magic that would send him down a third time and keep him there.

Summoning up what little energy I had left, I advanced on my opponent. All the familiar twinges of past street fights pulsated like electric shocks through my arms and legs. There was none of the lightness on my feet that had always been my trademark: instead, I fell back on raw fury, going for him like a madman with the rage that used to grip my dad as he bolted down the street after Des for no good reason. But Kaylor was ready. With a shark-like expressionless face, he moved towards me. Mouth pinched and baring his teeth, he sensed blood in the water and edged closer to tear at my body a little more before moving in for the final kill. For a split second, I caught a glimpse of his face and I could see that he was enjoying himself.

This felt like a final battle: the moment when a warrior knows that after a lifetime of victories he must face the grim prospect of defeat; all those who have laid at his feet rise up to take him down. I'd always regarded boxing as a kind of war, jokingly referring to the ring as the battlefront, but with Kaylor that feeling was taken to a whole new level: he truly was my enemy.

I was desperate not to lose in that place, at the end of Kaylor's fists, in front of those people. If I lost, this would only be my second professional defeat. Already, I could already hear the sportswriters preparing my obituary. Pub-goers all over the East End would cackle over their pints at my demise. Plus the jeers and sneers of all those who wanted to see me put back in my box since the days of my arrogant Ali shuffles. This was their night, the night Christie was finally buried.

The end came swiftly, in the eighth round. Kaylor pummelled into me with some hooks and a combination of a left, then a right and another left to my head proved too much to bear. Within me, a physical shutdown got under way as my legs refused to function anymore and the rest of my body followed suit. I fell down flat on my front.

'Christie sprawled all over the floor, crawling his way to the corner,' Harry Carpenter commentated.

As my future crumbled before my eyes, I grasped for the rope. A near-unbroken run of KOs couldn't end like this. In my mind, I could see an eight-year-old kid at the Standard Triumph putting on gloves for the first time, a teenage Schoolboy Champion effortlessly destroying everything put before him. My entire life's struggle was ending here in plain view of my enemies: how was it possible, how had I let things come to this? I could now hear the crowd's every growl, begging me to go down, to concede defeat for me and my race: to prove myself the upstart I'd always been.

Then came the dread of every boxer: to see the referee coming towards you with that demeanour which says, it's all over, son. Gibbs hovered over me like a malevolent presence but I wouldn't oblige him. No matter how pathetic a figure I was – there on my knees, shuffling across the ring, pleading with my body to rise – I wasn't prepared to give in so easily. I got up on one foot in the same genuflecting pose that Kaylor had adopted earlier on when I'd knocked him down. But then nothing happened – I couldn't get up.

'He's not got up, he's out!' Carpenter told TV viewers. Then the man who once announced the birth of my star summed up the fight with complete precision: 'Kaylor has won the grudge battle.'

Out of my field of vision, Kaylor now mounted the ropes and punched the air to the jubilation of the West Ham army. It was all over; Gibbs simply had to say the word.

I was counted out.

As the whole arena erupted in joy, McCarthy, for reasons I've never fathomed, went over and kissed Kaylor on the cheek – a point noted by Harry Carpenter on the night. Terry Lawless, out of good politics and nothing else, got Kaylor off the ropes and encouraged some polite applause for me. But little was forthcoming and despite the win that the crowd had just witnessed, a victory they'd so wanted, some of them still booed as I began the walk of shame from the ring.

Maybe I wasn't cowed enough for them. Shaking off the last vestiges of mild concussion, I refused to display the required level of humility. In front of this horde, I wasn't going to bow my head as if I should be ashamed. Nevertheless, I was feeling that way because of a performance that didn't measure up to the years of training and dedication I'd given the world of boxing and the promise so many had felt resided in me. In one night, I'd gone from world champ in the making to busted flush. I knew only too well that things were about to get very bleak indeed.

Back in the Christie dressing room, the mood was marked by a heavy and gloomy silence. The oppressive atmosphere made my defeat doubly hard to accept, the rats all contemplating the gang-plank. Then Burt rounded on me.

'How could you let that happen?

But I had no answer. All my brash talk of bringing a fresh, American style to the staid world of British boxing had come to nought. My ambitions were made to look pointless and absurd, back there in the Wembley Arena. Errol Christie, the dancer-fighter who reminded crowds of Muhammad Ali, had been swept aside by a brawler of a fighter – a mean and dogged puncher who lacked my flair, but made up for it with sheer staying power. In eight rounds, this man had swept away my life's work.

During the days and weeks that followed a certain madness descended on me. Little surprise that under this kind of pressure my father's genes would take me to the brink of insanity. I took to sitting at home in the dark – silent, with the curtains drawn, refusing to come out of my lair. Over and over again, in a cata-tonic rage I'd go over all the mistakes I'd made and the poor advice from those around me. Then I'd miserably gaze into a future of dwindling earnings and respect.

A return to Coventry loomed like a very real and nightmarish prospect. In the darkness, I tried in vain to close off my worst fears, to sink deeply and safely into myself. Proof indeed, that boxing is the loneliest of sports: no team members to help you through a defeat, to share the humiliation or cheer you up. I used to think of boxers as 'killer monks' – deranged, solitary figures, forced to rely solely on themselves whether training, sparring, fighting or sliding into the inevitable cycle of defeat and despair.

Eventually, that dark room had to be left behind. When I emerged, blinking into the light, it was to find the boxing scribblers who had once idolised me were now tearing me down, like a fallen idol. To my horror, some of them even dragged out the worst insult a boxer can face, a term of abuse always uttered with a malicious snigger: 'glass jaw'.

Kaylor took
some punishment
early on.

Mirrorpix (top),
PA Photos (bottom)

The 'grudge fight' – as the press dubbed it – never let up for a second.
Mirrorpix

8

THE LIGHT GOES OUT

'The world ain't all sunshine and rainbows.
It is a very mean and nasty place and it will beat you to
your knees and keep you there permanently, if you let it.'

Rocky Balboa (from *Rocky Balboa*, released 2006)

Overwhelmed by James Cook as my career fades, 31 January 1989.
PA Photos

The Michael Watson fight: not just a defeat but an embarrassment,
18 November 1990.

PA Photos

'Lawd Jesus, Errol – she's your sister!'

They were back: the Christie family had descended on me like a biblical plague. It's said that when everybody else has deserted you, you'll always have your family. But that's not necessarily a good thing – in fact, for me it was a burden.

In this instance, the burden in question was Annette. Mum wanted me to take her in and look after her for a while. She'd become a bit of a handful, back in Coventry. We still hadn't fully realised that this wasn't just a case of adolescent rebelliousness and that Annette was storing up serious problems.

So, my sister arrived in London. At first, it was pleasant enough having her around but it didn't take long for signs that the two of us would make stormy company to materialise. With bouts still coming up, I was getting up early to train and going to bed well before midnight but my sister was of a completely different mindset. Freed from the restrictions of Cheveral Avenue, there was no question of her sitting around most evenings at home in front of the telly – which was my life. Instead, she was intent on taking advantage of her new-found freedom in the capital and tasting the good life.

Aged seventeen, Annette behaved like a very irresponsible teenager. At this point, my parents should have exerted some control and I certainly didn't want to become her surrogate father. For a while, I tried to tolerate her being out all night, even slamming the doors as she came back in during the small hours. Very quickly, my patience wore thin. The home I had literally fought to buy was my sanctuary, somewhere to escape the world of boxing and all the hassles of everyday life. Like a lot of working-class blokes who get a bit of money and some security, I didn't want any instability in my life. My home was organised along predictable lines, with everything ordered how I liked it.

Like my mum, I was a stickler for cleanliness and things

arranged just right. When I was living with Andy Straughn in Brockley we'd briefly shared the flat with a white boxer called Pat Clinton. I'd ended up tearing strips off him over what I felt were his unhygienic habits, especially his version of washing the dishes. He probably thought I was being extremely unreasonable, but coming home and finding the sort of mess you'd get in student digs drove me nuts; that was never how I wanted to live.

Strangers in my home were another bugbear: when I opened the front door and stepped inside, I wanted to completely exclude the outside world. I didn't want to hear unfamiliar voices or have conversations that meant nothing to me – all I craved was a silence broken only by whatever was on TV or some music. Otherwise, it was complete calm in total contrast to the roars and shouts of the boxing arena.

After the Kaylor defeat, I took my yearning for privacy one step further by taking to closing all the curtains in the house. Reports had been fed back to me of ordinary black blokes all over London getting beaten up by white thugs, who now thought: yeah, we can smack these niggers, just like Kaylor. Freddie, a trainer I know, told me the streets of Hackney had become very unsafe for blokes like him – all my fault.

'They came for us. The East End was full of gangs of white boys, who thought yeah, we can all beat up black guys now, they're not invincible.'

With my name either cursed or mocked outside, I needed four walls to retreat behind – which was why Annette's behaviour wasn't well timed. One day, returning from training, I found a strange bloke stretched out on my sofa, like he owned the place. He was breaking so many rules in my eyes: disrespecting my property and disrespecting me. I was in no mood to make polite conversation.

'Who's he?' I shouted to my sister.

'I dunno,' she answered impudently, 'just met him.'

I felt a strong temptation to smack the guy around my living room for a while until I'd got all the anger out of my system. Instead, I turned to Annette and asked her to find somewhere else to live. My sofa was for me to stretch out on – not for her latest conquest, a bloke she couldn't even put a name to. And so she duly packed her bags and went off to live God knows where. But it didn't take long for Mum to ring. Something had gone seriously wrong in Annette's new pad – complete pandemonium when a man we knew nothing about contacted Mum to tell her that my sister had gone completely crazy. My mother was more furious with me than Annette because she'd send her daughter down to London on the understanding that I'd keep her under my wing. Instead, I'd turfed her out and now the inevitable had happened.

My naïve sister, had got herself into a situation with some bloke we knew nothing about. The man told Mum that Annette had gone bonkers and she was screaming the place down. The moment he put down the receiver, Mum was straight on to me, cussing that I had let this happen and now I must sort it out.

Grumbling away angrily to myself about never being left alone by my family, I nevertheless realised that Annette could be in serious trouble. Like a lot of teenagers, she thought she knew it all, but clearly she didn't. My fury diverted to the stranger and the thought that he might have raised a hand to my own flesh and blood. That thought began to nag at me and, once there was a bee like that in my bonnet, my level of indignation and anger rose rapidly. So, I rang my trainer's son, Ritchie.

'We're going to Brixton – come tooled up.'

Like Hillfields in the old days, I decided my fists would suffice to resolve the problem, but Ritchie was armed with a big stick. We stood in the entrance to a grubby residential block in Brixton, the area of south London where the riots had taken place in 1981. I told him to stay where he was while I went upstairs to the flat and found out exactly what was going on – I'd shout if I needed him.

I got to the flat door and pushed it open. Inside, a tall and reasonably built African was standing over Annette. She was jabbering away at him. The scene convinced me that this was, as my mother sensed, an attack on a defenceless young woman. With a murderous expression on my face, I strode over to him and prodded his chest, inviting him to take on a man, not a seventeen-year-old girl. But instead of defending himself, he began to blubber. Then, speaking in some kind of West African French accent, he told me: 'No, you are mistaken – I never touched 'er, you must believe me. Honestly, I did nothing. She went mad, completely mad.' Something about the way he was talking made his story credible. I turned to Annette, expecting her to denounce him as her abuser but instead, she just mumbled: 'It's true, leave him alone.'

'Unbelievable!' I snarled, as I grabbed Richie and got back in the car. He got an earful from me about how my family were trying to drag me down. Always, there was some drama that the Christies would try and suck me into.

When I arrived home, my mother got a shower of venomous abuse down the phone: I'd had it up to there with Annette. With all the stresses I was facing as a fighter, why did my family have to heap even more crap on me? I just wanted to be left alone. But Mum was ready with her stock response: 'Lawd, Errol – this is your sister!'

I felt like screaming back: 'Mum, this is my *career*, my future!' But there was no point: family came first.

It was only a matter of time before I found myself driving Annette to St Thomas's Hospital to have her baby. In the back seat, she gripped her abdomen and screwed her face up. I hurtled along the streets, eventually screeching to a halt outside the hospital. Leaving her in the capable hands of the nurses should have been the end of my woes but sadly Annette's behaviour became increasingly erratic and troubled the staff. Hers was a loud and furious labour, followed by a bout of post-natal depression.

At about the same time, Dad had finally been diagnosed as a schizophrenic. 'Tell me something I didn't know,' I'd responded when Mum called with the news. His driving had grown ever more dangerous, his building work so bizarre that he no longer had any clients. Now at least he might get the medication he so badly needed. But Dad wasn't the only unhappy soul Mum would have to care for.

My sister now left London and moved back to Cheveral Avenue – where her depression began to take a heavy toll. On her return to Coventry, she started to give all my old boxing trophies away to complete strangers in the street. For years, the proud records of my success had sat in the living room and now they were gone.

Not satisfied with erasing my past glory, she moved onto the family photo albums. With a pair of scissors or anything sharp to hand, Annette started scratching her own face out of every photo. Only *her* face, mind, not the rest of us – for some reason we were allowed to keep our identities.

On learning from Mum that my amateur boxing cups had disappeared, I raced back up to Coventry. As if to add to my troubles, the gearbox on the Porsche decided to malfunction halfway up the motorway, so I cruised all the way up to my hometown in third gear, thumping the dashboard furiously with my clenched fist. Clapped-out Porsche, clapped-out family, clapped-out boxing career: everything was going wrong.

Soon, I was staring at the familiar front door in Cheveral Avenue. Sitting in my Porsche, hands still on the wheel, gazing at the house that kept drawing me back. Wesley greeted me first as he was also paying a visit and he announced that we had to take Mum to a Birmingham prayer meeting in Andy's Sierra. My Porsche certainly wasn't up to the journey.

Now I really was back in the Christie family zone – driving my 'Lawd'-worshipping mother to yet another evangelical gathering in the big neighbouring city. A slight chill between Mum and me remained over the way I had treated Annette. Over the Bible clutched between her hands, I got a series of disapproving glances that spoke volumes. She felt I'd betrayed my own sister, put my selfish interests first.

'We'll talk later,' she assured me in the way that only a mother can.

While the convention thundered on, Andy, Wes and me amused ourselves in the car, catching up on what we'd been up to. Once Mum was through with Jesus, we drove her all the way back again. She climbed out and gave me one more guilt-trip of a stare before she disappeared into the house. From the driver's seat, Andy turned to me and suggested we go out and have some fun, just like old times. For some reason, I had a deep sense of foreboding.

My younger brother revved up the motor and stepped on the gas so hard that Wes and me were flung backwards. Out of Radford, we screeched and down towards the town centre to see what mischief we could find. This was exactly what I'd left Coventry to avoid.

Eventually Andy parked up, dragging Wesley and me into the Tally Ho for a few drinks. The pub always meant trouble and that day was to be no exception. Moments later, we were embroiled in a nasty stand-off with some mouthy local white guys. Having learned a few lessons during my time in London, I sensibly urged the others to leave. Surely we were big enough to ignore those idiots?

But we were in Coventry, a place where no insult could be forgotten and every grievance was nursed. So, the white guys started to follow us in their car. How the situation would pan out was anybody's guess. In the seventies, you never expected to die in a fight, but with the new decade, knives were much easier to come by, guns already trickling into the ghettos only to become a flood over the next twenty years. Even back then, it was easy to imagine a headline such as 'LOCAL BOXING HERO GUNNED DOWN IN RADFORD' on the front page of the *Coventry Evening Telegraph*.

Suddenly, Andy braked hard. He then grabbed my long trench coat which I'd been sitting on, with my legs folded up. Wrapping it around his forearm, he got out of the car. Bold as any Christie, he marched up to the offending vehicle full of white boneheads and pointed his arm at them. Completely covered by my coat, it bore an uncanny resemblance to a concealed sawn-off shotgun. The white guys were reduced to jellies.

'Get outta the car, right!'

'C'mon, mate – be reasonable.'

'Don't shoot, alright?'

'Oh, look! Don't kill us, right?'

Wesley got out to join in the practical joke and I felt obliged to follow. Surely the muppets would realise at some point that Andy wasn't armed? But that moment never came. On the contrary, they opened the window and desperately started to push banknotes towards us.

'Take the money, right?'

But I pushed it towards them and then indicated to my two brothers that we ought to go. Back in the Sierra, Andy laughed his head off and hit the gas once more. Eyes like fire, he went faster and faster until hitting a corner, he over-steered and smashed into two cars on the left-hand side. Trying to correct the car rapidly, he managed to hit yet another, this time with a horrendous crunch. Not content with that impressive display of road rage, he ploughed into someone's front garden, sending several gnomes flying for cover.

Wesley and I got out. The bumper, lights and wing mirrors hung off the vehicle and the engine sounded less than healthy.

'Get back in!' yelled Andy.

We did as we were told. Andy's foot back on the gas, we made for Cheveral Avenue accompanied by some alarming clanking noises from underneath the car. Pulling into a main road, he managed to smack yet another vehicle. Then, as he headed over a bridge near Stanley Lane, the long arm of the law finally caught up with us – I'd almost say I was relieved.

As we clunked past, a West Midlands copper stood on a corner, scribbling away in his notepad: three black men in a smashed-up Sierra, looking very sheepish. He didn't need a second invitation and started off in pursuit. Close to the entries, we abandoned Andy's car and darted off into that parallel universe of alleyways that we knew so well.

'*Shit*, Mum's stuff!' Andy cried out.

Darting back to the Sierra, he had seconds to spare before the copper panting towards us on foot would manage to catch up. The boot flung open, he grabbed Mum's Bible, hat and other bits and pieces. Then he fled to a friend's house while Wesley and me made our way back to the family home, hiding behind hedges each time we heard an approaching cop car.

'You coming in?' asked Wesley.

I shook my head. Without a second thought, I climbed into the Porsche and made my way back to London as fast as the failing gearbox would let me. Leaving Wesley on the kerb with my exhaust fumes in his face wasn't my proudest moment, but I just had to get away from the Christie clan. The afternoon at the Tally Ho had been too much of a trip down memory lane.

After the day back home, I was determined to get my boxing back on track. It was as if I'd needed a quick reminder of why I'd taken up the sport with so much passion in the first place. After Kaylor, a process of damage limitation took place. Biting his lip, McCarthy arranged some fights designed more to get me back on track than to mount any serious title bid. I had to get some victories under my belt to silence the sceptics and resurrect my battered hopes of becoming a world champion.

In fairly rapid succession, I floored three boxers: Hunter Clay, Carlton Warren and Adam George. Clay was a Nigerian boxer, who had been beaten by Herrol Graham four years earlier in his home country for the Commonwealth Light Middleweight title. About two years older than me, we went the ten rounds and I won on points.

The Warren bout was more satisfying. A Jamaica-born British fighter with three wins, he lost to Michael Watson three weeks before we met. I compounded his misery with a knockout win in five rounds. Slowly, I began to feel as if some form was returning, though I was still very much aware that I was on trial as far as the commentators were concerned.

Louisiana fighter Adam George gave me my next boost of confidence. The year before, he'd beaten Huddersfield boy and former light middleweight champ Prince Rodney, but now I would account for one of the three losses he suffered in his professional career, alongside twenty-four wins. We went the whole distance and the judges awarded it to me on points. Though this was another victory in the bag, points wins were not what I wanted: somehow I couldn't summon up the demon inside that once used to deliver clear knockouts before the spectators got too comfortable in their seats.

Within my camp, McCarthy could see that my physical problems were still very evident. My calves were now swollen to an abnormal size, like gigantic yams. Burt brought in a physio to look at them, but there never seemed to be an answer. Sooner rather than later, I would have to face a world-class opponent and the fear in the Christie camp was that my fight-scarred, over-trained body would turn me into a sitting duck.

I used to joke that my opponents were 'powder-puff punchers' because I couldn't feel their feeble-arsed attempts to stop my onslaught, but now I ached from every jab and cross that reached me. Also, my opponents were catching me out in ways that were once inconceivable to me.

McCarthy announced that to restore my rightful place in the boxing pantheon, I would have to destroy the Irish southpaw Sean Mannion. Six foot tall, he had an impressive record in the United States as a light middleweight. Nearly a year after Kaylor, in October 1986, my moment came to wipe the slate clean. At London's Alexandria Pavilion, I went head-to-head with Mannion.

It really was an almighty battle with the two of us thumping away relentlessly at each other. The crowd was left in no doubt that they'd got their money's worth with a full ten rounds of uncompromised fighting. Mannion really was a tough old boy – he just refused to stay down.

In one of the last displays of the classic Christie form, waves and waves of combination punches crashed down on the persistent southpaw as I delivered one of the most brutal beatings of my career. I couldn't allow him to win: this had to be a clear and uncompromising victory, with no room for question marks. But Mannion refused to lie compliantly on the canvas. Like a Terminator, he rose up, again and again.

I had to fight like a lion for that victory. Still only twenty-three years of age, I was already a veteran boxer. I'd been in the ring since the age of eight and even though my body looked good on the outside, I was an old man inside. Mercifully, Mannion eventually wilted under the pressure of pounding fists and the decision went my way. For one evening, I let myself believe that Errol Christie was completely back on track.

Just over a month later, Frank Warren welcomed fans back to the same venue to watch me take on Charlie Boston: 'Errol, having his fifth fight this year, is raring to go into action again.' Another southpaw, this time rated in the World Boxing Council's top ten. No doubt the American fighter was a worthy opponent.

With hindsight, although I see Kaylor as the beginning of the end that wasn't how I was viewed as I prepared to meet Boston. No, I was the comeback kid, back from the edge of the grave. Once more, I'd vindicated myself and Burt believed that if Boston could be seen off, then a world championship belt would be mine for the taking.

On paper, I still looked like a success story: TV sports reporters would always point out that I'd lost only two professional fights and had an incredible amateur record-breaking history behind me, but it was the unbroken tally of victories that made any defeat look that much more catastrophic. Another fighter might sweep defeat under the carpet, but for the country's top prospect, Errol Christie, to be floored was that much harder to explain away. Jose Seys had shocked the boxing fraternity, Kaylor punched a huge gaping hole in my reputation: the unconquerable Christie was now an idol waiting to be toppled.

'Never been stopped, never been dropped,' they said of New Jersey boy Charlie Boston. He'd been sparring with Sugar Ray Leonard and in the run-up to the bout his manager took to goading me with some pretty corny stuff: 'If Charlie reproduces his best form, then your Errol is in real peril. You remember that Boston Tea Party we had two hundred years ago, when we threw all that British tea in the harbour? This is going to be the Boston ChrisTIE party! Charlie will be aiming to hit Errol so hard he gets dumped in the Thames.'

As with Harlein 'Who is Errol Christie?' Holden, I let the bravado get to me. I went into the ring, fired up and determined to give Boston a piece of my mind, courtesy of my fists. The first two rounds went my way and I planned on more of the same. But in the third, things started to go wrong: it was like re-living the closing stages of the Kaylor bout. Once so well oiled and powerful, the machine was creaking at the joints. My management looked on as Boston got his tea party and Errol Christie steadily nosedived over eight rounds to a final crashing defeat. The return to the changing room had the air of a funeral procession. If I'd been a racehorse, they'd have taken me round the back and shot me.

In just over a year, I'd totally lost the look and feel of a world-class hopeful. No matter how much I raged that my defeats were inflated and my victories brushed under the carpet, there was also a sense of being thrown into the dustbin of sports history: Errol the also-ran, the heroic failure – he could've been a contender.

McCarthy rolled the dice on Boston: he'd taken a gamble that this would be the fight that would propel me globally to the top.

But the two sixes failed to materialise. Instead, he began to consider the unthinkable: he and I would now have to part company. For my part, I wondered whether we'd ever clicked as a partnership. In my darkest moments, I questioned whether turning my back on Mickey Duff had been the right course of action.

But McCarthy and I had walked the road together and nothing in our history could be reversed now. Two fights followed, in June and September of 1987, both of them at the Albert Hall. Neither was intended to make a statement about me to the wider world, simply to get Christie back on his feet, unleashing jabs, crosses and hooks. In five rounds, I took Tyrone McKnight to a technical knockout and achieved the same result in one round with Rafael Corona. Both were completely forgettable fights.

In November of the same year, I was pitted against Jose Quinones. He was not a world-class fighter, just someone I'd have flicked across the ring at nineteen years of age. This bout should have been – if things had gone to plan – just a mere signpost on the road to my recovery. However, in a very telling development, the fight wasn't televised. TV was clearly reaching its own verdict on my future.

Afterwards, McCarthy said that he'd wanted to see if the Boston bout was a low from which I could pull back. He'd been horrified at my performance and seen none of the previous flair. With Quinones, we were in the business of rebuilding me yet again, but my manager was also eyeing up the exit at the same time.

When you're asked to bounce back after a second setback, it's that much harder. In the months after Kaylor, I could assure myself that it was still only my second defeat and Errol Christie would return. But after Boston, I found myself getting into the ring with Quinones beset with self-doubt for the first time in my life.

The fight at Blazer's Night Club in Windsor was well attended. Quinones was no great shakes, but a careless approach by me from the start – similar to the opener of the Seyes' bout – saw me go down to a defeat in four rounds. This time, it was too much for those around me to bear: McCarthy decided to call it quits.

Burt says he called me into his office, but my memory is of going there myself. Whatever, the end result was the same:

'I don't think you should box anymore.'

Trying my hardest to compose myself, I glared down at the familiar comb-over: 'Boxing is my life, Burt.'

'I can't manage you, then – here's your contract.'

I'd never realised or imagined my pro career could be brought to a halt so easily. Hardly able to breathe, I asked if there was any TV money or other bits of cash that I was still owed, but there was nothing.

Walking through Hatton Garden and down into Holborn, I struggled to imagine where my life could go without the ring. As I pondered the likelihood of hanging up my gloves, a couple of fans said hello to me. Twenty-four years old, with no academic qualifications or job training, having failed the first year of my mechanics apprenticeship, now the only thing open to me was the dole queue and I had no intention of joining it.

Not too far under the surface, I was boiling with rage. I felt betrayed and let down by the whole industry. Maybe that was my problem: after leaving Coventry, I'd tamed my temper too much. In all the years since, I've regretted not exploding right there, right in front of McCarthy. I've also regretted that I didn't tell him how frustrated I'd felt for so long. Where were the top-class training facilities? The sponsorship deals, the TV rights? What about physios? Everything a boxer today takes for granted. All those concussed bodies on the canvas and nothing to show for it.

Financially, I was on the thinnest of ice. And as luck would have it, that ice decided to go right ahead and break. In late 1987, the stock market crashed. Eighteen months or so later, the property market sank with it. Interest rates soared and house prices collapsed. With no decent income on the horizon, I put the 'For Sale' sign up on my Dulwich home and flogged the Porsche. All the trappings and baubles from boxing days now fizzled into thin air. I was left as poor as the day I'd arrived in London.

Sitting in the dark, which had become a habit since the Kaylor defeat, I brooded endlessly on events over the last few months and years. Only by retreating into myself like this could I fend off the Christie family insanity that threatened to overwhelm me. My head throbbed as I went over things time and time again, trying to make sense of how my life had dive-bombed. Then came a knock on the door. Trevor Curry walked in and switched on the light.

'You can't live like this, mate,' he told me.

I lifted my head out of my hands and looked up at the bulky Commonwealth and British Heavyweight Champion looming over me. His career was by no means over, though the best days – as he would find out – were arguably behind him. He'd still get to the finals for the two titles he'd won before but not walk away with either belt.

'What do I do, Trev? How do I *live*?'

He pulled up a chair and began to recite the boxing facts of life. When a man finds himself in the position I'd found myself, there's only one thing he can do. Boxers are feared and respected people, even the ex-fighters: there's always work for professionals like us, most of it in the security game.

'*What?* A bouncer?'

Curry nodded. The money wasn't so bad. He'd got involved in an outfit called Scorpion Security and recommended I don their jacket and get some cash in my pocket. Trevor was always a good talker with a warm personality. Basically, he was telling me the game was up and I had to examine other avenues to survive. Instead of drinking champagne in clubs at the manager's expense, I would have to stand out in the cold at the door, turning away troublemakers. This was a tumble all right, but his words were a lifeline out of the pit of depression I'd fallen into. At least I'd escape this dark room: I'd be with others of my kind, albeit in a twilight world where the sport's broken men cling together. So, I went to Scorpion's offices to pick up my jacket and sign on with the firm. Arriving, I kept my head down, not wanting anybody to recognise me. But at that time, it was too much to hope for. Years of ITV Saturday night coverage couldn't be so easily left behind.

'You Errol Christie?' one of the guards said smiling up at me.

'Yeah.'

'Blimey! 'Ere, should 'ave seen what I did, Errol. Other day, these blokes jumped me, right, outside this club, yeah? So I'm throwing these fantastic punches: pow, pow, pow!'

Though I listened politely, all this boasting fight talk was unbearably tedious. After all, I'd been the real thing. Nice of him to share his fantasies with me, but all I wanted to do was get through a shift and pick up a wage. Later, another guy swaggered up.

'Errol – my brother, he met your brother once.'

That gave me an idea.

'I *am* Errol's brother,' I replied.

'Oh.'

And he was off in seconds. So that's what I'd do from now on: I'd cease to be Errol Christie. I'd become a regular geezer, like 99.9 per cent of the other men in Britain – an ordinary bloke, nothing special, not well known, never been on TV. A big nothing, really – I'd be back where I'd started out. There was no point in trying to keep a grip on the fame I'd once enjoyed – that was all behind me now.

Trevor had been doing security work for a little while and was keen to impart his unorthodox crowd-control techniques. The knack was not to get too close to the thugs and idiots who mouthed off, always keep a safe distance, just like in a boxing fight. Only he had a little friend in his pocket that had never been there in his time as a heavyweight. He produced a canister and brandished it at me proudly.

'What's that, then?' I asked.

'CS gas.'

Years after this, he explained why he carried the stuff around with him in those days. It was all about making sure the punters knew who was boss without further questions. Even if we were outnumbered, the gas would settle the argument in our favour. Nobody would stick around when it got to the eyes and mouth. In his humble opinion, CS gas was the doorman's best friend. It was even better than having a gun because you didn't run the risk of killing anybody, unless you were extremely unlucky.

Not only did Trevor take to carelessly tossing these canisters into any bunch of hooligans that bothered him, he also experimented on himself. This mighty ex-heavyweight would sit at home and deliberately spray CS gas on his face. But his wasn't a route that I intended to follow. Like my time in the squats of Hillfields, I resolved to let my fists do all the talking. A warm Christie smile to psychologically disarm my opponent, followed by a mighty silencer; it never failed me.

The bouncer in overall charge was a small man with the dictatorial ambitions of Adolf Hitler. Time and again, he would wind up the punters unnecessarily. This reminded me of the bubble-perm idiots who used to refuse me admission to Tiffany's. I couldn't see any reason to annoy kids who had only come to spend their money on a fun night out, but a lot of the bouncers enjoyed wielding their tiny bit of power to insult the boys and girls in the queue. However, they paid the price for it. More times than I care to mention, the cars of unpopular bouncers were scratched and dented by disgruntled punters. Worse still, some of the club-goers might lie in wait and jump a bouncer they didn't like in the car park as he made to go home. Frequently, I saw bouncers with bruises and teeth missing, having been attacked by youngsters lying in wait. If they lived locally, they were in even more trouble: walking up to their own front door, bully-boy bouncers could get knocked to the ground and given a thorough going-over. It really didn't pay to aggravate those who paid our wages.

My view was that if nobody provoked me, they'd get a friendly face and be ushered through the door with no grief. That's what I'd always wanted as a teenager. In my new position, I'd do unto others as I wish had been done unto me. Once, a grateful youth pointed at the little Hitler in charge of us and whispered to me: 'Problem ain't with you, mate – it's that wanker you work with.'

Things got so bad for our power-mad superior that one night he approached me, looking more than a little shaken.

'Errol, you … you wouldn't mind walking me to my car, would ya?'

'Nah, mate,' I responded gleefully, 'walk to your own car.'

Terrified out of his wits, he wandered off into the dark.

One night, I found myself at a south London club in my Scorpion jacket, hands jammed in my pockets, bobbing from foot to foot to keep out the cold. All the time I was telling myself that this line of work wasn't so bad: the money was OK, I was with other ex-boxers and we understood each other. But it was no good. No matter how positive a spin I tried to put on the situation, I was a man in his mid-twenties who had lost everything.

More and more often, little pangs of desperation would hit me and the only way I could overcome them was to goof around with the other bouncers: tell my habitual corny jokes, behave like that kid who used to be the life and soul of the changing room at amateur boxing bouts all over the UK, the irrepressible adolescent who won all those trophies.

One night, as I cheered myself up, I caught sight of an object that froze me to the spot. A kid in the queue had produced a gun from inside his coat. He must have been arguing with one of the bouncers and was about to take his revenge in some style. Without uttering a single word, the youngster pointed the gun at the crowd outside the club and then he fired. Not into the air, but directly at the punters; everyone hit the deck.

With not a word exchanged, all of us bouncers lunged upwards from the pavement towards him and brought the juvenile psychopath crashing to the ground. Fear gave way to fury as we tore him up with our fists and feet. Thanking our lucky stars to be alive, we were bent on punishing our would-be killer. It didn't matter how young he was. Fortunately for him, the sound of police sirens soon filled the air – otherwise, several ex-boxers might have ended up serving prison sentences for manslaughter, even murder.

Some scenes in those clubs I'd rather forget, but Trevor vividly recalls everything: 'Me and you saw people dead in clubs, being taken out on stretchers; people getting shot, chopped in the head, people getting beaten up, loads of things going on. And boxing is useful when you're a doorman 'cos we can look out for ourselves. We knew things that were about to happen, we could even dodge bottles being thrown at us.'

When we did spot kids with guns, we tried to avoid handling them ourselves: getting our fingerprints on the weaponry wasn't a smart move. Trevor recalls telling one kid to throw his shooter away in a nearby bin and then he could come in. If we asked those punters why they were armed, they'd usually claim somebody was after them; it was always for self-defence. Once I encountered a bloke who had quite an impressive collection of knives, a gun and various other bits and pieces on his person.

'You going to war, mate?'

The club owners liked having boxers on the door – they seemed to think we were in some way invincible, as if our sheer strength created a force field around our bodies. If it just came down to using fists by the Queensberry rules, they'd have been correct but one thing even we couldn't do was to deflect bullets and sharp knives. Like any other human being, boxers' bodies don't take kindly to being shot at or punctured.

Trevor knew one ex-boxer-turned-bouncer who committed the capital crime of knocking a drink out of a thug's hand. It wasn't intentional, but when the drunk demanded another beer, the ex-boxer ignored him and walked on. None of us liked being bossed around by street scum, no matter how far we'd fallen ourselves, but the response was to produce a gun and fire point-blank into the ex-boxer's back. With that, one of my sporting comrades hit the ground and died. Trevor was devastated:

'He was a nice guy, Francis – a boxer and a fellow bouncer. Just thirty-one and he had kids, a black guy from south London. If one of us on the door gets killed, it's very sad. I didn't go to his funeral. The police kept his body in a freezer for so long, six to eight months, it felt like I'd said goodbye to him already by the time they buried him.'

Sometimes it felt as if we were being sent into the front line against the nation's thugs and morons. George Henry, the Coventry and London club-owner who used to race me down the M1 motorway, became my employer for a while. He operated a Soho-based club called Limelight, where I stood at the door and decided who could and could not enter. One turned-away punter decided to vent his grief in the old fashioned way.

'Can't come in yet,' I told him.

'Who you talking to? You black bastard!' was his reply.

It was seven years since that fateful day in 1981 when I'd seen a man's head stamped on, the day when I'd decided Errol Christie and the street fighting had to go their separate ways, yet there I was, confronted by the old enemy – a German. Could I let his insult go completely unpunished? As I mulled this over, the white guy continued to stare angrily at me. Knocking his teeth out might not be a smart move, I concluded. George Henry wouldn't want that sort of bad publicity. So, with one quick-as-lightning move, I slapped him hard around the face – so hard in fact, that I felt his skin folds between my fingers.

Two coppers wandered over, having heard the cracking sound, but they were unable to make out what it was. A little dazed, the punter still stood before me, but now with a large red welt on the side of his face, shaped like a huge hand. He was a little tearful with shock and might have needed a filling replaced.

'Everything alright here?' the copper asked.

'Yeah, it's all fine,' I said.

But the racist couldn't seem to talk: his expression was completely blank. Losing interest, the coppers drifted away, as did the idiot. Lost in a mental fog, he was unable to walk in a straight line, still trying to work out what had just happened.

After complaining to Trevor that my debts were mounting up and bills needed to be paid, he got me some bodyguard work. This involved walking several paces behind a rich client as he went about his daily business. I found the work itself pretty straight-forward enough, though the sight of a black man tailing an obvi-ously affluent white man raised a few eyebrows, particularly when I shadowed him into a bank. He'd be taking out money at a till while all the clerks nervously eyed me up. Was I there to rob the bank? Would I mug him? Why was I just standing there? The fear was written all over their faces.

Bodyguards are supposed to blend in and look inconspicuous, but it's difficult when you're a middleweight boxer tailing a much smaller, well-dressed gent round the aisles of Sainsbury's. As I walked a few paces behind him through biscuits and cereals and onto toiletries, I had the unnerving sensation of being watched myself.

Unbelievably, the store detective was checking me out. There I was, tailing my client while I was being tailed myself. This was getting ridiculous. Suddenly, the store manager appeared in front of me.

'Can I help you, sir?'

'Nah, I'm fine.'

'You don't seem to be doing any shopping. Can I ask what you're doing?'

But I couldn't breach a client confidence and so I kept my mouth firmly shut. Thankfully, my wealthy friend strolled over and explained the situation but that broke my cover for the day.

Added to the bouncer shifts, this kind of bodyguard work would help keep me afloat for the next ten years, but it wasn't always enough. By night, I could guard the clubs but I needed to find another way of making money during the daylight hours. It didn't matter if I never had time to sleep, I was a chronic insomniac anyway and the collapse of my boxing career only made kip nearly impossible. The moment I put my head down on the pillow, the memories of my many fights came flooding back. Once again, I was in the Wembley Arena with Kaylor, re-living every round of the bout, particularly the last moments, trying to analyse how I'd snatched defeat from the jaws of victory when so many had expected and hoped for me to win.

At some point in 1987, eighteen months after the Kaylor defeat, I found myself browsing through the stalls in Lewisham market. This was near my only remaining house, which I'd bought as a little rental property, but was now my home. They called the main drag in Lewisham the 'black market' because that's where my community came to buy cheap goods. Places like this in the Midlands had clothed me as a kid and put crockery and cutlery on the table at Cheveral Avenue. I wasn't really shopping, though – just floating from stall to stall in a gloomy daydream until something caught my eye.

Her name was Kelly.

During my boxing years, one thing I'd never managed to hold down was a relationship with a woman. There had been a succession of one-night stands and short-term flings, but the life-style didn't seem to lend itself to monogamy. The intensity of my training schedule and a narrow focus on boxing ruled out any other commitments. Also, I wasn't about to copy certain boxers' 'champagne and nappy runs'. This malarkey involved dropping a jumbo-size packet of nappies and a bottle of champagne on the doorstep of some poor girl left holding the kid by a shag-a-round fighter. I never put myself in a position where I'd have to shell out for a bottle of Moët and some Johnson & Johnsons. I'm not painting myself as a virtuous role model for all black men, I just didn't think it was nice to leave a litter of kids around town, all asking where Daddy was.

On this particular day, though, I couldn't take my eyes of the girl in front of me: young, maybe mixed race, and petite. Trevor Curry and Lloyd Honeyghan were always telling me that I wasn't cool with women. They'd try and give me advice on how they thought the opposite sex should be handled: don't look too keen, pretend to be disinterested, be a bit aloof at first. All this was wasted on me, I dived into any chat-up situation with my mouth running ten to the dozen:

'Haven't seen you before round here? What you looking for, then? Not that crap over there, I hope! Oh, you *are* looking for that. Yeah, that's nice, that is. Buy some of that myself. Fancy seeing a flick – go to the cinema, you know? No? Oh, alright – not my thing, either.'

So, I took out a scrap of paper and scribbled down my number.

'Can I have yours?'

'My *what*?'

'Number.'

There was a slight hesitation. I held out another scrap of paper that I'd fished out of my pocket. Then she wrote down those all-important digits.

'See ya soon.'

'Yeah.'

Smiling, she glided away and all the time my eyes were on her. Adoring every last inch of her body: the curves, the way she moved. If anything would finally help me shake off those post-boxing doldrums, it would be the lovely Kelly.

Smitten, I sat at home waiting for her call, pacing up and down the kitchen and staring at the phone. Lloyd Honeyghan and Trevor were right: I just didn't do cool detachment. After a few hours, I couldn't take it any longer. Picking up the phone before I smashed it against the wall, I dialled her number and waited. Eventually, after what seemed like an eternity, she answered.

'Hello?'

'Hi, it's Errol. Remember me? Met ya in the market. How are things? Fancy meeting up?'

With the same determination that I went after an opponent in the ring, I cornered Kelly and wouldn't let her go. In my chosen sport, I'd always regarded myself as something of a perfectionist

– every move had to be just so, every opportunity seized with both gloved hands. When it came to women, I was similarly focused – and very, *very* picky. Kelly was exactly what I desired: nobody else would be allowed to place their arms around her waist or kiss her lips ever again. She was going to be mine, end of story.

As I guessed, she was mixed race. Kelly's dad was African and her mum was white. For reasons not automatically apparent, her mum's parents had brought her up. They had refused to attend their daughter's wedding, but ended up bringing up her offspring. I was intrigued to find out what was going on, so I went round to her grandparents' house in deepest south London.

Bob and Brenda were white, but their surname was Black. They were typical white working-class Londoners, who loved their boxing and knew exactly who I was. Sitting in their living room on a very comfy sofa with the fire toasting my feet, I made small talk and felt strangely relaxed. Being at ease wasn't a sensation I'd felt for a long time. I had a warm glow at the thought that not only would I soon have a beautiful girlfriend, but some hospitable and kind in-laws. Everything seemed to be going swimmingly.

While Bob gabbled over his mug of tea, I slurped at mine, listening to his stories about life in Lewisham over the years and how things had changed – some for the better, more for the worse. As I looked up from the warm refreshing liquid, I couldn't help noticing something rather odd over the fireplace: a sight that destroyed the feeling of ease I'd been slipping into. Staring back at me with big wide grins on their faces was a row of golliwogs with red trousers, white waistcoats and fuzzy black hair.

'You collect Robertson's jam jars, then?' I murmured.

It's been a few years now since Robertson's withdrew their rather offensive logo from products, but in the 1980s, the company still cheerfully stuck golliwogs onto strawberry preserves. I seem to recall that if you got enough stickers, they'd even send you a golliwog badge.

My personal history with golliwogs wasn't so happy. 'Golliwog' was the name my mother was called by a little kid every time she went to the back yard to fetch some fuel. With that painful episode in the back of my mind, I took slight exception to being stared at by a row of them. But Bob remained nonplussed: 'Nah! Funny, ain't they?'

Determined to win my prize and slightly disarmed by Bob and Brenda's kind manner, I tried to ignore the golliwogs. I'd address the issue on another occasion. But now I spotted something far worse: screaming hatred up at me from the living-room floor was a pile of British National Party pamphlets.

'Fucking *hell*! You don't support that lot?'

Bob coughed awkwardly, before replying: 'See, fing is, Errol – it's like this: my old dear, right, she got mugged by a black man. Now I'm not saying you're like that, Errol, but there's plenty that are so that's why the BNP get my support. 'Ear what I'm saying?'

So, I was in deepest German territory, sipping tea with the enemy. I hadn't understood why they'd refused to attend their daughter's marriage to an African but now everything was crystal clear: the mixing of the races clearly wasn't acceptable.

Then a thought crossed my mind.

'Don't you think it's strange?' I said.

'*What?*' asked Bob.

'You two being called the Blacks and you support that lot?'

Unexpectedly, he laughed. Infuriatingly, I was finding it very hard to dislike him although all my urges, rational and otherwise, were to hate his guts. He was far too friendly and open to be a proper German. In turn, they seemed to think that I was the acceptable face of my race. Time and again, that old chestnut was trotted out: 'You're alright, it's the others I can't stand!'

These weren't uncommon views in south London at that time. In fact, I'd say most white people would have broadly agreed with Bob. They couldn't quite accept the idea of living cheek-by-jowl with blacks and Asians. Indeed, it has to be said that some of them were extremely hostile to the notion.

In 1977, a massive riot – 'the Battle of Lewisham', as the media dubbed it – had taken place between National Front supporters and their opponents near where I was now living. The pitched street battle sucked in about 20 per cent of the Metropolitan Police and certainly put our Coventry riot in the shade. I'd missed that particular altercation, but tensions between blacks and whites could still be felt there in Lewisham, as if we were all living under a truce that might break down at any minute.

The Black family was prominent in Lewisham market. Bob had a stall, Kelly's aunts, Linda and Janet, had stalls, her parents had their own stall and so on. It really was a family affair. I never expected to be invited into this very insular world until one day, Bob did just that: 'You fancy having a stall, then?' He went on to explain that Linda wanted to sell up and move to Spain with her husband.

'What would I sell?' I asked.

Bob leant over conspiratorially: 'Baby-wear.'

Well, I hadn't come to London to sell booties and bonnets but then I hadn't anticipated the premature demise of my career boxing, either. Baby-wear, it would have to be. Bob's view was that Kelly wasn't up to running the stall on her own: she couldn't – or wouldn't – lug heaps of merchandise from the East End wholesalers to Lewisham. I also got the impression that Bob really didn't think Kelly's heart was in the whole enterprise. Over the next few days, I talked myself round to the idea. Desperate to find a daytime money-spinner to complement my security work at night, I agreed to take on Mothercare in my own small way. Getting involved in the market would, I calculated, bring me even closer to Kelly – I'd be a part of her family's business.

Kelly started going out with me and very soon, she moved into my house but things were stormy from the start. There was a clash at the very root of our personalities. I'd been brought up to expect nothing, but Kelly was spoilt rotten. In my old fashioned way, I'd come back from the market or security work and expect to find the Lady of the House had kept the place neat and tidy, maybe a little scrubbing and cleaning in the manner of my own dear mother, but I could have whistled for it. I'd run my finger along the sill and pick up a small pile of dust, then stare gloomily at the grease marks on the window. Having been bullied by Mum into trying to achieve impossible levels of domestic cleanliness, I found Kelly's slovenly ways intolerable.

'This your idea of tidying up?' My question was greeted with a 'So, what are you going to do about it?' stare. She didn't see herself as a housewife and wasn't about to slot into the picture of domestic bliss I so wanted to create – a new security in which to wrap myself after the collapse of my boxing dreams.

There was also an age problem. When I first met her, I'd had Kelly down for a couple of years younger than me, but in fact I was in my mid-twenties while she was in her late teens. It turned out there was a seven- or eight-year gap and at that stage in our lives, it really showed. Nevertheless, I was desperate to make our relationship work and if love was slow to blossom, lust certainly wasn't. The sex was frequent and fervent.

Pregnancy was almost inevitable. When she announced the news to her dad – the African guy – he was the most hostile of anyone. Whether he thought Kelly was too young or I was inappropriate in some way, I had no idea but he did his level best to create an ugly mood. Nine months later, Lou Christie was born at Lewisham Hospital and later baptised a Catholic. I'm not entirely clear why we chose Catholicism but I seem to remember it being the nearest church on the high street.

Now that I was living with his granddaughter and running a baby-wear stall, Bob Black and me ended up spending a lot of time together. We'd drive off in his big white van to the East End to meet the wholesalers. All our gear would be picked up from warehouses and backstreet factories in Tower Hamlets, then driven back across the river to Lewisham.

The irony of the whole set-up was that despite the National Front screaming we needed an all-white, Anglo-Saxon Britain, London had long depended on the different races trading with each other to survive. The East End wholesalers were mainly Asian. They sold their gear – all sorts of stuff – to predominantly white market traders, who then flogged it to mainly black customers. At the bottom of the heap were the new African immigrants, some of whom worked for the wholesalers. I once saw a Bangladeshi wholesaler talking to his African assistant as if he'd just bought the poor guy from a slave ship, which raised my hackles sky-high.

'You shouldn't talk to your workers like that – they're people. You talk to me like that and I'll knock your block off!' I told him.

One wholesaler even turned to Bob and pointing to me, complained: 'That boy is very aggressive.'

I swiftly corrected him on my social status by going nose to nose and snarling into the now-petrified man's face: 'I'm not his boy!'

On journeys, Bob would pass the time discoursing why blacks, give or take a few, were basically inferior and needed the guiding hand of their white superiors. 'Taught you lot how to read and write,' he'd inform me. 'We civilised you. If we hadn't come along, you'd still be in huts, mate. Hear what I'm saying?'

Because I wasn't about to correct him with my fists as I had so many other Germans, I developed an interest in black history. Every week, I'd voraciously read the *Voice* newspaper. I began to find out about what Afro-Caribbeans had done for the British Empire and even discovered that ancestors of mine had fought in the First and Second World Wars, things I'd never been taught at school.

So, I hit back at Bob: 'What about the muggers of our people? Coming to our countries, taking the goodness out, raping our women, leaving it like shit, measuring out our land so we couldn't go where we wanted then dividing it up with barbed wire? Taking us as slaves?'

One day, Bob watched a black kid crossing the road in front of us and muttered: 'Up to no good, I dare say.'

We had another one of our exchanges but then I exploded in no uncertain terms: 'You know, Bob, I never came to London to rob or steal. I came here to work, that's all I wanted to do – make some money, have a house like my mum and dad did – but I ended up getting mugged by the boxing industry, that's how it feels to me. And they were all white, every last one of them!'

After that last outburst, Bob drove silently home, aware he'd just trampled on an extremely raw nerve.

As it was, I hadn't completely finished with the world of boxing, not quite yet. 1988 saw three fights of mine, including one at the Albert Hall against Winston Burnett. He'd just been duffed up by Nigel Benn – in both 1987 and 1988, losing both times – and also, Chris Eubank. The dapper boxer had taken him apart six months earlier, in March 1988, at Hove Town Hall. Now it was my turn to tear into Burnett amid the fine surroundings of the Albert Hall. After a shaky first round, the fight ended up in my hands.

Those bouts were more like battles for survival rather than the start of any world championship bid. I had no qualifications and only the market stall, plus some security work, to fall back on. Unless I got back in the ring a few times a year, we'd struggle to make ends meet. After Burnett, I faced James Cook. The 6ft Jamaican boxer was no slouch or mediocrity – this man would go on to become British and European Super Middleweight Champion. Once more, I had a chance to pull myself back up.

York Hall was a venue that had been supported for years by Frankie Fraser and we did battle on 31 January 1989. But I was inadequately prepared for the encounter and fell victim to Cook's remorseless uppercuts. Nine months later, I met France's Martin Camara at the same venue. This time, I lost on points after eight rounds. Camara went on to become French Light Middleweight Champion.

The losses led one wag to quip that the champions of tomorrow were using me as a staging post along the way. Not only had my world belt hopes gone, but I was now a punchbag for those still in the ascendancy, or so it seemed – never a good way to be forced to view oneself. Around this time, the only consolation I had was to knock out the Arizona cruiserweight Thomas Covington at the Albert Hall in May 1990. By this stage, he was recording one loss after another and so the win provided just a small boost to the flagging bank account and not much else.

Burt McCarthy had thrown the dice on Charlie Boston and now I was to gamble on a truly big name that was emerging through the ranks. The mighty Michael Watson and me would face off in the ring. When the bout got the thumbs-up, I was inexplicably in seventh heaven. After four years of being treated like a joke, I was to bounce back on 18 November 1990.

Convinced I could stage the boxing comeback of the decade, I got into training with Chris Eubank, who I'd met at the Thomas A' Beckett. I became one of his main sparring partners, following him down to Brighton where he lived. Like Fashanu, Eubank was another black sportsman who had figured out his finances and was brilliant at self-promotion. He revelled in the showman side of boxing, which was undoubtedly my major weakness.

I would go to the gym and do some sparring while he would take over a hotel, set up a ring and get some photographers along. The whole thing became a training session and media event at the same time. Part of the new breed of sports celebrities, he knew exactly what the journalists and fans wanted.

Chris was always into fancy clothes, the poshest stuff he could find. Even before he made big money, somehow he managed to look a million dollars. In all the years I have known him, he has never changed. Eubank would be mocked for his monocle and plus fours but that was him from day one. And I noticed no one mocked him to his face: he could always give a first-class account of himself with his fists, the smartest pounders in the business.

His boxing style matched his clothes – flamboyant and stylish, though a bit too showy for my taste. He had what I called his 'Cobra routine', where he would fix you with a stare and bob around a lot while he was thinking what punches to deliver. In the run-up to the Watson fight, he gave my boxing a little dose of magic.

Unfortunately, in one sparring session I managed to knock out one of his front teeth. I was unaware of what had happened – there was no blood and his gum shield held the tooth in place. Days later, he took me to one side to inform me of my unwanted dental work. I apologised and told him that I normally reserved that treatment for skinheads only.

As I steeled myself for the encounter at Birmingham's huge National Exhibition Centre, my private life took a decided turn for the worst. Kelly and I had simply not clicked. We'd meet in the bedroom, fuck, put our clothes back on and go about our separate lives. For her, that involved an increasing amount of partying that I didn't want to get into, especially as I struggled to get in shape to meet Watson.

After a couple of rows in which both of us plumbed our abilities to say the most terrible things to each other, I decided to call it a day. She and Lou could stay in the house and I'd rent somewhere else. To make a living, she could have the market stall while I would stake everything on the Watson fight. I packed my bags and got ready to leave my own home.

I was dismayed to discover, as my dad had done thirty years before, that there were still plenty of Britons who didn't want to rent to men with black faces. After calling up landlords, over and over again, I'd turn up to be greeted with: 'Oh, Mr Christie ... erm, actually, the flat has gone now.' Eventually, I found someone prepared to give me a room and moved my stuff in.

November 1990 rolled round. Once more in front of the nation's TV cameras, I walked calmly into the ring to do battle. 'Make or break for Errol Christie,' the TV commentator correctly noted. Watson had a similar professional record to mine and an equal talent for knockouts but where we differed was that he was seen as the global champ of tomorrow – the way I myself had once been viewed.

Accompanied by some rap music, Watson skipped up to the ring in a red dressing gown, looking serenely in control. I still know him now and his voice is calmer than the sea, a soothing baritone that completely belies what he could deliver in the boxing fight.

I entered the arena more aggressively, my brow furrowed and jolting my shoulders as my fists jerked about. No doubt there was some over-compensation going on for what I knew was being said about me. It's a good job I couldn't hear the BBC commentator when he wryly observed that I'd been around and experienced six defeats against opponents who wouldn't have troubled me once upon a time.

In the red corner, Watson from Islington accepted the adulation of the crowd. Meanwhile, in the blue corner, I thumped the air, replete with quiff and goatee. We both did the obligatory stare towards the centre of the ring but I found it difficult to be too mean – I had great respect and admiration for Watson. He was a good boxer and a fundamentally decent man. Naturally, I gave him some verbal, to which he listened with good grace.

The bell rang and I advanced on him, knowing this was the final gamble. Anxious eyes in the front row looked up, wondering if I would stay the course. Meanwhile, the TV commentator at last conceded that I was actually quite a good fighter and had looked impressive sparring with Eubank. But the words barely left his mouth before Watson sent me sprawling down to the canvas.

We were still in the opening seconds.

I stumbled to the corner of the ring using the heavy-padded post to slide back up to a vertical position just as the number 'Eight!' was shouted in my face by the referee. Like a true hunter, Watson wasn't going to waste any more time. Refusing to allow me out of his reach, he used the full extent of his arms to land a volley of punches on me. Much as I would once have done, he met his opponent's obvious weakness with murderous intent.

Reacting defensively and finding myself moving backwards, I realised the old eye wound had decided to open up yet again. With blood in my eye and the arena spinning round, I sensed the whole fight slipping away from me rapidly.

Watson was fresh and vibrant, while I was rotten to the core of my broken body. Occasionally, I'd give him a run for his money, unleashing a succession of punches, but this was no Kronk performance. For one happy moment, I landed a good strong jab, which whip-lashed Watson's head. Feeling that things might conceivably go my way, I re-doubled my efforts and the second half of the first round began to look more equally matched. Returning to the blue corner, I resolved to gain the initiative in the second round and cruise from there to a stunning win.

Round two saw no breakthrough for either of us, though a good display of skill that kept the crowd entertained. Finally, I'd shaken off the daze from Watson's early near-knockout punch but the cut above my eye was severely irritating.

In what was billed a ten-round fight, round three saw my world finally collapse. The power to defend and attack just ebbed away. Lumbering around the ring, I felt less like the Errol Christie of old, more akin to a zombie. A superb right-hand from Watson spelt trouble and once more, I backed away from my opponent. Another right hand caused the referee to take a closer look at me. How much longer could I remain standing?

Then a third right-hand punch sent me down to wild cheers. The dreaded countdown from the referee filled my ears: 'One, two, three …' I *couldn't* let this happen. Turning onto all fours, I crept to the corner post. There was a big *Daily Mirror* logo emblazoned on it. I began to climb. 'Six, seven, eight …' Now I was up again. I turned round to the referee.

'I've beaten the count.'

But Watson came over and slung an arm around me. Even in my semi-concussed state, the will to slug on was still there. For a few seconds, I wandered round the ring, trying to figure out what had just happened, unable to fully comprehend how badly I'd lost. To millions at home, the commentator delivered the fatal verdict.

'And that, I think, might well be the last time we ever see Errol Christie in a professional boxing ring. He had the chance tonight to re-establish himself at the very top of the tree, but Michael Watson proves that he is still a force to be reckoned with.'

I returned to Lewisham a truly desperate man: generosity was now off the agenda, so I moved back into the house. It was my property and I was damned well going to live there. Kelly got the hint and days later packed her belongings and fled with Lou. I then got word that the market stall had not exactly prospered under her management and so I seized that back as well.

Then I quietly fumed. The house was back in my hands, the stall was mine again, but my son had been taken away. The fact constantly grated. Eventually it even crowded out the appalling events in Birmingham. Now all I could cling onto was the hope that the little boy I'd brought into the world with Kelly would make more of his life than his old man had. But first, I needed Lou back and I resolved to get him by whatever means necessary, so I kidnapped him.

The next time I saw Lou without Kelly around, I put him in my car and sped off towards Coventry. Even though Andy and me had been through good times and bad, it was in his hands that I left Lou. My brother now had a partner and kids of his own, so I figured he'd provide a safe family environment for my son to stay in while I tried to work out my next move, though truthfully, I had no idea what that might be.

It was not exactly a well-thought out strategy. Stuck in London, with the market stall and security work, I hardly visited Lou and he began to ask Andy where his mummy was. Then a letter arrived, full of threats from Kelly's solicitor. With a heavy heart, I handed my son back. Needless to say, I haven't seen much of Kelly over the last twenty years. The incident drove a big fat nail into the coffin of our relationship and the lid has been firmly on ever since. Strangely, her family and me are still on very good terms – particularly Bob and Brenda.

Despite the botched kidnapping, I was still allowed access to Lou and one day the two of us were wandering round a Sunday fair on Blackheath Common – a huge stretch of parkland in south London with magnificent Georgian houses dotted round the edge – when I felt a finger jab in my shoulder.

It was summer and I had treated the public to a rare look at the Christie legs. Normally, outside of a boxing ring, I always wore tracksuit bottoms, jeans or trousers; shorts were only for the ring. But the heat had climbed unseasonably high and so London got an eyeful of my gigantic calves.

As I was browsing the stalls, I felt this unexpected finger jab. Turning round, some military type was standing there, pointing at me. Major so-and-so from the nearby Woolwich Barracks, as it turned out. He gestured to my legs.

'They must be painful,' he barked.

'Yeah, they are.'

'Come along to the barracks and I'll get the Army doctor to give them the once-over.'

Curiously, the military officer had no idea who I was. This was a completely random act of kindness, the sort that makes life worth carrying on. Hours later, I was lying on my front in a medical unit deep inside the barracks, having fluid pumped into my calves.

'Interesting,' the doctor conferred with the Major, before turning to me. 'Do you know that you have Compartment Syndrome, Sir?'

'Nah – what's that, then?'

'Blood can't move round because your muscles are far too big, must be in agony. Ever thought about having something done about it?'

I didn't know whether to laugh or cry. Finally, the great hulking elephant-sized legs that destroyed my dancer-boxer ability had been diagnosed. Where the boxing industry failed, the British Army had come to the rescue. I made a mental note to buy a box of poppies every Remembrance Sunday, from there on.

The following day was Lou's fifth birthday and it fell to me to keep him entertained. As ever, I set up the baby-wear stall and resolved to look round the market for a present later on. First of all, though, I'd take him for breakfast in the nearby Wimpy.

As we tucked into our sausage, egg and chips, there was a

sudden and almighty commotion outside: police sirens and then yelling and the stamping of heavy-duty boots down the street. I told Lou to stay put while I went outside to find out what was going on – I wanted to keep a beady eye on the stall. Most of the other stallholders seemed frozen to the spot as riot police stormed down the road. Then, completely by surprise a copper lunged at me from behind a rack of leather jackets. Shocked at first, I realised he was trying to force my arm behind my back.

I'd never been handcuffed as a teenager and it wasn't about to happen now. Filling the air with expletives, we wrestled each other to the ground. I hadn't found myself in a situation like this since Mark Kaylor and I brawled in front of the press, all those years ago. The policeman rolled round with me on the filthy tarmac. Then some more joined in, all trying to restrain me.

From inside the Wimpy, little Lou looked on. It was surely the weirdest birthday of his short life. There was Daddy, taking on the Metropolitan Police single-handed and cursing like a trooper.

'Get off me, you fucking bastards!'

Very soon, I'd disappear under a small mountain of blue uniforms. Every so often, my fist or foot would break through. The writhing mass of struggling bodies went this way and that, watched by a highly bemused crowd. My blood pressure surged to bursting point as one of them pushed my head backwards. Through the chaos came a familiar voice.

'Don't resist them, Errol. There's too many of them.'

Kelly's aunt Janet hovered nearby. She was right – the best thing was to let them take me and then find out what the hell was going on. They were clearly determined to cuff me and chuck me in their van. I just had to swallow my fierce pride and let them do it. Moments later, there I was, glowering in the back of a cop wagon as it moved off at some speed towards Ladywell Police Station.

Eventually, the van screeched to a halt and the doors were flung open.

'Get out!'

'*You* put me in here,' I snarled, '*you* take me out!'

The coppers left me for a moment or two while they went off to have a confab about what to do next. One of them disappeared, but returned with a secret weapon: a black policeman. But if this was to make me play their little game it wouldn't work. In the 1980s, it's fair to say black guys in the Met were regarded as something akin to collaborators.

'What difference is *he* going to make? He's probably worse than you lot! He'd have to be – wearing *that* uniform! Gotta prove himself, hasn't he? Be much worse than the rest of ya to earn his stripes.'

That tactic gone up in smoke, they ended up carrying me into the station. It wasn't dignified, but I was past caring. I sailed through the doors in the arms of the boys in blue and found myself dumped in front of the main desk.

'Name?'

I rose up in front of the duty officer: 'You tell me why I'm here! Take law-abiding blokes off the street and leave the criminals behind, that's what you lot do.' For a while, I went on in a similar vein.

'I'm just doing my job, Sir. Name?'

But I wasn't going to give up my name so easily: 'You're all the same! Got a uniform, you're just like the rest of them.'

There was an uneasy little stand-off. The copper began scribbling before glancing up officiously to inform me of my heinous crime: I was being charged with armed robbery. Now it's not often I'm struck dumb, but this was one of those rare occasions. They'd found a gun, there'd been a chase and my face fitted the description. They'd seen me run from the Wimpy and assumed I was making some sort of getaway.

If I'd been white and middle-class, I would have given them a long speech about my rights and demanded a phone call to my lawyer. But being black and working-class, I just swore a lot. So then it was time to be carted off to a cell, again carried by a gang of coppers. Inside, they forced me to kneel on the floor and one of them placed his foot firmly on my back. My nose touched the floor. Then they removed the cuffs and bundled out of the cell door as fast as their legs could carry them – a wise move on their part, as I sprang up, slamming the thick metal door with my fists. The clanging sound echoed down the corridor.

'Bloody Germans!' I screamed. 'I'm a hard-working black man!'

After a short pause, the little shutter on the door opened. The copper seemed slightly confused: 'Who's a German?'

'You are!'

He shook his head, not knowing what I was going on about.

'We'll let you cool down, eh? Then we'll all have a chat.'

Chewing at my fist, I slumped onto the hard bed behind me. Nothing was going right in my life. If the gods hated me, they were certainly letting me know. In short order, I'd been made a fool of in the boxing ring, lost my worldly wealth, seen my girlfriend and son walk out on me and now I'd been flung in jail. I was sure Janet and the rest of the family would have rescued Lou. What must he have thought to see his old man being manhandled away like that?

Hours passed. Intermittently I'd march up to the door and declare how fucked-off I was, in loud and uncompromising terms. For those who have never been inside a police cell, it's comparable to being a caged animal: pacing up and down in a small space, never knowing if you'll enjoy your liberty again.

After what seemed like an eternity, a key rattled in the lock. Then the door ground open with a loud whining. Before I could even consider knocking out the constable on the other side, he quickly muttered: 'You're free to go now.' As if I should somehow be grateful.

Striding back to the main desk, I found an altogether different reception. There had been some big misunderstanding: all my mates had been ringing the cop shop to say who I was and even the manager of the local C&A had called to give me a good reference. I now learned that some of the police officers were big boxing fans, though obviously not eagle-eyed or knowledgeable enough to spot Errol Christie when they wrestled him to the ground.

Kaylor supporters all of them, I surmised, as they now affected a jolly bonhomie. Back slaps and goodwill all round, even the offer of a lift home in a police car.

'No, thanks,' I growled back.

Some fresh-faced specimen stepped forward: 'Shake your hand?'

'Fuck off, you German!'

Hardly one of my better days, and I'd had quite a few bad ones of late. Being carted off in front of Kelly's family and my customers was not good for business or my mood. Unprepared to let the matter drop, I reported the whole incident to the Crown Prosecution Service but my militant behaviour on being arrested was held against me and the whole matter dropped. The only funny point was that the CPS report bemusedly noted my frequent use of the word 'German' in the police station.

My mood was dark but if I couldn't cheer myself up, a friend suggested, I might want to try amusing other people instead. The burgeoning black-comedy circuit beckoned. Whatever possessed me to think I might be the new Lenny Henry, let alone Richard Pryor, is anybody's guess but seeking a new role, I nonetheless launched myself into it. Very soon, I discovered that what raises a few laughs in the changing room doesn't necessarily work in front of an audience of paying punters.

'We had to leave off sex before boxing. You can see that with the heavyweights when they're grappling each other like wrestlers, all the hugging. Referee breaks them apart and then they're doing it again in seconds, so sex-starved they're going for each other ...'

Yeah, I bombed. But for a while, I toured the country, raising just enough giggles and guffaws to stay on the bill. Eventually though, I found myself at a south London venue when, in mid-gag, some loudmouth yelled: "Ere – it's that geezer from the market!'

I choked. My mouth was still open, but nothing came out. Years later, I told a journalist that compared to boxing, stand-up comedy was a hundred times more terrifying. There were only two of you in a boxing ring and you didn't have to talk – and when you died in the ring, at least you were concussed.

While on the comedy circuit, one of the acts tried to convert me to a new movement sweeping through the black community at the time: The Nation of Islam. He was a 'general' in the organisation and I once saw him dressed in the required bow tie and black coat, surrounded by his lieutenants. It wasn't difficult to understand the attraction of this group to a directionless black youth and their strong anti-drug message certainly had its appeal, but it wasn't for me.

The leader of the movement, Louis Farrakhan, had some controversial views that I didn't agree with. He'd also fallen out with my hero Malcolm X and an enemy of the great man could be no friend of mine. Hilariously, Burt McCarthy asked me at the start of my career before I signed up with him, if I was in any political organisations. I should have told him the Black Panthers just to see the blood drain from his face.

On 19 March 1993, I made a terrible mistake and ventured back into the ring. This was to be my last bout as a professional boxer. At a venue in Manchester, Trevor Ambrose knocked me out in two rounds.

A full two and a half years after the beating I'd had from Watson, I should have learned my lesson but, like so many fighters, the call of the arena proved too strong. The adrenalin rush that always surged through my body as I marched through the crowd was a sensation I'd missed for too long. Then there were the cheers that you drink in, not to mention the booing you try and screen out. Bright lights above, gangsters and managers in the front row, the stare-out with your opponent before the first round and the sound of that bell summoning you out of your corner. It had been my life and I still couldn't accept it was gone.

So, I came, I saw and I was slaughtered.

9

AND IN THE BLUE-BLOODED CORNER...

'Look at where football was in the seventies and eighties. It was ruled by thugs – you'd never consider taking your family to a match. Now it's clean. We're doing the same with boxing. We're taking it upmarket.'

Alan Lacy, founder of The Real Fight Club, quoted in the *Independent*, 1 August 2005

ol Leavers' Open E
6th February, 4 - 6

'I SHOULD HAVE BEEN A CHAMPION'

Errol Christie, currently talking to youngsters about the perils of knives and guns around London, tells **Tris Dixon** he could have been more than a contender

Boxing News follows me to Hackney Community College as I tell kids to put down the knives, 15 February 2008.

Boxing News

Teaching junior school kids that boxing can keep them on the straight and narrow.

Tony McMahon, personal collection

In 1997, a *Daily Mail* reporter tracked me down to the baby-wear stall in Lewisham market. He was on a mission to discover whatever had happened to the pro boxer whose name had once been so casually linked to legends like Sugar Ray Leonard, Tommy Hearns and Roberto Duran.

At the time Frank Warren was busy promoting a hot new talent from Sheffield – Prince Naseem Hamed, a young, flashy and gifted fighter who had every reason to expect global glory. It seemed my name had cropped up at a press conference and a comparison had been drawn between the big money Hamed was raking in now and the pittance I'd got from the game back in the eighties.

As the *Daily Mail* later put it:

While Hamed has more luxury cars than most households have cutlery, Christie's was a story which could be repeated by countless boxers who have retired with scarred, damaged bodies and vacuum-filled wallets.

It seemed I was now a benchmark for how far a fighter could fall from grace. As if sports reporters were looking into the abyss of boxing failure only to find Errol Christie looking up from the bottom.

The newspapers didn't need to tell me about such grim realities though, I was living them every day.

I explained to the reporter that Prince Naseem was lucky that times had changed. Here was a young talent, who could now reap huge rewards and get rich very quickly; that same opportunity had never been on offer to me. The reporter pretty much concurred with everything I said and when he wrote up the story, he added: 'While Hamed, with his millions might not agree, whoever said boxing was the cruellest of sports got it about right.'

But raking over the disappointments and frustrations of my career became the least of my concerns as bitter news came from Coventry – Dad was dying.

Travelling up to my hometown, I felt numbed. Finally, the big man who had picked yams in Jamaica, travelled to England in the hope of a better life and then lost his sanity in the process was shuffling off this mortal coil. Though I wasn't very religious, I hoped there was a choir of angels ready to take him on high, to give him the peace he'd never known on earth. It was hard to believe such a life of unending grind and anguish couldn't have some sort of reward at the end of it. Dad believed in God and I'm sure, in his more lucid moments, he was convinced this short spell of hell on earth would have its compensation in an eternity of bliss. Even in his final years, Mr Christie hadn't lost his ability to throw a good temper, but the physical strength that once overawed us had ebbed and gone.

I'd never had much to say to Dad. In fact, it's impossible to think of a day when the two of us sat down and had a normal father–son talk – it just wasn't that sort of a relationship. We'd always been at war, twenty-four seven. He was unapproachable, a man quick to anger and incapable of reason, but before he bowed out, I couldn't resist asking him a few questions, things that had always bugged me. Like, how he met Mum for a start.

In a halting voice, he told me all about writing to Jamaica to get a woman, then buying the wedding licence which prevented Mum from even thinking of going back to her native country, not after he'd gone and spent all that money. Then on to the petty injustices he'd faced after arriving in Britain – the guesthouses that turned him away and the building sites that refused to employ him.

I wanted to know if he'd fallen out with Mum because he'd found out about Paulette, her child born out of wedlock. Had that caused a distance between them?

'Me did know about dat,' he insisted.

So, Paulette was nothing to do with the anger between them. It was just they weren't suited, simple as that. In those days, you made do with the partner you ended up with: fate dealt its card, and that was that. Once kids appeared there was no escape and if you were trapped in a marriage made in hell, tough. Not that I'm saying it was a loveless union; I don't doubt they grew into each other, but there was no affection or warmth.

The struggles and hardships their generation went through scarred them deeply and took a huge toll on their personalities. My parents were people who couldn't afford to stop long enough to think about romance. Candle-lit dinners, boxes of chocolates, holding hands in the moonlight ... Maybe Mum and Dad managed to grip each other's hands once – on the pier at Weston-super-Mare – but never again.

A few days after my last chat with Dad, the Christie brothers found themselves standing round a mortuary slab, a large metal tray where a familiar cadaver was laid out in front of them. There he was, our chief tormentor: stone cold and speechless. The medics had given his body a thorough examination and the cause of death was asbestos-related. After all those building sites in the 1950s and 1960s where he'd toiled, the choking dust had filled his lungs and eventually finished him off.

But I didn't feel like crying: that just wasn't the way things had been between Dad and me. Our relationship hadn't been a close and loving thing. So, I was more than a little surprised to see my brothers breaking down – particularly Wesley. He sobbed like a baby. Were they crying for themselves or him? I knew that if I cried then it would have been more from self-pity than anything else and that's a sin I refuse to give into, so I stayed resolutely dry-eyed.

The funeral saw all the local church bigwigs turn up in their finery. One of the elders popped by to pay his respects, though he was glancing at his watch a little too much as he did so for my liking. Andy was there, dressed to the nines. He loved occasions like this – opportunities to act the big man, without the money to back it up.

Annette showed up as well. By this time she'd got involved in some sort of charismatic movement. Dressed from head to toe in bright and very colourful African robes, she stood before her family. As the hearse moved off to the cemetery, she refused a seat in one of the cars, preferring to run along in front of the hearse. Some Rasta guy she'd shown up with accompanied her all the way from the church to the graveyard and it was a reasonable distance. In death, as in life, the Christie clan couldn't help but make an impression.

Annette had brought three children into the world – Jubiah, Daniel and Tabitha. But somehow Mum got wind that Jubiah had burned himself in Annette's kitchen, down in Brixton. A careless accident hleft the kid badly scalded. Horrified, my warrior mother hurtled down from Coventry to Brixton and took the three youngsters back with her to Cheveral Avenue. Even though she'd spent the best part of her adult life rearing a brood of eight and could have enjoyed some peace at last, Mum took on the burden of Annette's trio. And even though she's well into her seventies now, those kids are still living there. Which is why I've taken to calling my Mum a genuine warrior. In her way, she's fought as many battles as Alexander the Great and Julius Caesar combined, but her battles are fought against unruly kids, her main weapon a sharp tongue used to devastating effect.

Before he died, Dad had taken massively to Tabitha, in particular. He'd loved her to bits and shown her a level of affection that he'd denied any of us. Maybe he was finally mellowing with age. Whatever the reason, there's no doubt Annette's little girl gave him a joy his own children never had.

The deaths of others make us think what our own lives are all about and now I realised there was only one way that my life would have a purpose again: somehow I would have to return to boxing. Not climbing into the ring to receive a pummelling from a younger fighter, though. At this stage, I'd have been little more than a particularly immobile sitting duck and I had no wish to see my head smacked about, ending up the punch-drunk butt of cruel jokes.

The solution was to become a trainer, to admit to myself the glory days were well in the past and now my best option was to impart the skills I'd learnt at the Standard Triumph to a whole new generation. My style of boxing, the Ali-influenced dancer approach, was still in demand. And frankly, the gyms of London were still full of blokes who were giving the most uninspired, sometimes downright incompetent advice on how to box. If I was to make sense of who and what I was, the gloves had to go back on.

In no time at all, I found a gym near my home and the Eltham Boxing Club soon resounded to the barking voice of Errol Christie as he ordered pasty white kids to jab, jab, jab: 'Give me a cross! Those are lazy legs! Move your legs with your punches! You been eating pies? Give me an upper cut! And another one! Work that bag! Ten jabs – now!' And so on.

The younger kids were fun to work with and very keen to learn. Like the junior boxers at the Standard Triumph, they raced to get to my lessons on time, changed quickly and emerged enthusiastically to start working over the bags or each other. But the older lads at Eltham were a different matter, often late and surly with it.

'This is a *war*! War for fitness! What time do you call this?'

I'd always regarded training as an experience akin to a military exercise: a boxer was a soldier – you were recruited into the world of fighting. This wasn't a hobby, like stamp collecting or some sort of evening class, like upholstery or learning French: you came to a boxing class because you'd been recruited into the world of fighting. This was a vocation, something that seeped into every pore of your body; it would obsess your mind, take over your entire life. There could never be half-measures or slack attitudes in this sport, so I hated the sight of those kids sloping in late whenever they felt like it, mumbling verbals in my direction when I took issue with their attitude. There was an unfortunate undercurrent at play here and it had a lot to do with the area.

Eltham is next to Lewisham. It's just another little district south of the river Thames in London. I decided to work at the gym there because I could jog from home and I'd be warmed up by the time I arrived. But in spite of Eltham's convenience, it might as well have been a million miles away. Whereas my part of London had become increasingly multi-ethnic, Eltham was resolutely white and still largely hostile to blacks moving in. The area was referred to as 'Heltham' by some, owing to its ultra right-wing tendencies.

Black people had to be on their guard. There were pubs you were ill advised to enter, if your skin was less than lily-white. Also, streets off-limit late at night, estates where black families lived at their peril. This wasn't 'casual racism'– it was completely in your face. Other, more enlightened parts of Britain might be shedding the 'nigger' talk of ten and twenty years before but in this overlooked part of the capital no quarter was given to so-called political correctness. Blacks were still to be spurned and regarded as less than equal.

Not that this stopped me teaching in the midst of these Germans. In fact, by this stage of my life, I wanted to confront such demons head-on. Nobody in the 1990s was going to tell me where I could walk; nowhere in London was off-limits. Segregation was a given when I was growing up: black and white kids never mixed on the streets, in the school playground or the discos of seventies' Coventry. Well, I'd had enough: bloody-minded as ever, I would venture into Eltham and stake my claim on their club.

There were a few danger signs that should have warned me that at some point things would come to a head. The National Front had its headquarters in Welling, just down the road. In September 1993, the British National Party had its first-ever councillor elected in Millwall, a stone's throw away from the gym. That sort of politics wasn't about fears over jobs, either. Many people in Eltham just hated the idea of having a black person next door – there's nothing more profound to it than that.

Given this was 1993, not that long ago, what happened while I was teaching at the Eltham Boxing Club should make any decent person's blood run cold. A black kid called Stephen Lawrence was studying design at the Blackheath Bluecoat School. He dreamed of one day becoming an architect. Lawrence was part of the new wave of black youth who believed their prospects might be better than those that had been on offer to their parents, my generation.

Waiting for a bus home on a street in Eltham, he would have had no idea that his life was about to end. A gang of white youths – and all the witnesses confirmed this was a gang and white – set about him for no reason, inflicting multiple stab wounds. After running over a hundred yards to get away from his attackers, he breathed his last.

The black community was horrified, as were most Britons. Suddenly, working as a boxing trainer in Eltham became a major talking point among my mates. Why was I giving *them* any help?

Why teach *them* how to box? Why not come and train black kids? They needed the support, not those bastards … and so on. Not that all kids in Eltham were racist, even the ones on the streets, but the area now became a byword for intolerance. It wasn't helped when the reporters who went down there to interview the locals heard them moan in a way that suggested they had more sympathy for the killers than their victim.

I'm not going to recite the events of the Stephen Lawrence case here. The facts are still well known: the botched police investigation, the private prosecution by Stephen's brave mum and then the inquiry in which the Met was accused of institutional racism.

I used to see Doreen Lawrence walking through Lewisham market quite often, looking very embittered. She set up a community centre to honour his memory and it still helps kids from poor backgrounds to become architects or town planners. Unbelievably, the centre had six windows smashed in February 2008 while the memorial on the spot where her son died has been subject to repeated attacks, including one in 1998, when a hammer was taken to it. What happened to Stephen was a nightmare but race-based politics is still live and kicking today, even growing in strength. The rising support for the BNP and other far-right groups means the old fights must be taken up again, though I think my fighting days are over, so I'll have to give way to others in the future.

But what depresses me now is that, in the face of a new racist menace, many of our youth spend more time shooting and knifing each other, playing into the hands of our enemies. I sometimes say that the fascists don't have to bother anymore because we'll do the killing for them, damage ourselves first. The strange thing is that today's youth are better educated than I was, back in the Stone Age of the 1970s: they can use the spoken and written word better than I ever could, but instead I have to read about another death over who has the best bling or who didn't show enough 'respect'.

So, the attraction of Eltham quickly dimmed, but fortunately another door opened just as that one was closing. A man called Alan Lacey had made a very interesting discovery in Manhattan. On a trip to New York, he was amazed to find boxing had gripped

Wall Street, but it wasn't just a matter of watching the sport – those investment-banker types wanted to do it for themselves.

They were sticking their expensive suits in lockers and donning wraps and gloves before smacking the hell out of each other. A sport you'd once have searched for in working-class Harlem, the Bronx or Brooklyn could now be found on the Upper West Side and other swanky parts of town. Corporate lawyers were jabbing and crossing, derivatives traders practising their upper cuts on the bags.

What appealed to these guys was the competitive and brutal nature of boxing: they saw the sport as a physical reflection of what they were doing on the dealing-room floors – beating each other up, sending their opponent down, leaving victims out for the count. After a day of mental warfare, they wanted physical warfare. And so white-collar boxing was born.

Lacey came back to Britain and set up The Real Fight Club in 1996. The idea was to get City of London types off the golf courses and into the boxing rings. And sure enough, his astute move paid off. Queues of thirty- and forty-something public schoolboys and rich kids from the Square Mile soon formed to sign up. Some were fit blokes who had done other sports more suited to their social background, while others were big fat bastards hoping to work off their long lunches with a spot of aggression.

The boxing grapevine hummed and I liked what I heard, it was different. Anything new in boxing always grabbed my attention. But now there was also the opportunity not only to teach, but also to make a half-decent living out of it. In the nineties, the City boomed and it would continue to do so until the credit crunch.

The boys working in their Canary Wharf skyscrapers, with multi-million-pound apartments in Kensington and Chelsea, wanted to be put in a situation where victory boiled down to the use of their fists: they were eager to be stripped of all the civilised niceties that normally surrounded them. The thrill of literally smashing your enemy in the face or body was something they couldn't do at work but now they could get away with it in a boxing ring. Those guys really believed in the survival of the fittest and, through this sport, they would prove that they had achieved the right to survive. Not surprisingly perhaps, the British Medical Association and the Boxing Board of Control took a slightly different view. The Board of Control was highly vocal in its opposition to white-collar boxing while the BMA warned that middle-aged men were putting themselves at risk in taking punches to the head. However, this was a phenomenon that refused to be put back in its box.

In the late 1990s, Brad Pitt starred in a Hollywood classic called *Fight Club* – about men who take up no-holds barred fighting. The film became required viewing for millions of ordinary men, mostly office types who wanted to project another version of themselves to the outside world. Adopting names like 'Bomber' this and 'Hitman' that, they led double lives. Like Jekyll and Hyde, they were respectable by day and murderous by night.

It fell to me to transform middle-class blokes into gritty, no-nonsense fighters. Suddenly, my life was taking a major turn. And for once, this was a turn for the better. In several gyms, I discovered my name had not been entirely forgotten and my style of fighting was still admired by men I'd never met. In no time at all, I had a roster of wannabe white-collar boxers on my hands and so I was spending morning, noon and night back in my favourite place – the boxing ring.

I even ended up training the billionaire producer of *Fight Club* and other Brad Pitt movies, Arnon Milchan. Boxing with him in his suite at The Savoy or jogging with Arnon and his wife down the Victoria Embankment. And he wasn't the only film-industry type to knock at my door: a movie producer called Simon Franks was among my keenest students, very quickly picking up the basic skills and showing a remarkable degree of flair. What I didn't reckon on was Simon using what I'd taught him to deck Hollywood star George Clooney. But that's what happened in 2005.

I got a call from the *Guardian* newspaper to say that Clooney had been at the première of his latest movie, *Good Night, and Good Luck*. At some point, he and Simon exchanged words over a deal that had gone wrong and they had a bit of a standoff. The report said that some shoving took place and then Simon let fly with his fists. A very concerned *Guardian* reporter asked me what I made of my student's behaviour. 'Did he use his left hook?' I asked, and was promptly quoted all over the national media.

Having been taught boxing in a no-frills sort of way at the

Standard Triumph, I saw no reason to sugar my approach with these wealthy types. If they really wanted to box, they had to develop the right attitude – a killer instinct that would drive them to keep on hammering their opponent, even if he was already heading down onto the canvas. 'Never stop fighting,' I thundered at them. 'No retreat, no surrender!' Day after day, those Churchill-like words of mine could be heard echoing round the walls of the gym.

I started with Alan Lacey at the Real Fight Club, then moved to a gym in Camden named after the Kronk, before finally moving onto Gymbox in 2003, when the chain of boxing gyms first opened. I'd met the founder, Richie Hilton, at a white-collar boxing event and he invited me to be the face of his new operation. Flattered, I could hardly refuse and I'm still making the walls shake at his new outlet near the Bank of England. In fact, the gym is in what was originally a massive safe for storing huge amounts of gold and money.

Not all my students wanted to develop such an instinct. One, in particular, found my constant bawling-out technique a bit tiresome. He was in the ring, doing some sparring with me, and the obligatory aggressive verbals were flowing:

'Those are lazy legs … Laziest legs I've ever seen!'

'Lackadaisical – that's what you are!'

'Does yer Mama know you're here?'

'What am I feeling there with my fist – cake, fried chicken!'

'Give me ten press-ups for being late – *now*!'

He wasn't enjoying this at all, but I continued to alternate our full on sparring with some impromptu, vigorous exercises.

'Touch the four corners of the ring. Ten star jumps – *now*! Give me two jabs, cross, upper cut, upper cut, hook to the body, hook to the head. Now run and touch that wall, now give me a jab. C'mon, jab like you mean it!'

He was doing as he was told, but with maximum resentment as if I'd no right to presume on him.

'Got five seconds on the clock, get round that ring!'

Now he was glaring.

'Back in your stance – give me a jab, cross, hook, upper cut, upper cut!'

Then the clock stopped.

'That clock loves you, son. I never seen such a bad effort. Does yer Mama know you're here? *Does* she? She'll be sending the Red Cross by the time I'm finished!'

The student was the singer Seal and while he didn't say anything to me as he sloped out of the ring, I was told by another trainer later on that he thought I was completely over-the-top. Seal, who clearly felt as if he'd nearly been culled, had a bit of a moan about yours truly in the changing room: 'I'm not a fighter – he's trying to *kill* me!'

While I never saw Seal again, I enjoyed a long period training *X Factor* presenter Dermot O'Leary – a splendid geezer – and Gianluca Vialli, player-manager at Chelsea Football Club from 1998 to 2001.

Then came an opportunity to mix with true royalty. A good friend of Princes Harry and William, Hugh Van Cutsem, asked me to sit in his corner at a big charity white-collar boxing contest at the Boodles Boxing Ball. This was a £100-a-ticket bash, where the cream of British society donned black tie to watch public-school-educated gentlemen beat the crap out of each other.

This was about as far as you could get from an ABA bout in Whitley Bay, circa 1977. No Kia Ora orangeade, just champagne on tap. And no Scotch eggs and sausage rolls, either, but delicate canapés and petit fours. It was the sort of food my big hands crush just picking it up. And instead of puny working-class kids, here were well-fed and well-spoken young adults squaring up to each other.

Turning up to help Van Cutsem, I did a double take. Among all the well-dressed boys and girls were two very familiar figures, both looking extremely excited at the prospect of watching their buddy put on his wraps and gloves. Princes Harry and William were, as one journalist at the *Daily Telegraph* later put it, in the 'blue-blooded corner'. Royalty has always had a soft spot for boxing and these two were truly pumped-up.

Van Cutsem had taken the name 'Hunter' for the evening. His opponent was a chartered surveyor called Huw 'The Welsh Whirlwind' Williams. I leant behind the ropes in Hunter's corner and whispered advice in his aristocratic ear. Van Cutsem had been preparing for a long while and took his preparation very seriously. He told me later:

> All my brothers and friends were at the fight and the Princes. The guy I was up against was much bigger and stronger than I was. He was a Cambridge Blue so I'd had to over-prepare for this fight. For months, I'd been waking up at five-thirty in the morning and training at the gym, four days a week, two hours at least each time. I knew you from Gymbox and though you weren't my trainer, you always told me where I was going wrong. You were great like that.

Kind words.

Looking back, that night I finally began to erase the shame of my downfall. Through passing on what I'd been taught from a very young age, at long last I could re-connect enthusiastically with the sport I loved, the only sport that had ever really meant anything to me.

The Welsh Whirlwind was short and stocky and could do Hunter some damage if he got close. He was a pint-sized powerhouse with well-built arms that Van Cutsem would do well to steer clear of.

'He's a big guy, Hugh, but he's not tall. Use the reach you got with them arms, keep him at a distance. Don't let his jabs get close,' I told him.

As the bell rang and they went for it, Hunter seemed to have the advantage. But the more he punished the Welshman, the angrier the little guy got. Hunter's hot headed opponent came back ever stronger through the first half of the fight. But Hunter said that, in retrospect, he never saw defeat as an option.

'I don't want to sound arrogant, but I was confident of victory – you have to be. In the first round, I could see in my opponent's eyes that he was surprised I could box at all. In the second round, he got angry. And then in the third round, he was determined to knock my head off. If I'd connected with his right, I'd have been sitting four tables back with the Princes. If I'd lost the match, I'd never have known about it.'

But the Welshman showed Hunter no respect. He was intent on using the Princes' mate as a punchbag.

'Keep cool,' I barked into his ear. 'You got one more round to go. Just don't let him get in range – he'll tire himself out.'

Sure enough, the Welsh Whirlwind huffed and puffed, but Hugh kept him at bay with his long arms. It was a measured performance and I couldn't have done better myself. That's no empty compliment: Hunter had the right instinct, which you might not expect, given his background. In fact, I never thought I'd witness the day when a toff would remind me what good boxing looked like.

The judges' decision came: 'Hunter' Van Cutsem was the winner! As the place erupted, the two princes punched the air, red-faced and glassy-eyed, mouths wide open and shouting their approval. The victor told me that before that night he thought boxing was just about two meatheads beating each other up, but at Boodles he learnt that my chosen sport involved loads of skill. He described it as a 'mental chess game'.

At another white-collar boxing bout, I had an encounter that I could never have predicted. A multi-millionaire American businessman in his sixties had come over to take part in a London white-collar boxing night – just one of several bouts taking place that evening. I turned up to see if this very rich guy's fists would last the duration. With a little fanfare, the American walked in and wove his way through the dinner tables with suited guests to the ring in the middle of the venue. And behind him came a very familiar figure: a little older, but instantly recognisable.

I didn't know whether to say anything at first, but the other man broke the silence, spotting me as he walked close to my table.

'Errol! What are you doing here?'

The Virginia drawl hadn't changed. There was the same twinkle in his eyes and warm smile. I stood up and shook hands with Emanuel Steward. Two decades had elapsed since we'd spoken or seen each other – a whole river of pain had flowed through my life.

'You gonna be my second – get in my corner and give this guy some advice.'

Suddenly, I was back in the Wrecking Crew, taking orders from the big man. I hopped to my feet and sat in position by the ring. Steward's man was tall, with very long arms. In spite of his age, he moved like a trooper – the Kronk training methods had clearly paid off. I kept up my usual level of encouragement, yelling the same kind of advice I'd given Van Cutsem, and the combination of my constant verbal barrage and Steward's genius ensured our man came out the victor. Steward and I indulged in a bit of mutual back slapping while privately, I wondered how my life might have turned out differently had I stayed at the Kronk and never come back to Britain.

While teaching the rich how to box restored my spirits and boosted a slightly dented sense of self-worth, I felt there was something I needed to give back to kids who came from my sort of background. Living in south London, with a son now in his late teens and memories of Eltham still keen, I was only too aware of how lost so many young people had become. Many of them were falling into knife crime and, even worse, gun-related crime. I'd always been reluctant about tooling up with weapons but so many of today's youth seem unable to resist the temptation or at least they feel they have to for protection.

So, in recent years, I've turned to the schools. In 2008, I was invited to speak to several classes at Hackney Community College. They were to be brought together in the college's lecture theatre to get the Errol Christie treatment. When I arrived, the first thing that made me realise how different school and college is for kids today was the airport-type security at the entrance. To get in, I had to walk through a metal arch that scanned me for knives or guns.

In the lecture theatre, I was confronted by rows of hooded, sullen teenagers, who didn't know who the hell I was. The deputy head, a lovely woman called Sonia, put me at my ease and advised me to talk candidly about my life and boxing. So, standing at a lectern, I began telling the kids about the stormy life of Errol Christie.

I'd never been so nervous in my life: I certainly lacked the overbearing authority of Elder Nicely – and unlike him, I didn't have a 'rod of correction' to hand. I'll be completely honest here and admit that speaking in front of fifty couldn't-care-less young people was infinitely more terrifying than boxing in front of 10,000 at the Wembley Arena.

Of course, the kids instantly sniffed out my unease. They began shuffling about in their seats and stifling yawns. Pulling myself together, I launched into all the details of my upbringing in Cheveral Avenue, raising my voice to command their attention: my father hitting us for no reason, me hiding under the stairs as a little kid to avoid his fists and the cries of my younger brothers as he trapped them upstairs and gave them a relentless walloping. A journalist from *Boxing News* who was in the lecture theatre later described this as a 'pin-drop moment'.

Just speaking frankly and openly about my mad dad and his random acts of violence quickly shut them all up. Clearly, I'd hit a nerve they related to. Maybe many of them had been victims of similar abuse. Or unlike me, perhaps they didn't have a father around at all, even to beat them. Whatever was going through their minds, they were now listening. I begged these youngsters to find the sense of community they seemed to have lost. Even in the violent decade in which I'd grown up, the much-maligned 1970s, there were still factories, trade unions, gyms and other organisations that brought people closer together, but the work and activities that used to turn boys into men had long vanished.

At one point, I told the kids to shake hands with the person sitting in the next seat, to try and feel a sense of kinship and responsibility for those around them. Not to exist like lonely little islands, ignoring the needs of others. It was this selfishness, this mistrust of the world around them that led to shootings or knifings over who had the most 'bling' or who felt they hadn't got enough 'respect'.

I ended my speech with a plea: 'So, I say to you guys, get your education. Go forward that way, forget about gun crime: be patient. Your mum and dad, they made sacrifices for you, they want you to succeed. You've got to fight, not each other, but those who keep you down.'

There was no applause at the end and just a few questions, but looking into those kids' eyes, I felt I'd managed to plant a seed, something that hopefully would stop them going down a path that would leave them behind bars or bleeding in a gutter.

It's sad to say that not long after my speech in March 2008, a student from the college – Devoe Roach – was stabbed to death.

In the trial that followed, it emerged he'd been killed for looking at another youth in the wrong way. The word 'senseless' doesn't seem to sum it up.

Seeing those kids at the college brought it home to me how much I'd changed as a person. Many of them were as angry and resentful as I had been, growing up in Coventry – fighting every day of the week, being called names all the time. But now, as a father and an older man, I've been through so many stupid and needless wars that I realise no matter how much hatred is inside you, it's not possible to take on the whole world alone.

Back in Coventry, the name Errol Christie equalled fighting, whether on the streets or in the ring. The first positive move was to leave Coventry for London, otherwise I'd have ended up walking the streets of my home city like a deranged crazy, jabbering away to myself. People would have pointed at me, saying, 'There's that nutter Christie.'

Even though my professional boxing career didn't go stellar, it tamed me. I signed up to McCarthy as a street-savvy wild animal and emerged an approachable and more thoughtful person, someone who uses his brain more than his fists. Sometimes I regret losing that certain sharpness, a ghetto sensibility, but on balance I wouldn't want to be the turbulent soul I once was.

Being a father, I can see the problems my son is going through and I try and guide him away from the mindless violence that beset my youth. Luckily, Lou has never had to experience the constant taunts and abuse that was my daily diet in the 1970s. There may be other problems now but at least I can see he has his self-respect intact in a Britain less bigoted than it once was.

The Errol Christie who trains wannabe boxers these days is thought of as a joking, always-smiling character, someone who tells corny gags and is never down, the life and soul of the party, so this book may come as a huge surprise to those who have only known me in recent years as a beaming, upbeat bloke. But to the skinheads and rude boys who remember me from decades past in Coventry, they will appreciate that I'm a transformed man: the lid has been slammed down on my once-boiling aggression.

In 2001, Tom McGarry retired from Standard Triumph. He'd been secretary of the club since 1967 and the man who was once the rock of my life was now in fading health. I'd bolted away from him the moment I went professional, I left Tom and Coventry behind. Eager to make something of my life, I'd callously thrown him to one side: ambition ruled my heart and my head.

Now I was at his front door for the first time in many years. I knocked and was shown in. Sitting in the living room was a Tom I'd never wanted to lay eyes on – he was a shadow when once he'd been a giant. The cancer was taking its toll and I could see he was losing control of his bodily functions. I sat down and peered into those familiar eyes, now tired and faded, the light gradually going out of them.

'When I get better, I've got to sort out the club,' he said, tapping me on the hand.

Talking required some effort, so there were spells of silence during which memories came flooding back: the holidays to Rhyl in north Wales that Tom organised every year for all the boys of Standard Triumph at the end of the season: a mixture of boxing training and horsing around, staying in those rudimentary chalets dotted round a field. It was the closest thing I got to a proper holiday.

After working up an appetite, Tom's wife Sally would cook bangers and beans on a gas fire – a meal we'd all gobble down as if we'd just been through a famine. Tom would bark at Sally a lot, but he never meant a bad word.

'Sally, what you doing?' his gruff Lanarkshire voice would boom across the field as she rustled up dinner. We would then descend like locusts on the tummy-warming food.

My mind drifted back to Tom at the amateur boxing bouts, grabbing a drink after the fights were over and declaring: 'It killed my mother, it killed my father – *revenge!*' He'd then gulp the family enemy down his throat. Unfortunately, this meant he wasn't always sober on the drive back home to Coventry. This being thirty years ago, we all found his unpredictable road manoeuvring hilarious instead of downright dangerous. We would laugh in the back as one of the trainers grabbed the minibus wheel, yelling: 'Keep it straight, Tom!'

Then there were his huge eyebrows, which resembled those of the 1970s' British politician Denis Healey. They were never trimmed and allowed to grow like a bush in a wild garden. Underneath them, two glassy eyes glared disapprovingly if his young fighters didn't do as they were told in the gym and below that a big gut held in by a blue nylon anorak, his hands plunged into the pockets.

The best memory of all was Tom giving me the key to the gym, which also meant giving me another key to the main factory gates so I could get access any time of the day or night. This was an ultimate act of trust on his part: to allow a poor black kid access to an industrial premises with valuable equipment and cars parked up, then in the gym, all those boxing bags and gloves lying around. But Tom knew I was no thief.

'Ay, Errol, I can see you're dedicated,' he said, handing me the spare set of keys, 'train whenever you want.'

Sally McGarry died first and that hit him hard. Without his beloved wife, he began to lose his own will to carry on. I could see that he wanted to say something now. His hand rested on mine.

'How come, Errol … How come you never came back to see me? Why did you never come back?'

But I just bowed my head. I couldn't replay those years: they were what they were, my one big chance to make something of myself. As I knocked out one pro boxer after another, I'd seen those victories as steps away from my background. If I could forget where I'd come from, I almost hoped I'd never return. As a seventeen-year-old rising star, I hadn't looked back for a second when I fled Coventry for London.

'I didn't think, Tom. I was just focused on the boxing.'

'I know, Errol,' he replied, 'I know.'

Shortly afterwards, Tom died. I carried his coffin and then spoke at the funeral service. 'Tom didn't recognise any colour except the blue and white of the Standard Triumph boxing kit,' I told the congregation. It was a pity there hadn't been more like him in those days, men prepared to give kids like me a fair crack of the whip.

A year after the funeral, I watched as the Standard Triumph was levelled to the ground to make way for new housing. It broke my heart to see the place that had given hope to my brothers and me destroyed by a wrecking ball. The walls caved in so easily.

The world represented by that place was now gone: the car factories with shop stewards like Tom who could click their fingers and halt a production line, the armies of skinheads who ruled and terrorised the streets throughout the 1970s – and black kids like us, in our ragamuffin clothes, being chased home every day in blind terror. All gone. And until now, almost forgotten.

ACKNOWLEDGEMENTS

Thanks to my fellow boxers and mates, Andy Straughn, Trevor Curry and Michael Watson, who shared their memories, as well as some kind words from Lloyd Honeyghan; Emanuel Steward, who took time out from nurturing the next generation of champs to talk about me as if I'd been at the Kronk yesterday; Eddie McGarry, who helped with the book; and I salute the family of my late amateur boxing trainer, Tom McGarry.

Thanks to 'Hunter' Van Cutsem, an excellent white-collar boxer who can still hear me shouting: 'No retreat, no surrender!' in his ear; Alan Lacey from the Real Fight Club and Richie Hilton of Gymbox, both of whom have given me amazing support. Neville Staple of The Specials for sharing his childhood memories; and Bob Brolly from BBC Radio Coventry. Also, my teenage buddy Simon Daffern and all the Mighty Seven, some of whom I couldn't get in touch with.

Thanks to Frankie Fraser for an entertaining afternoon in 2009, when we recalled the good old days and he laughed at all my jokes; Burt McCarthy for a steady stream of e-mails; and Frank Warren; also ex-Coventry FC footballer Garry Thompson, whose stories of racism in football still shock me now.

Bob and Brenda Black get a special thanks for extending a helping hand when I was at my lowest ebb and agreeing to be open in this book about their political views, which never got in the way of our friendship.

Most of all, thanks to the Christie family, including my dear departed old man and my mum, who helped out with some of those childhood stories, and my nephew David who is writing a rap about this book. Finally, one big mention to my brother Michael, now a minister in Tottenham and a calming influence on us all.

INDEX

Page numbers in *italic* refer to photographs